RILEY POOLE'S
BOOK OF
SECRETS

MORE ON THE SUBJECT

NATIONAL TREASURE HUNT
BY AUBREY R. PARIS AND EMILY M. BLACK
(2023)

THE MIDAS TOUCH
BY GARY GROSSMAN
WITH CHARLES SEGARS AND OREN AVIV,
THE CREATORS OF *NATIONAL TREASURE*
(2026)

RILEY POOLE'S BOOK OF SECRETS

HISTORY FOR
NATIONAL TREASURE HUNTERS

AUBREY R. PARIS

TUCKER
 DS
PRESS

Cover by Aubrey R. Paris
Edited by David Bushman
Book design by Scott Ryan

Published in the USA by Tucker DS Press
Columbus, Ohio

Contact Information
Email: TuckerDSPress@gmail.com
Website: TuckerDSPress.com
Instagram: @fayettevillemafiapress

Library of Congress Control Number: 2025918927

To my parents

CONTENTS

–FOREWORD–

While spending years and years being told that *National Treasure* would never work, never get made, never make any money, I constantly heard the same things over and over.

"History is boring."

"No one cares about these things."

"People like World War II and Civil War stories, but everyone hates the Revolutionary War."

All I kept thinking after every rejection was that these criticisms were absolutely, 100 percent true, not because history was actually boring, but because everyone's history *teacher* was boring. If you had a crappy history teacher, of course you grew up to hate the subject. I can't tell you how many people rolled their eyes at the idea of making the movie *Titanic* for that same reason.

A good film or a good TV show can make any subject exciting. That's what's so great about movies and television: they turn the mundane into something fascinating or funny or exciting or romantic. And they do it by telling stories. They do it by humanizing the characters and making the subject matter have at least a tiny connection to *you*.

Movies we love that are heavy in history connect with us and hold our attention only if they make us care about the people who are making history. Or, in *National Treasure*'s case, care about the people who care about the people who are making history. And to care about them, we need to know what they want, why they are worthy of it, and who's getting in their way. The best way to do that is to tell a story in the present tense.

History books take place in the past; movies are always in the present. The "present" may be 800 BCE, World War II, or 1776, because the story is being told as if it is happening right before your eyes. And since it feels like it's happening as you watch, it also feels like the ending is undecided. When you sit in a boring history class, the ending can't change. In fact, history classes usually start with the ending and then tell you all the facts that got you there. Snore. Tell me a story!

This is where the fun of the conspiracy theory comes into play. A conspiracy theory exists to tell you that perhaps the ending is *not* set in stone. Perhaps you've got it all wrong, and as the saying goes, there's more to the story. It's the story that you're focused on; the story is still alive. Until the mystery is solved, the true end is always up for grabs.

For a guy like Riley Poole, the craziest conspiracy theories are his special domain that separates him from Ben Gates. While Ben knows all the real facts, Riley likes to think that he himself is the one with the greater knowledge, elevating his contribution and status on the treasure hunt. But that also means that Riley is us. We like feeling smart, even though we all know we're kind of dumb. Riley mentioning his belief that the aliens built the pyramids triggers our own response: "I saw a show about that! I know things too!" This makes us feel better when confronted by actual historians who really *do* know things—things that are often much more mundane than aliens.

Believing aliens built the pyramids makes us think we're smarter than the archaeologists. Believing all elections are rigged and that the Illuminati chooses the president makes us think we have greater wisdom than the press, the politicians, and, well, math. Riley likes feeling smarter than Ben because, frankly, Ben is really annoying! He knows so much and is right about everything. (Unless, of course, there's a *National Treasure 3* in which he is very, very wrong about something . . .)

The fact is, while alternative conclusions can be mysterious and fun, today we have completely destroyed and corrupted the idea of the "conspiracy theory." Now someone just makes stuff up, and other people find themselves believing any nonsense that comes their way so long as it's different from the "official" story. Those aren't conspiracy theories. Those are called lies, and they're meant to trick you, confuse you, or control you.

So stop believing the nonsense and become a detective—a historian.

If there really is more to the story, and you can prove it, then *that* is the story. Just remember that most conspiracy theories seem true because we *want* them to be true. We don't want reality to be boring, and we want to think we're smarter than everyone else. Well, you're not.

But Ben Gates is.

Jon Turteltaub
Producer and Director
National Treasure and *National Treasure: Book of Secrets*

–CHAPTER 1–
Motive and Opportunity

As an expert on Disney's *National Treasure* franchise, I've spent more time than I care to admit thinking about its storylines, puzzles, and characters. Throughout the course of my research, I've learned almost everything there is to know about the Nicolas Cage-fronted blockbusters.

For instance, I've discovered how story creators Charles Segars and Oren Aviv initially envisioned Will Smith in the lead role, and that at one point Disney offered the part to Julia Roberts. I've unearthed behind-the-scenes secrets, like how actors Sean Bean and David Dayan Fisher, who played two of the franchise's initial villains, furtively rung the Centennial Bell at Independence Hall while filming in the bell tower. I've helped members of the creative team remember and revisit elements of the films' plots that had been long forgotten.

But as hard as it is for me to believe, there was a time when receiving an Instagram direct message from *National Treasure* creatives reading "Did the President in *National Treasure 2* have a name?" was not on my bingo card of life. What started as a passion project (born out of the COVID-19 pandemic) has quickly turned into a second career of sorts, as *National Treasure* has functionally taken over my life. I wouldn't have it any other way.

For years now, my research on the franchise has been preserved in both podcast and book formats. Interviews I've conducted with director Jon Turteltaub and screenwriter Ted Elliott have been the source material for reports by global media outlets. I've covered a red-carpet premiere, essentially torturing the cast of 2022's *National Treasure: Edge of History* with deep, character-driven questions that they frankly should not have had to answer on a night of levity and celebration. (Catherine Zeta-Jones, a seasoned professional, effortlessly pivoted and answered her *preferred* question rather than my own.) The screenwriting and showrunning duo of Marianne and Cormac Wibberley have called me a historian of *National Treasure*; I like to think I've earned the title.

I suppose I share these anecdotes as a way of presenting my bona fides. I'm making a case for why I hope you'll buy into the thesis that has motivated much of my work related to this cult-classic franchise. Namely, *National Treasure* can be a strategic tool for galvanizing interest in American and world history, because—contrary to popular belief— the vast majority of the films' plotlines are inspired by actual people, places, and events from the past.

Don't believe me? As proof, I'll point to the fact that I've lectured about *National Treasure* at the US National Archives, Library of Congress, and President Lincoln's Cottage without mortally wounding the souls of the historians, archivists, and conservators on staff. Perhaps they would even agree with my longstanding opinion that a franchise so entrenched in history and with such potential for inspiring a love of history deserves its own history *book*.

Developing a history book for *National Treasure* Hunters, as I've affectionately dubbed fans of the franchise, makes even more sense when considering the creative team's goals for their films. Motivated in part by a desire to increase visitation at historical landmarks and museums, *National Treasure* embraces the concept of "edutainment": engaging audiences so creatively and effectively that they don't even realize they're learning something. Sneaky. Plus, story writers Segars and Aviv were captivated by the concept of ubiquitous treasure hunt clues that could be found in everyday life—whether that be your backyard or your back pocket. To pinpoint an example, look no further than the film's fictional treasure hunt clue preserved on the real one hundred dollar bill via an etching of Independence Hall's clock tower.

If you ask Turteltaub, he'll expand upon the nature of *National Treasure*'s edutainment value by speaking to the very source material referenced in the films. As a veteran director, he observed how action-adventure treasure hunt flicks typically take place outside of the United States, inadvertently implying to viewers that history is only interesting or exciting if it predates the United States. In helming *National*

Treasure, Turteltaub sought to overturn this assumption, proving that stories associated with America's founding and its subsequent years as a fledgling nation could inspire a compelling Hollywood treasure hunt in the same way that Egyptian, Roman, and other ancient civilizations regularly do.

But painting an intriguing picture using US history as a palette demands precision and care. After all, centering historical figures that students are tired of hearing about would be a recipe for boredom, but evoking completely *unknown* figures would elicit a similar lack of interest. Storywriters are handed an impossible task in trying to strike a balance.

Yet *National Treasure*'s creative team rose to the challenge. Instead of belaboring points about Thomas Jefferson, who famously drafted the Declaration of Independence, *National Treasure* opted to shed light on Charles Carroll of Carrollton, the document's last living signer. In lieu of another story about Benjamin Franklin's Poor Richard pseudonym, *National Treasure* made his lesser-known pen name, Silence Dogood, central to its plot. And in service of avoiding yet another tale about the well-known Oval Office, *National Treasure* made the Resolute desk, housed within, the star of the show when depicting the White House. Based on these examples and many more, we can define what *types* of history constitute "*National Treasure* history."

National Treasure history includes any story from the past that is missing from a stereotypical classroom setting. It consists of tales implicating famous figures and secrets whispered about historical events, most of which have been lost to time (or the recesses of the Internet). *National Treasure* finds a moment from a bygone era that's missing a single, defining puzzle piece, then takes the liberty of filling the blank in a way that appeals to intergenerational audiences.

What topics, then, would fill the pages of a *National Treasure* history book? Charles Carroll, Silence Dogood, and the Resolute desk are obvious answers, but the franchise already tells their stories shockingly well (as does my first book, *National Treasure Hunt: One Step Short of Crazy*, if I do say so myself). To prevent such redundancy, inspiration must be taken from elsewhere within the movies' well-worn scripts.

To author a book about history that is truly "*National Treasure*" in scope and style, a writer would do well to consider the second-most-famous text featured in the franchise itself: *The Templar Treasure and Other Myths That Are True* by fan-favorite character Riley Poole. Indeed, peering inside *this* book's pages would lend valuable insight into the types of historical moments the franchise holds dear. The only problem? *Templar Treasure* doesn't exist.

Riley purportedly wrote his book in the "offseason" between *National Treasure* (2004) and its sequel, *National Treasure: Book of Secrets* (2007). The text claims to tell the true stories underpinning myths, legends, and mysteries that have seeped into popular culture, and it conveniently offers key information to progress *Book of Secrets*'s hunt for Cibola, the lost city of gold. The film kindly informs viewers about the contents of precisely two chapters, but the remainder is itself a mystery. How poetic.

Luckily, I happen to believe that mysteries are meant to be solved (I was a murder mystery enthusiast long before venturing into the action-adventure genre). I strongly suspect that conducting a close read of Riley Poole, informed by his on-screen demeanor paired with little-known source material, will allow fans of the franchise to understand not just what motivates the character, but why. This information would surely offer hints about the types of historical topics Riley would choose to feature in his own book. And if we can successfully identify these hints, then we might just be able to write the definitive book on history for *National Treasure* Hunters.

–CHAPTER 2–

Who Is Riley Poole?

In my years of deep diving into the franchise, I've closely studied the intricacies and nuances of *National Treasure*'s key characters. If I'm honest, this hasn't been a terribly daunting task, since the principal cast is relatively small. Such studies have always left me impressed by the sheer *density* of the traits written for a character like Benjamin Franklin Gates, the franchise's hero. Viewers certainly don't know even a fraction of Ben's personal backstory, but every detail to which they are privy—from Ben's expertise in American history to his studies at the US Naval Diving and Salvage Training Center—is a piece in the puzzle of justifying how he can accomplish seemingly impossible treasure hunt tasks.

On the surface, when considering Ben's right-hand man, tech genius Riley Poole, viewers are treated to a similar lack of backstory. From a practical perspective, at least some information about Riley's employment history is necessary to convince a rapt audience that the character will be capable of accomplishing his many technical tricks. But a closer examination of Riley's demeanor and dialogue in certain scenes, paired with the outcomes of his publication journey in *National Treasure: Book of Secrets*, provides viewers substantially more insight into the quirks of this likable, familiar figure.

It's no accident that loyal viewers of *National Treasure* see themselves in Riley. Known for delivering quippy lines, Riley provides comic relief but was also written to serve as an audience stand-in. Recognizing that most audiences would find Ben's historical prowess and clue-cracking abilities unrelatable, and clocking the ridiculousness of his stated goals ("I'm going to steal the Declaration of Independence" comes to mind),

Riley was introduced to challenge the status quo—to challenge *Ben*. The result is just the right combination of skepticism ("You *are* gonna go to prison, you know that?"), realism ("It can't be done. Not that it *shouldn't* be done; it can't be done."), and pleading ("Let me prove it to you."). Once Ben has convinced Riley ("This might be possible."), the viewer buys in too.

This relatability is another reason why understanding the likely contents of Riley's book would be a great starting point for crafting a *National Treasure*-inspired history text: if Riley is representative of *National Treasure*'s audience, then his interests are likely to align with their own. So what do we know about Mr. Poole, what can we infer, and how might these details inform his choice of historical tidbits to include in his debut book?

When embarking on such a character analysis, one must first consider the available source material. In the case of *National Treasure*, we have at our disposal the movies themselves as well as final filming scripts, previous drafts (when they do not conflict with the final on-screen product), one novelization (for *Book of Secrets*), and exactly four little-known prequel books. Since 2022, we also have the fourth episode of the short-lived Disney Plus streamer series *National Treasure: Edge of History*, which reintroduced audiences to a present-day version of Riley Poole.

Right off the bat, I feel confident in asserting that prior to his pursuit of the Templar treasure, Riley would not have considered himself a particularly adventurous person. As Ben points out in the bowels of the *Charlotte*, Riley handles stumbling upon the skeletons of the ship's ill-fated crew poorly. True to function, his startled reaction is that of an innocent bystander, such as the movie's viewer, but this grisly find is not exactly unexpected given the context within which Riley is operating (i.e., on a long-lost ship frozen in the Arctic). Riley's willingness to push himself and take on such an adventurous task—something so out of character—means he is strongly motivated by *something*. Before considering the obvious motivation, let's examine the less obvious.

Many *National Treasure* fans—and even Riley himself—would be surprised to learn that adventure is figuratively encoded in the character's DNA. According to the *Gates Family Mystery Series* of prequel books, authored by Catherine Hapka, Riley's exploration gene traces back to the first members of the Poole family who settled in America. In the late 1700s, a young Franklin Poole and his father immigrated from Ireland to the East Coast of the nascent United States. The elder Poole found a job building a little structure that would later come to be known as the White House. But the job would prove perilous, as he was struck and killed by a falling stone during construction, leaving Franklin orphaned. On his own in an unfamiliar land, the boy saved up for a one-way ticket to Pittsburgh.

Another fact that may surprise audiences is that the Poole and Gates families have been intertwined for more than two centuries. The prequel series establishes the lore that Franklin Poole befriended Adam Benjamin Gates and his twin sister Ellie in Pittsburgh in 1804. Thick as thieves, the trio spent years following the expedition of Meriwether Lewis and William Clark in search of a northwest passage to the Pacific, following a treasure map along the way. Their search uncovered a handful of sentimental family heirlooms and trinkets dating back to the lost Roanoke colony.

The prequel series shares that adult Franklin Poole moved to New York City, where he raised his son Seamus. As a kid, Seamus seemed like someone Riley Poole would have befriended, since he was fascinated by secret societies and the conspiracy theories surrounding them. In 1848, a teenage Seamus joined James Monroe Gates, Adam's son, on a trek west in pursuit of riches during the California Gold Rush. Not only did the pair find plenty of gold in the so-called Golden State, but the young men opted to settle there permanently. It turns out that like adventure, treasure hunting is buried deep in the recesses of Riley Poole's DNA.

But I don't think Riley always knew about this hobby of his ancestors; otherwise he probably would have been diving deep into history and searching for treasures his entire life. In fact—and this might be controversial—I'd wager that a school-aged Riley Poole was *really* bad at his history classes.

Consider his dismissiveness even after participating and succeeding in the Templar treasure quest: "Someone did something in history and had fun. Great. Wonderful." Riley clearly finds the concept of learning about old men sitting in old rooms arguing over old words written on old parchment—in other words, the drafting of the Declaration of Independence—unstimulating. I could literally imagine him critiquing the entire vibe of the dawn of America in July 1776 as reeking of sweat and horse manure, a statement that contains all the sarcasm and snark of a characteristic Riley line delivered by actor Justin Bartha.

Of course, for young students, an unstimulating learning environment often translates to classroom challenges. Maybe, as a result, Riley risked failing his courses focused on bygone eras of the pre-1900s. If I had to predict the only "traditional" history class topics to resonate with young Riley, I'd put my money on pirates (because of treasure, obviously), ancient dynasties (because of luxury, obviously), and World War II (because of the attendant Nazi gold legends, *obviously*).

But we must tread lightly when analyzing Riley's academic past, since the events of *National Treasure* prove without a shadow of a doubt that our sidekick character is something of a tech genius. How often have you witnessed a student gravitating toward one subject and detesting subjects that seem to be its opposite? It doesn't seem like a stretch to surmise that a history-disinclined Riley would have a particular proclivity for science, technology, engineering, and mathematics (the "STEM" fields). STEM subjects would hone his puzzle-solving skills— just not the type of *historical* puzzles he'd encounter later in life. To put it bluntly, while Riley probably couldn't tell you the fourth or the seventh presidents to save his life, he could likely rattle off forty-seven digits of pi without batting an eye.

If Riley was as technologically gifted in youth as he proves to be during the timeline of *National Treasure*, he was probably considered the "smart one" in school. Based on his desire to partake in *rewarding* teamwork as an adult, fellow students likely clamored to be paired with him on science fair projects but never remembered him when doling out invites to the weekend's hottest parties. It was perhaps this lack of popularity that prompted Riley to develop his typical sarcastic, snarky humor—primarily targeted at others—as a social coping mechanism.

As such, Riley could have conceivably viewed college as an opportunity to start anew. He could rebuild his image as the guy who was too cool for school and excel without even trying. I like to think Riley majored in computer science, a field with classes he could pass in his sleep, because he was no longer eager for an academic challenge but rather a social one. Maybe he wanted to land a girlfriend using some combination of his trademark humor and the promise of a lucrative information technology job after graduation. The latter would serve him on multiple levels; we know beyond a shadow of a doubt ("Why can't they just say . . . 'here's the treasure, spend it wisely'?") that Riley enjoys the idea of being well-off financially.

But would this have been enough for Riley? If he struggled in high school classes that he found topically boring, would *unchallenging* classes—a different kind of unstimulating—be any easier to withstand? I suspect he would have quickly realized his mistake, finding basic computer science coursework just as boring and unstimulating as learning about Thomas Jefferson's early drafts of the Declaration of Independence. I can envision him sitting in class and longing to conquer a particularly difficult Sudoku or master a new Rubik's cube. Fresh out of academic inspiration, he might have discovered a newfound joy (and an intriguing way to merge his passions) in a turn-of-the-century phenomenon known as Y2K.

Disclaimer: this is entirely my own personal theory, but I do believe it tracks. Based on Riley's age in *National Treasure*, Y2K could have been his first exposure to the world of conspiracy theories, especially given its technological ties. There he was, a brilliant, impressionable young adult studying computer science and preparing for a job in IT, and society at large was losing its collective mind over the impending end of the world to be caused by his chosen field. I'm sure the public's fears sounded ridiculous to tech-minded Riley, but it would be hard for him to deny (and probably equally hard to stop thinking about) the chokehold the Y2K threat seemed to have on people from all walks of life. Y2K captured imaginations in unimaginable ways.

This could have easily been a formative experience that ultimately led Riley to develop his well-known fascination with conspiracy theories and superstitions. Y2K may have propelled Riley down a rabbit hole of learning everything he could about myths and legends, quenching a newfound thirst for understanding the unexplained. What a convenient source of stimulation this would have been to quash the tediousness stemming from an academic discipline he once loved, especially given the sheer breadth of conspiracies available for study. Seamus Poole would have been proud.

Based on previous script drafts, we know that after graduation, Riley was bored to tears *again* working a nine-to-five desk job out of a windowless cubicle at Intel—probably the job of his dreams according to the outdated goals of his youth. So when a strange man by the even stranger name of Benjamin Franklin Gates and his rich friend Ian Howe waltzed into headquarters (that's how I picture the scene, anyway) and asked to speak to Riley, a lowly analyst, he probably picked his head up off the desk, wiped the drool off his chin, and took the meeting. Such a setup sounds like the stuff urban legends are made of, so he could hardly pass up the opportunity.

National Treasure canon states that Ben "found" Riley in this job, so the two soon-to-be teammates couldn't have known each other previously. Perhaps Riley had read a bit about the legends associated with the Knights Templar and Freemasons thanks to his personal research, but Ben likely would have been the one to clue him into the Gates-led, centuries-old hunt for the Templar treasure. Maybe Ben shared stories of great Gates-Poole duos of history that had been passed down in his family for generations. I personally like to think Ben tracked Riley down *because* of these stories—and what a pleasant surprise it must have been for Ben to discover that his contemporary was a techie, the exact role he needed filled for his hunt.

And with that, Riley was offered the perfect career pivot at the perfect time. Quitting his corporate job would give him the chance to investigate a real-life legend by applying his real-life talents. Since his new partner was a history whiz, Riley probably believed he wouldn't need to think about his least favorite subject very much. Plus, Ben and his family had already done so much work pursuing the Templar treasure that it was only a matter of time until they found it; Riley would contribute minimal work and still rake in a ton of cash. Perhaps he'd gain some fame to boot.

We all know what happened next. Riley packed his bags and moved to Washington, D.C., to join the treasure-hunting team. Ben solved the history puzzles, Riley solved the tech puzzles, and Ian wrote check after check. Ben didn't care about the legends and myths that Riley held dear, and we are led to believe Riley cared equally little about the historical facts around which their hunt revolved. The two intellectuals were perfect complements to each other, probably spending many days doing their respective research in the hallowed halls of the Library of Congress.

Did Riley need to develop any new skills during the hunt? I'm sure his myriad tech capabilities were already established at Intel and back in college, but they may have been rusty from disuse, or he may have needed to apply them in new ways. For example, I can't imagine Riley had much relevant experience when he was tasked with geolocating an old ship lost somewhere in the frozen tundra of Canada, requiring him to craft tracking models with GPS coordinates and meteorological data. Throughout the treasure hunt, Riley would end up flexing numerous technical muscles: tapping security feeds, developing surveillance software, disabling alarm systems, and hacking a database or two.

Since all of that is super illegal and Riley is a pragmatist, he must have either been *that* bored in his corporate job or he was convinced by Ben that doing the wrong thing for the right reasons—the franchise's calling card—was not just morally sound, but legally sound as well. While this idea is by no means guaranteed in the real world, *National Treasure* validates the concept when the FBI lets Riley off scot-free after the Templar treasure is secured.

Through all his renegade, white-hat hacker appearances in the franchise, Riley proves that regular Joes with unique interests can save the day. Like Ben, he demonstrates that "geeks" and "nerds" can be not only cool, but wholly aspirational. His role in discovering the Templar treasure was more than just doing something clever with a computer; it was also to bring his teammates back to reality by verbalizing the questions they were all thinking but too afraid to voice. In a sea of fearless optimists, Riley was risk averse, a critical characteristic when pursuing treasures concealed beneath rickety wooden beams decimated by centuries of termite damage. He may have developed that characteristic as a cog in a corporate wheel, but because it has saved his life a time or two since meeting Ben, Riley likely owes Intel a hearty thanks.

Ultimately, our heroes find their treasure and live to tell the tale, an event Riley ultimately commemorates by writing his first book, *The Templar Treasure and Other Myths That Are True*. His authorship indicates that in addition to being monetarily motivated, he is at least somewhat fame driven (and disappointed in the *lack* of fame he has earned as evidenced by a *lack* of a line at his Borders bookstore display). After all, Riley is meant to represent a typical audience member to whom wealth and fame would seem, if not actively attractive, at least somewhat intriguing.

But much like your average moviegoer, Riley is more than surface-level superficiality. Thanks to our deep read of his character, I envision

Riley's book as an homage to the historical legends that got him through his moments of boredom and ultimately changed his life. After all, in his pursuit of the Templar treasure, Riley learned how to truly appreciate history—the subject that was once the bane of his existence. The second he laid eyes on the Templar treasure and watched dozens of sarcophagi, coats of armor, paintings, and statues appear in the light thrown by his torch, he discovered that nothing makes history more interesting than proving it to be true.

According to *National Treasure*, everyone in the respected historical community vowed the Templar treasure was a legend. A myth. Something believed in by only the superstitious. But in this one case, Riley and his team proved the naysayers wrong, capturing the imaginations of millions of film fans of all ages and walks of life. With imagination comes the determination to pursue lesser-known stories, seek evidence, and have adventures that encourage those existing in the present to engage with the past. Imagination makes history come to life in the tales that live forever.

So, to return to our initial question, what topics would fill the pages of a *National Treasure* history book? The answer is simple, really. The topics would need to meet the incredibly high bar of piquing the historical interests of Riley Poole. The book would examine mysteries obscured by time while scrutinizing what we know and—importantly—what we don't. And since said book would be an homage to a franchise well-known for inspiring mass interest in very real yet lesser-known people, places, and events from the America of yore, it would be less focused on *actual* conspiracies and more dedicated to stories that *sound* like conspiracies if you'd never heard of them before. In short, it would probably look a lot like *The Templar Treasure and Other Myths That Are True.*

What follows is an unauthorized *National Treasure* history textbook that I think Riley would have been eager to learn from—one that would have transported him out of Independence Hall's Assembly Room in 1776 and onto a ship navigating the coastline of North Carolina's barrier islands at the beginning of the American story. Or a campsite on the day the Corps of Discovery happened upon its first prairie dog. Or an unassuming cabin during some of the most decisive peace talks in world history. It's a book that dedicates whole chapters to topics that most history classrooms gloss over with a single bullet point in a slideshow, and it considers those topics holistically by weaving together moments of science, literature, culture, and controversy. And if you close your eyes, you might even be able to imagine Riley's voice bringing life to the words on the page.

A Brief Guide to the Reader

The following "textbook" is—I hope—unlike any you've learned from before. For chapters whose topics are new to you, my goal is for you to enjoy a glimpse into a niche, little-known past. For those that already ring a bell, I invite you to think about the latest interpretations of their attendant mysteries—and their often surprising social or cultural implications. Regardless of the subject, I think you'll find yourself considering history in new ways when presented with complementary context from science, literature, pop culture, and more.

Each chapter is divided into two sections. The section titled "Hunt Down That History," an homage to Ben Gates's earnest plea to Dr. Abigail Chase in her office at the National Archives, aims to make clear the definitive story of the topic at hand. These are the facts as they are currently known to historians, archaeologists, and the public. The second section, "Listen to Riley," addresses the mystery or intrigue associated with the chapter's theme, summarizing our present-day understanding and inviting you, the reader, to draw your own conclusions. Based on this information, how would you go about furthering the hunt?

Chapters also include text boxes that relate the subject matter to our character-based inspiration for this book: Mr. Riley Poole. Consider why Riley might be curious about the chapter's theme, pinpoint his favorite (often surprising) historical detail, and hypothesize how the topic could fit into Riley's future treasure-hunting pursuits (read: *National Treasure 3* plot ideas).

I hope you discover inspiration in these historical mysteries. You might just find that you have more in common with Riley than you ever imagined.

Chapter 3

The Templar Treasure

What makes a story a legend? I'd say that legends are tales passed down over centuries, generations, or at least a handful of years. They are considered by many to be incontrovertibly true, but they have not been (or cannot be) validated. Yet no matter the length of time a legend has existed, or how much verifiable fact underpins its existence, all legends tend to have one thing in common: their story has been popularized. Legends are people, places, things, or events that are famous—perhaps even infamous—and I daresay some amount of mystery or intrigue inevitably surrounds them.

Not all legends are created equally. Some are more compelling than others, blessed with the good fortune of their tales being shared by well-known storytellers, virtually ensuring their persistence through time. Some are at least inspired by—if not entirely based in—provable historical reality, while others are colored by religious context or peppered with supernatural explanations. Some legends have drawn substantial attention and, as a result, have been more thoroughly investigated. Some have spawned books, movies, entire TV series...If I didn't know any better, I'd think "investigating legends" was its own media genre these days; there are still entire channels dedicated to the premise in these dying days of network television.

But in my humble opinion, what makes a compelling legend is the perfect ratio of fact and fiction. A legend whose premise is entirely factual, such that you can hardly deny at least the origins of its story, is bound to persist. I also believe physical evidence should exist to support a particularly potent legend, but that evidence must never fully explain the story. The evidence must be incomplete, or it might *seem* complete, until the end of the story and then *BAM*; just as the legend reaches its conclusion, that final piece of the puzzle is missing. There's just enough intrigue to ensure audiences cannot dismiss the story outright, for that would require throwing cold, hard facts out the window. Yet that same audience cannot in good faith accept the legend as entirely true, since that would deny the obvious—the unshakable feeling that things simply don't add up.

Based on this description of a compelling legend, the Templar treasure can surely be considered one of the greats. I may be biased, but the Templar has all the key ingredients: a centuries-long shelf life, plenty of historical premise, and a long list of explorers who have tracked every possible lead in an attempt to finally solve the mystery. But when it comes to a legend as longstanding and grandiose as this one, it can be challenging to separate myth from fact and speculation from reality. All at once, the Templar treasure is Schrödinger's cat—both existent and nonexistent at the same time—unless, of course, one knows where to look.

> **Why Riley Would Care:** As someone who can't quite compete with his fellow treasure protectors' historical prowess, Riley would be keen to establish his authority on a subject with which he has firsthand experience.

HUNT DOWN THAT HISTORY

If we are to believe it, the story of the Templar treasure begins nearly one thousand years ago at the advent of the First Crusade. The Holy Land was under Muslim control, and Pope Urban II was frankly not having it. He instructed western Europeans to venture to the Holy Land and seize control of the region, and they ultimately succeeded. Christian crusaders led by Godfrey of Bouillon took Jerusalem in 1099, opening the proverbial doors to western Europeans who sought to make the long trek to pay the Holy Land a visit. Enter the Poor Fellow-Soldiers of Christ and the Temple of Solomon, a group that would eventually be remembered in history by a much shorter moniker: the Knights Templar.

The Knights Templar organization was established around 1118 or 1119 by Hugues de Payens, a French knight who opted out of returning to his homeland following the First Crusade. Instead, he stayed in the Holy Land and began practicing as a monk. To best serve Christianity, de Payens proposed that he and his fellow monks become personal security guards for Christian worshippers—after all, these monks had been crusaders who were trained for battle, making them well-versed in the protective practices of the day. To this end, de Payens suggested formally establishing a group of soldiers tasked with ensuring European pilgrims to the Holy Land met no harm during their 7,500-mile, multiyear journey, which included passage through Muslim-controlled territories and a route that was rife with robbers.

De Payens's idea was met with enthusiasm by Jerusalem's ruler, Baldwin II, who officially established the Knights Templar with nine men (including de Payens himself). The group was given refuge in Jerusalem on the Temple Mount near the Al-Aqsa Mosque, a structure that had been captured during the crusade. At the time, the crusaders believed this location was synonymous with the ruins of the Temple of Solomon, which, in its heyday, was thought to house the Ark of the Covenant, relics from Jesus's lifetime, and, by some accounts, the presence of God.

Beyond its religious implications, the Temple of Solomon was purportedly the hiding place of King Solomon's robust treasure. But the temple was pillaged in the sixth century BCE, rebuilt in the first century, and destroyed once more in 70 CE. The eventual presence of the Knights Templar spawned a breeding ground for new legends, most of which were associated with the organization's abrupt and, by some interpretations, *mysterious* accumulation of wealth. More on that later.

The Knights Templar existed for around a decade before its role—and accumulation of riches—became clear. Around 1129, the group received formal written support from French Abbot Bernard of Clairvaux. Apparently, "street cred" was a thing back in the twelfth century, and Bernard's backing lent the Knights Templar a newfound, positive reputation as warrior monks who won coveted endorsement from the Catholic Church during the term of Pope Honorius II. Another decade later, in 1139, Pope Innocent II issued a papal bull that granted the Knights Templar additional rights. The Catholic Church effectively gave the order a formal go-ahead to recruit more members, raise funds, and use military tactics to preserve the Christian states in and around the Holy Land.

But that wasn't all the church's support allowed. The Knights Templar would be exempt from paying taxes, could not be pursued or prosecuted by state institutions, and would be held accountable only to the pope himself. They were also given the right to select their own priests and grand master. Under circumstances like these, it's no wonder that some outsiders viewed the Knights Templar with raised eyebrows, sharing rumors and stories about the organization's activities and status.

The Knights Templar soon got to work defending Christians' occupation of the Holy Land. On the battlefield, members of the order were said to be unyieldingly brave. When captured by their religious rivals, they adamantly refused to convert to Islam, typically resulting in their execution. During combat, they were not permitted to retreat unless the odds were overwhelmingly stacked against them. These characteristics are some of the reasons why history has largely remembered the Knights Templar with a martyr-like legacy, but as is often the case, this recollection is overly simplistic. To be fair, it should be noted that the Knights Templar could be almost vicious in battle and were frequent purveyors of raids.

But who were the men (*never* women) of the Knights Templar? The order's symbol, two knights riding a single horse, lends some insight into how they hoped to be perceived. At its core, the Knights Templar operated under monastic rule, which required members to commit to a life of poverty, chastity, and obedience. They were not permitted to drink, gamble, or swear, but they were permitted—required, really—to engage in thorough prayer, with emphasis on the Virgin Mary.

The Templars' lengthy code of conduct was formalized in a text called *The Rule of the Templars*, which encompassed what members could wear, how they should eat (in addition to *what* they should eat), guidelines governing sleeping patterns, rules of engagement for battle, how to travel and behave in public, what they were (and were not) allowed to own, conditions for their leisure activities, and more. The first draft of *The Rule*, written in 1129, included sixty-eight individual mandates, but the list expanded over time as the wealth and size of the organization grew. The final version contains hundreds of rules, including portions that describe how members should be punished for failing to comply. These consequences ranged from corporal punishment to expulsion from the order.

To fully grasp the nature of the Templars' code of conduct, we must examine a few examples of strict guidelines governing day-to-day activities. For starters, members were permitted to eat meat only a few times per week because meat consumption—or "flesh" consumption, per *The Rule*—was believed to corrupt the human body. While on the topic of eating, those facing punishment were forced to take meals on the ground. In the garment category, Templars' clothes could only be white, black, or brown in color, and their shoes could not be pointed or laced. A shocking number of mundane, daily tasks, including bathing and taking medicine, required explicit permission, while other activities, like playing games, were expressly forbidden. Permission was also required for individual Templars to keep their own money or purchase goods.

Interpersonal relationships were strictly monitored, as members could not embrace women, including their female relatives. Naturally, misogyny was plenty ripe in these early years, as women were seen as "[leading] many from the straight path to Paradise." Perhaps unsurprisingly, Templars were also prohibited from having children and were encouraged *not* to take on the role of a godfather! (Yes, that recommendation was explicitly noted.)

The Knights Templar were *not* allowed to do, frankly, most things. The time they spent not doing those things was instead dedicated to attending mass and praying as well as practicing their combat skills and tending to their horses. While they were influential in the military sphere, the Templars had no control over broader military policy. Their own policy was set and executed by a grand master, who governed for the duration of his life, alongside a cadre of commanders scattered throughout Europe and operating from outposts known as "commanderies" (read: monasteries). In and around Jerusalem, the Knights Templar lived in fortresses.

Despite their strict rules and regulations, the Knights Templar weren't a terribly exclusive group; any man could choose to join, regardless of his preexisting wealth. Those who joined as aristocrats were deemed part of the knight class, while poorer members made up the sergeant class. If you thought joining the organization and committing to a life of poverty would make the aristocratic and poor members indistinguishable, think again. Members of the knight class wore white coats adorned with red crosses (symbolizing purity and chastity), while sergeants sported simple black habits.

After the Knights Templar gained credibility thanks to Bernard of Clairvaux's stamp of approval, the order began receiving money and land from wealthy, religious patrons, though it also collected riches when defeating adversaries in battle. These funds were used to facilitate the Templars' military training, stock their equipment, and send them to the Holy Land. But the money also allowed the Knights Templar to build and maintain massive structures, like castles and churches, as well as hire local support soldiers, provide transport services to pilgrims, and donate to charity. Soon, the Knights Templar began using commanderies as branch offices to manage, facilitate, and centralize these new functions.

As you might have guessed, while the individual knights were poor as a rule, the organization was soon rolling in cash. Commanderies housed individual treasuries—tapped to provide loans to European monarchs—and operated the medieval equivalent of safe deposit boxes. Many pilgrims to the Holy Land gave their money to the Knights Templar for safekeeping. In return, the commandery issued the pilgrim a letter of credit that could be given to a different commandery located further along their route, allowing them to withdraw their money. Some believe these letters of credit contained ciphers to confirm authenticity. However the Knights Templar managed to prevent fraud, the efficacy of their system and quantity of their holdings became the envy of secular rulers.

Like any good legendary organization, the Knights Templar had a bona fide rival: the Knights Hospitaller (later known as the Knights of Malta), which provided hospitals for pilgrims. Also like any good legendary organization, the Knights Templar eventually encountered a series of trials and tribulations. By the late 1100s, the Muslims had taken Jerusalem, requiring the Knights Templar to relocate numerous times. Once Acre fell in 1291, the Muslims had regained control of the Holy Land in full, so the Templars became obsolete: they had been established to protect the Holy Land's Christian states, which no longer existed. The order returned to Europe and, by 1303, headquartered itself in Paris.

What purpose did the Knights Templar have anymore? Many Europeans began asking this very question, especially as the idea of conducting military operations in the Holy Land fell out of favor. Not one to miss his moment, France's King Philip IV saw growing skepticism of the Knights Templar as a grand opportunity. By some accounts King Philip IV was dangerously in debt to the Templars (as one of their banking clients), while others claim he thought the order was growing too powerful, wealthy, and therefore threatening. The king also found himself in a battle of wits with the Templars' papal supporters. Regardless of his primary motivation, King Philip IV wanted to bring an end to the Knights Templar, and social conditions were ripe for him to act.

The king had gotten wind of some pretty serious accusations against the Knights Templar, which ranged from spitting on the cross to worshipping cats to conducting fraudulent business activities. These and other supposed actions were considered immoral at best—heretical at worst—which begs the question of where King Philip IV had gotten his intel. Supposedly, a prisoner named Esquieu de Floyran had heard the scandalous stories from his cellmate, a former Templar, and the rumors spread like wildfire. King Philip IV wasn't the only one who caught wind of them; the pope did too.

But the French king chose not to wait for the conclusion of the papacy's formal investigation, and on Friday the 13th in the year 1307 (October, for those keeping track), King Philip IV arrested all the Knights Templar in his country. Once apprehended, the prisoners were tortured to elicit false confessions corroborating the many allegations against them. What followed was the systematic suppression of the Knights Templar throughout Europe, with Pope Clement V prohibiting the organization from operating in Christian states in 1312. All assets and properties of the Knights Templar were given to the rival Knights Hospitaller (which is a major burn, if I do say so myself), though some believe King Philip IV and England's King Edward II might have kept some of the wealth themselves.

> **Riley's Favorite Fact (Probably):** The Knights Templar organization met its demise on Friday the 13th in the year 1307, which could make the group's fate one of the earliest known examples of this unlucky superstition.

You may be wondering what happened to the imprisoned former Templars, particularly those who confessed to crimes under duress. As was often the case in tales of historical heresy, many were burned at the stake. Some were permitted to retire to monastic life, while others escaped. At least one became a pirate, because why not? In March 1314, the last Templar grand master, Jacques de Molay, continued to proclaim the order's innocence as he was burned at the stake, an event that marked both a formal and symbolic end to the Knights Templar.

LISTEN TO RILEY

In more recent times, the Catholic Church has admitted its yearslong persecution of the Knights Templar was unwarranted, asserting that Pope Clement V ultimately disbanded the organization because he faced pressure from European monarchs. In the early 2000s, historians uncovered evidence that Pope Clement V had absolved Grand Master Jacques de Molay and other Templar leaders of the religious charges for which they had been found guilty.

Despite the formal dissolution of the Knights Templar, theories of their perpetual existence have swirled for centuries. In the 1700s, for instance, the Freemasons and other organizations seemed to revive many symbols and traditions formerly associated with the Templars, even though these newer organizations are not directly descended from the monastic order. Even today, many people from around the world belong to associations that purport to live by key Templar values.

Another question continuously surrounding the Knights Templar is what became of the organization's riches. After all, the vast monetary wealth and properties the Templars managed from their outposts could certainly be considered treasure worthy. Of course, after their disbandment, the Templars were formally required to hand their assets over to other organizations, but it is unclear how much monetary wealth remained with the Knights Templar by the time King Philip IV called for the arrest of their French members on that unlucky Friday. At the time, some believed the Templars had been tipped off or warned of the impending arrests, leading them to make plans to smuggle their money out of the country. According to legend, this "treasure" was loaded onto ships at the French port of La Rochelle, or perhaps somewhere along the Seine River.

This story was fueled by the account of a Templar named Jean de Chalon during an interrogation. According to de Chalon's testimony, Gérard de Villiers, a regional Templar commander, had managed a caravan of fifty horses hauling cargo out of Paris around the time of King Philip IV's Templar persecution in 1307. Allegedly, de Villiers loaded the cargo onto eighteen ships, which swiftly sailed out to sea.

The record of de Chalon's testimony, written in Latin, reveals that he was not actually an eyewitness of the ships; he had heard about them secondhand. His account also did not mention the commonly cited port of La Rochelle, so it is unclear when and why this harbor became attached to the story. Some have speculated that because the Knights Templar had a known presence in La Rochelle, it would be logical to assume this was the location from which de Villiers's supposed ships departed. Yet others argue that if the ships were indeed meant to surreptitiously smuggle wealth out of the country, it would have been ill-advised to use a known Templar outpost to conduct the covert operation.

Then there's the question of whether observers of history should believe de Chalon's account at all, because his purpose for testifying was to lend credence to the Templars' alleged corruption. Whether completely true, completely false, somewhat exaggerated, or somewhere in between, the story he shared certainly supported his goal. Either way, we'd probably consider him an unreliable narrator by today's standards.

For completeness, allow us to consider the possibility that ships containing the Templars' material possessions really *did* depart French soil in 1307. Where could they have gone? Plenty of theorists propose that the ships docked at least temporarily elsewhere in Europe, such as Malta or Portugal, while others suggest they continued to North America. But maybe the Templars' wealth never left France at all. Another idea purports that the treasure was stashed at Rennes-le-Château and found by François-Bérenger Saunière in the late 1800s. Saunière was a local Catholic priest who came into sudden wealth, which could only be explained by outsiders as the result of him stumbling upon the Templar treasure hidden somewhere in his village.

As society has become increasingly fascinated with "secret societies," hobbyists have increasingly suggested that the location of the Templars' wealth isn't a secret at all. These theorists believe the treasure's location is known to the Freemasons, other modern fraternal organizations, or even orders to whom assets had been formally granted following the dissolution of the Knights Templar. When it comes to stories that exist somewhere on the spectrum between legend and conspiracy theory, this is where the real fun begins for people whose historical interests align with Riley Poole's.

One order that received physical remnants of the Knights Templar was the Portuguese Order of Christ. Prince Henry the Navigator, made famous for his role in European westward exploration in the early 1400s, would eventually become a member. One niche theory suggests that a surviving member of the Knights Templar—or a descendant of one—informed Prince Henry of the existence of the Americas since the Templars had already hidden their wealth there. In this version of events, Christopher Columbus didn't *really* make a mistake when he sailed the ocean blue and "discovered" America in 1492; he knew where he was heading all along.

A related theory claims Scotland's Henry Sinclair, Earl of Orkney and rumored Templar associate, led an expedition to Greenland and North America way back in the 1300s. And yet another iteration suggests that the treasure-smuggling Templar ships took refuge in Scotland until they could proceed to Iceland, then Greenland, then Canada. This story would also imply that the Knights Templar preceded Columbus in North America. If any version of this theory holds, Columbus was anywhere between fifty and one hundred years late to the party.

> **Riley's Next Hunt:** Riley already found the Templar treasure, of course, but he might still be enticed by the theory that European treasures predated Columbus in the Americas. Implied connections between US and world history would make this hunt a bona fide candidate for inclusion in future installments of the *National Treasure* franchise.

It is worth considering where the Knights Templar may have docked if they really did reach North America. One of the most popular hypotheses states that their treasure is hidden on Oak Island off the coast of Nova Scotia. According to local legend, Daniel McGinnis, the first known settler of Oak Island, found a suspicious ditch while he was searching for suitable farmland in 1700. This prompted a treasure hunt that is, to some extent, ongoing to this day. An old, somewhat hidden pit characterized by neatly constructed shafts at repeating ten-foot intervals was soon found on the island. This discovery makes clear the need to emphasize the word "known" when describing McGinnis as Oak Island's "first known settler," as someone else had clearly constructed the pit on the island sometime earlier. Who that person was, what they were doing, and both when and why they were doing it remain a mystery.

That hasn't prevented treasure hunters, who assume the pit was built to hide something like the Templar treasure, from trying to answer those very questions. Exorbitant investments have been poured into the pit (figuratively speaking) in an attempt to (unsuccessfully) reach its bottom, earning the site a moniker of the "money pit." But the pit's exploration has been far from fun and games. Some people who have pursued its depths have died in the process, prompting yet another local legend—or perhaps superstition—aptly dubbed "the curse of Oak Island."

Theories like these are certainly intriguing, but they rest on numerous assumptions that can be investigated by consulting historical fact. For instance, the Knights Templar secreting away their wealth by water would require the organization to have had ships. It turns out the Knights Templar were known to rent merchant ships (plus their captains and crews) when needed, typically for sending knights, pilgrims, horses, and supplies to the Christian states in the Holy Land. If necessary, these merchant ships would be commandeered as warships in times of battle.

For maritime transit purposes, the Knights Templar frequently departed from ports in Marseilles, France, and Barcelona, Spain, ultimately disembarking in Acre, Israel. They used the port at La Rochelle as a hub for the shipment of wine and other salable products, which was a Knights Templar side hustle. And despite its frequent status as a ship renter, the order owned at least a handful of its own vessels, as evidenced by paintings at Templar churches and written records cataloguing their battles at sea. While the exact number of ships they owned remains contested, at least some students of the order believe the Templars may have owned quite the sizable convoy in their heyday.

One interesting story about this fleet involves a ship dubbed the *Falcon*. The *Falcon* was captained by a Templar named Roger de Flor, who had risen in the ranks following his humble start as an onboard apprentice. De Flor was skilled at raiding adversarial ships, and he gave most of his raiding profits to the Knights Templar. Eventually, however, the order became suspicious that de Flor was not passing along a fair share of his spoils, so they moved to arrest the sketchy captain. Instead of going quietly into the night, de Flor resisted arrest by opting out of the organization entirely and eventually establishing an infamous band of mercenaries, the Catalan Company.

Despite our best efforts to prove the possible veracity of Jean de Chalon's secondhand (or thirdhand) account of ships disappearing with Templar wealth, and our consideration of the prevailing theories regarding said wealth's possible location, we reach an impasse. Historians tend to agree the Templars never possessed a "treasure" in the pop culture sense of the word, even though the mythical Templar treasure is one of the most longstanding and famous legends propelling the long-disbanded organization into our modern-day consciousness. But there is simply no definitive evidence in support of a Hollywood-style treasure having ever existed.

The origins of the Templar treasure legend are actually not very mysterious. When the Knights Templar were first granted refuge on the Temple Mount, and for about a decade thereafter, the order went quiet, failing even to complete its assigned responsibility of protecting European pilgrims to the Holy Land. This led some people to suspect the Knights Templar were quietly searching the Temple Mount—particularly the area under the stables that once housed King Solomon's horses—for the ancient ruler's lost treasure. And while modern historians agree that the order's seemingly sudden wealth was the result of a chain reaction—beginning with Bernard of Clairvaux's vocal support and ending with the establishment of a sophisticated banking and loan system—it was easy (and tantalizing) for outsiders to chalk up the organization's monetary holdings to the secret discovery of treasure.

But historical facts don't always make for the most compelling story. That's why, for years, individuals have speculated about what the contents of a mysterious Templar treasure could look like (because isn't it more fun to create legends than quash them?). Speculations have been informed by archaeological excavations on the Temple Mount, which began during the Victorian era and unearthed numerous Templar artifacts, including a sword and cross. Objects most commonly asserted to be part of a mythical treasure include the Holy Grail (the ancient dishware from which Jesus drank at the Last Supper), the Ark of the Covenant (a chest containing tablet-etched versions of the Ten Commandments), pieces of the cross on which Jesus was crucified, and the Shroud of Turin (a cloth believed to have enrobed Jesus's body after his crucifixion).

Yet not all proposed treasure components are religious in nature, and every time a Templar-era artifact is discovered, a new wave of theories bursts forth—reigniting the fire of a legend that can't seem to be stamped out. In particular, one modern collector, Hamilton White, has made headlines for his decade-long search for—and alleged discovery of—lost Templar relics.

White claims to have compiled more than one hundred artifacts of the Knights Templar that date back to the organization's peak in the 1200s. Put another way, this is more than $130 million worth of relics—a treasure indeed—and what makes them *invaluable* is what they might tell us about the culture of the order, including who these men were, how they worshipped, and more. Given that White would probably be an inspirational figure for someone like Riley Poole, it's worth taking a moment to explain how White came to be the proud owner of all this history.

To tell the story, we must venture to Portugal, which was (if I may remind you) one of the theorized docking places of the Templars' real-or-imagined treasure-smuggling fleet. In the 1960s, a stash of Templar-era artifacts was discovered in the Portuguese city of Tomar. This so-called "Tomar hoard" contained several iconic items, such as a sword adorned with three Templar crosses, an obsidian chalice thought to have been crafted in Byzantine times, a marble libation cup, and an early 1200s reliquary box. Another key item was a helmet in the Great Helm style popularized by medieval kings; it is believed this helmet was once in the possession of Heinrich Himmler, an agent of Adolf Hitler, who had once searched for the Templar treasure at Tomar.

At the time of the Tomar hoard's discovery, no one understood its significance, so its components were sold across the world. Hamilton White hunted down the history, relocating the artifacts over a period of ten years, and he now stores them at an undisclosed location. In his own words, the treasure trove is "so valuable [that] it's impossible to insure." White might just be in possession of the only historically acceptable version of a true Templar treasure. He has even wondered whether the obsidian chalice could have been seen as a representation of the Holy Grail, considering how the Holy Grail and Templar treasure are, for better or worse, often referenced in the same breath.

But if historians' pleas for people to stop believing in the Templar treasure have fallen on deaf ears, White's very real discovery, which has been popularized in television shows and news articles, certainly won't convince hobbyists to halt their quest for a much more stereotypical stash. Perhaps the true value of the Templar legend is to pique the public's interest in history, and to amplify archaeological discoveries that will continue to teach us about infamous orders of military monks whose place on a historical timeline seems unfathomably distant.

For instance, archaeologists are still searching the natural (and perhaps augmented) tunnels and caverns beneath Sinai House in England for evidence of Templars past. Monks from a nearby abbey (who bore little allegiance to the pope, potentially making them willing allies of the disbanded Templars) had taken over Sinai House around the time of the order's departure from Jerusalem. The inland location of the house would have made for an ideal place to hide anything the Templars may have wanted or needed to hide. As another example, in 2019, light detection and ranging (LiDAR) experiments in Acre, the last known outpost of the Knights Templar in the Holy Land, revealed previously unknown buried tunnels and a guardhouse. It has been suggested that these tunnels, which may have connected a long-gone fortress to the port, were once used to transport gold into the fortress's "treasure tower."

Could this have been the last known location of the Templar treasure? What Templar artifacts are next to be found? And what will their value be? Regardless of the as-yet-unknown answers to these fanciful questions, one thing is certain: the monetary worth of any discovery is sure to pale in comparison to the historical and cultural insights it will inevitably provide. *That* is intrinsic value—a quality that will always make for a compelling and timeless legend.

Chapter 4

Lost Colonists of Roanoke

Have you ever stopped to think about how the textbooks you read growing up were inextricably linked to the years during which you were a student? Some of the most common school-derived adages that unite your generation and seem so common or formative to you might mean absolutely nothing to someone who was a student a few decades earlier or later. Consider the phrase "the mitochondrion is the powerhouse of the cell," a scientific metaphor permanently burned into the brains of no fewer than all Americans who identify as either Gen X or millennial.

If you had grown up in the early 1950s, however, this phrase would never have been uttered in your biology class, as it was not popularized until 1957. And thirty years from now, will it have the same memorable impact on children who might not be nearly as familiar with the term "powerhouse" as it pertains to energy? What we learn in a classroom—and how we learn it—is intimately tied to the world's understanding of a given subject at a given moment in time. This reality is significant to no subject more than it is to history.

Our understanding of history is constantly evolving, not just as new artifacts are discovered and theories are tested, but also as we apply a modern lens to how we interpret events of the past. Even so, there are some historical tales that have been told so many times and occupy such a permanent position in our collective imagination that it can be difficult to think of them changing. One such story is that of the lost colonists of Roanoke—one of the few lessons I could see Riley Poole genuinely caring about during his grade school tenure because of its undeniably mysterious nature.

If you can relate, it might be surprising to learn that even this legend has shifted over time, due largely to changing social and cultural attitudes in the centuries that followed the now infamous event. And the version that has become common in American classrooms—the version that was told when *I* walked the halls—isn't even close to the complete picture. The biggest mystery surrounding the Roanoke tale is probably why we keep telling it this way, because you see, dear readers, the lost colonists of Roanoke were never considered lost. Not really. And if I were to put words in Riley's mouth, he'd like his metaphorical money back.

> **Why Riley Would Care:** Since Gates-Poole duos of the past discovered lost artifacts of the Roanoke colonists, Riley could take a page out of Ben's book by continuing his ancestors' work and furthering our collective understanding of this historical mystery.

HUNT DOWN THAT HISTORY

We should begin with what my old history textbooks got right. England began its exploration of the islands off the coast of present-day North Carolina in 1584 under the direction (from a distance) of Sir Walter Raleigh. Raleigh was a wealthy man in the good graces of Queen Elizabeth I, so she quickly accepted his proposal to create an English colony in the New World. Raleigh was granted a charter to establish said settlement on any chunk of land his expedition came across that was not already settled by Christians (read: other Europeans).

After all, other European explorers had begun staking claims along the East Coast of North America—including North Carolina's barrier islands—earlier in the century. Giovanni da Verrazzano, who had been exploring on behalf of King Francis I of France in 1524, sailed past the Outer Banks, and one year later Spain's Pedro de Quejo breezed by the same area as he sought out the Chesapeake Bay. Spanish explorers would end up docking at and exploring the Outer Banks in 1566, but they made no effort to colonize the string of islands situated in the shallow coastal waters.

Both France and Spain ultimately chose to busy themselves elsewhere on the continent, with the former occupying parts of present-day Canada and the Great Lakes region and the latter colonizing Florida and the American Southwest. Not to be outdone, English explorers Martin Frobisher and Sir Humphrey Gilbert had tried to claim land for their country in Canada's Inuit territory and Newfoundland in 1578 and 1583, respectively; both attempts were unsuccessful.

But the English couldn't just give up on creating colonies in the New World if they wanted to compete, especially with Spain. At minimum, England needed to establish outposts for their privateers to use when taking a breather from attacking Spanish ships. Plus, England didn't want to miss out on the chance to discover valuable natural resources in North America or—even better—to be the first to find a water-based route to the Pacific Ocean from the New World's Atlantic Coast.

For these reasons, Sir Walter Raleigh felt that 1584 was an opportune time to arrange a scouting expedition (which he would not personally attend) to identify a suitable location for England's first North American settlement. After crossing the Atlantic, the expedition landed at Roanoke Island in present-day Dare County, North Carolina, and the crew's leaders, Philip Amadas and Arthur Barlowe, named the land Wingandacon. During this exploratory trip, the English mingled with local Algonquin Native Americans, including the Croatoan and Roanoke tribes, who became trade partners and shared their cultural traditions.

In retrospect, some believe these reports of positive relationships with the local native communities might have been exaggerated to make Roanoke Island seem more appealing to future English settlers. But whether the accounts were embellished or accurate, Manteo and Wanchese, men from the Croatoan and Roanoke tribes, respectively, joined the 1584 expedition on its journey back to England. Manteo and Wanchese helped the explorers explain to Raleigh the status of different tribes and resources in the region. They would later become translators between Native Americans and the English who, unsurprisingly, sought to make a return trip to the New World.

Amadas and Barlowe wasted no time convincing Raleigh that a second voyage was warranted. This time, they argued, the expedition should make England's presence more permanent by putting down roots for a settlement, and they knew the perfect location: Roanoke.

They asserted that Roanoke's position between the mainland and the Outer Banks would offer the colonists security. Plus, the soil was fertile, game animals were abundant, and they had already established friendly relations with the island's native tribes. Frankly, the results of the previous expedition seemed so successful that Wingandacon was renamed Virginia after Elizabeth I, the virgin queen, who knighted Raleigh for his efforts. Raleigh proceeded to arrange the second expedition.

But like so many sequels, the 1585 journey performed far worse than its predecessor. Raleigh's cousin Sir Richard Grenville was assigned to lead the voyage, which formally sought to establish a military colony before allowing civilians to move in. Grenville was accompanied by around six hundred soldiers and crew aboard five large and two small ships, and the cohort immediately tried establishing itself on numerous North Carolina islands. But large ships like these could not easily maneuver in the shallow waters, requiring the ships to dock some distance offshore without protection from storms. As you might expect, the ships didn't fare well in the conditions, and most of the essential supplies stored aboard the vessels, including food, were lost.

Grenville was left with little choice other than to make a U-turn and steer the ships back to England for restocking purposes, and he figured he'd round up supplementary settlers while he was at it. Before departing for home, Grenville selected a war veteran by the name of Ralph Lane to serve as governor of the new colony, comprising 108 men who would be left behind to choose a location and put down roots for England. And just like that, Grenville and the ships set sail, and Lane and the settlers got to work.

Lane and the colonists built a fort, small houses, and a metal-working shop on Roanoke Island. Their principal goal at this early stage was to ensure they were protected from the Spanish while simultaneously moonlighting as attackers of passing ships. But they also occupied their time searching for valuable metals and other natural resources, as well as scouting Chesapeake Bay. They declared the bay a better location for permanent English settlement due to its deep waters (which behooved English ships) and easier access to the inland (which housed resources they desperately wanted). Not immediately successful in the agriculture department, Lane and his men primarily obtained their food from nearby tribes led by a chief named Wingina. Wingina's generosity was paramount in ensuring the survival of the colonists during a challenging winter.

It didn't take long, however, for the English to overstay their welcome. Wingina and his community felt their resources growing increasingly scarce, and they noticed their fellow tribal members dying from mysterious diseases (i.e., smallpox) that had seemed to crop up only following the colonists' arrival. By spring of 1586, Lane had heard that Wingina intended to stop providing the English with food, and that a Native American attack on the English settlement was possible. Lane opted to act first. The colonists killed Wingina and several other native people in June, severely damaging their relationship with all local tribes.

Left with little other recourse due to his utter failure to establish a self-sustaining settlement, Lane convinced English explorer and privateer Sir Francis Drake, who was serendipitously passing through the area by ship, to take the remaining colonists north to the Chesapeake Bay. But early on the route, a storm damaged Drake's fleet and rations, leading the entire cohort to begin the long journey back to England. Only a few weeks after the colonists' departure, Grenville finally returned to Roanoke with his long-awaited supplies, only to find the island abandoned. He left fifteen of his men behind to guard the settlement's structures while he reversed course and sought England yet again.

You'd think such a disastrous attempt at colonization might inspire the English to cut their losses, but inexplicably the opposite happened. Lane convinced Raleigh that the right location for a settlement wasn't Roanoke after all (whoops), but rather Chesapeake Bay. And so, a *third* expedition was planned, departing England in the summer of 1587. Somehow the previous two expeditions (and perhaps a "third time's the charm" mentality) gave Raleigh enough confidence to send not another military cohort, but rather a group of 115 normal people to establish England's first permanent settlement in the New World once and for all.

This was a significant step. As discussed, there had been plenty of prior European expeditions to the New World, but this 1587 expedition would be the first earnest attempt to establish a real population, complete with women and children. The group of settlers consisted of approximately ninety men, seventeen women, and eleven children under the formal supervision of a man named John White. Original

Native American ally Manteo also remained involved with the group.

Per Lane's recommendation, Raleigh's intention was for the colonists to establish their settlement somewhere near Chesapeake Bay. All the voyagers survived the journey across the Atlantic, and their first task was to make a temporary stop at Roanoke to gather the small group of fort-protecting Englishmen from the prior expedition left behind by Grenville. Upon arrival, however, the colonists were surprised to find that all fifteen men were missing, presumably killed by nearby Native Americans (per Manteo's reconnaissance). Plus, within days of the third expedition's arrival, yet another colonist succumbed to an attack by a local tribe. Clearly the relationship between the English and the Native Americans had only continued to sour following Lane's earlier decision to murder their chief.

Unfortunately for the latest group of settlers, they would not have the opportunity to escape the negative relations established by their predecessors. The captain of their fleet, Simon Fernandes, who had piloted the flagship of each of Raleigh's three expeditions, refused to continue onward to the Chesapeake, but there are conflicting theories as to why. John White believed Fernandes sought to get back out to sea quickly so he could raid Spanish ships on his way to England. Others have claimed there were fears about how the colonists would fare against unknown tribes in the Chesapeake Bay region, while another theory states that Fernandes believed it was too late in the season to continue northward.

Regardless of Fernandes's rationale, the colonists were forced to develop their settlement using the remnants of the fort on Roanoke Island, but the timing of their arrival could not have been worse. It was too late in the summer to begin growing food, and within weeks they were desperately in need of resources to support their fledgling community. As if that wasn't problematic enough, the region was experiencing a drought, and relations with the native tribes certainly weren't improving. In fact, they became *even worse* when the English attacked the suspected village of the tribe that had killed their fellow colonist, but an innocent tribe—the Croatoans—were occupying the village at the time of the ambush. The colonists seemingly couldn't make a good decision to save their lives (literally).

> **Riley's Favorite Fact (Probably):** The Roanoke colony that infamously disappeared wasn't the first or even second instance of England trying (and failing) to establish a permanent presence in the New World. The third time certainly wasn't the charm either!

As the governor of the colony, John White would soon be expected to take action to alleviate the settlers' struggles. White was adequately prepared to lead the Roanoke colony, as he had sailed on Sir Walter Raleigh's previous expedition in 1585. White was an artist, explorer, and cartographer, and during the 1585 journey he created many sketches and paintings of the local terrain, Native Americans, and wildlife. When the last colonization attempt failed in 1586, he returned home to England.

Fully buying into England's settlement goal, on this latest return trip to the New World, White brought along his wife, Tomasyn Cooper, and pregnant daughter, Eleanor White Dare, who gave birth on August 18, 1587, at Roanoke. Her daughter—White's granddaughter—was named Virginia Dare and was officially the first child of English descent born in the New World. Virginia Dare's name lives on in history books for this very reason, yet despite her fame, very little is known about her. In addition to her lineage traced through the White family tree, we know she was baptized on August 24 and that her father, Ananias Dare, was employed as a bricklayer. The reason the Dare family chose to settle in the New World remains uncertain, though some believe they sought religious freedom.

Tomasyn, Eleanor, and Virginia stayed in Roanoke when John White ultimately made the difficult decision to depart the colony en route to England in late 1587 to replenish Roanoke's severely dwindling supplies. White himself was opposed to this course of action, but his colonists begged for it. Unfortunately, White's return trip to Roanoke would be lengthily delayed by a war that inconveniently cropped up between England and Spain. Queen Elizabeth I ordered all English ships to lend a hand in battling the Spanish Armada, preventing White from piloting his craft back to the fledgling colony.

By spring 1588, White had received permission to sail two smaller ships to the New World, but on his way out he was attacked by French privateers. White made it back to Roanoke in August 1590—exactly three years after his settlement was first established. Despite the time that had passed, he was shocked at what he found upon his arrival. The colony—both inhabitants and structures—had vanished. Any remaining heavy objects, like iron bars, were overgrown with vegetation, suggesting that the colonists—wherever they went—had been gone for quite some time. White also found scattered chests containing his personal effects, including drawings, maps, and books, that seemed to have been dug up by local tribes.

But the most significant discovery—the one that has stood the test of time and ignited the imagination of countless students over the years—was the word "Croatoan" carved into a wood post near the former fort's entrance, as well as the letters "CRO" etched into a tree.

LISTEN TO RILEY

For years, history enthusiasts have pondered what these mysterious clues could mean and, more importantly, what became of the lost Roanoke colonists. No shortage of theories has been proposed, some of which are more historically based than others.

One of the most common is rooted in the local geography. At the time of the colonists' disappearance, modern-day Hatteras Island, located about fifty miles south of Roanoke, was called Croatoan Island and was the home of the Croatoan tribe. Some therefore believe the "Croatoan" and "CRO" carvings were indicative of the colonists having been killed or kidnapped by this tribe.

But the Croatoans and other local communities weren't the only ones who may have wanted the colonists gone. Some have proposed the colonists' demise had little to do with the Native Americans, and instead the Spanish, hailing from nearby Florida, might have been wary of the new English outpost and killed its inhabitants. Then there are the theories suggesting the colonists met their end all on their own. Perhaps they had tried sailing back to England by themselves and got lost or were capsized at sea. Maybe they were waiting patiently for White's return and died one by one at the proverbial hands of disease, starvation, a hurricane, or another natural disaster.

But who says the colonists perished en masse during White's absence? After all, upon his return, White found no human remains at the former Roanoke settlement. This makes the supposition that the colonists were attacked by Native Americans or the Spanish seem wholly unlikely, and the same rationale can be used to negate disease, starvation, or a storm wiping them out. Instead, the absence of human remains suggests that the colonists departed Roanoke—either willfully or unwilfully, peacefully or under duress.

Years later, in the twentieth century, a discovery was made that seemed to breathe new life into the longstanding Roanoke mystery. In 1937, a man named Louis E. Hammond was met with media frenzy when he announced that near North Carolina's Chowan River he had found a stone inscribed with messages allegedly written by Eleanor White Dare for her father. Hammond's stone detailed both Ananias and Virginia Dare's deaths in 1591 and asked whoever stumbled across the stone to share it with John White. On the opposite side of the stone was carved the story of the lost colonists' fate: that native tribes had killed all but a group of seven colonists, which included Eleanor herself.

In the years that followed Hammond's revelation, forty-seven additional "Dare Stones" were reportedly discovered and handed over to historians. It turns out that Hammond's original stone also alluded to the fact that at least one other stone existed to mark the grave of a handful of colonists, including Ananias and Virginia Dare. Following a lengthy analysis, all forty-seven of these additional stones were proven fake, with their origins tracing back to a single Georgia stonecutter by the name of Bill Eberhardt.

Yet no one has been able to definitively prove or disprove the authenticity of Hammond's initial stone. One piece of evidence supporting its veracity is the fact that its text is etched in the style of Elizabethan English handwriting, making it at least appear temporally consistent with the era in which it was purportedly crafted. Today, Hammond's stone and the forty-seven fakes are housed at Brenau University in Gainesville, Georgia.

> **Riley's Next Hunt:** It's not hard to imagine Riley and his fellow treasure protectors finding the second Dare Stone, corroborating it with modern geological tools, and ultimately locating the grave of the missing Roanoke colonists.

After all these years of theorizing, can anything be said with certainty about what became of the lost colonists of Roanoke? Plagued by hunger, disease, challenging weather conditions, and perhaps other difficulties of which we have no record, the settlement may have tumbled into chaos and broken into several factions or survivor contingents. If the colonists had chosen to leave the island and travel as one large group, it would have been much more difficult to find a nearby tribe that might be willing to part with such a great quantity of supplies to aid them. A large group of colonists might have outnumbered many tribes too, making the group appear threatening to the very communities whose help they so desperately needed.

One contingent of colonists may have traveled north toward Chesapeake Bay—where their colony was supposed to have settled to begin with. They knew the reputation of the area's resources and its access to critical waterways, potentially making it an attractive option for both relocation and encountering passing European ships. Plus, English Captain John Smith would later record that his interactions with Native Americans in the Chesapeake area revealed that Europeans had frequented the region before his arrival in the early 1600s.

Another Roanoke contingent might have moved west, deeper into the mainland of North America. Given the amount of time the colonists had spent on a difficult-to-reach and equally difficult-to-resource island, they may have been attracted to the idea of a secure and stable inland settlement. This theory is fueled by a map from the 1500s, once owned by John White, that is now housed at the British Museum in London. Relatively recently, the map was reexamined using modern imaging techniques, revealing fortlike symbols on the map that are invisible to the naked eye. These newly discovered map features became a guide that facilitated the discovery of Elizabethan-era artifacts, including brass and pottery, in present-day Bertie County, North Carolina.

The idea that these artifacts may have belonged to the Roanoke colonists is supported by the testimony of White himself. Before his resupply mission, colonists allegedly shared with White their contingency plan to migrate "fifty miles into the main" if conditions arose that required them to abandon the settlement. Some historians have interpreted this plan to mean that the colonists vowed to travel fifty miles inland. However, claims that the Bertie County artifacts are evidence of the Roanoke colonists have also been met with healthy skepticism, mainly because the area where the artifacts were located was occupied by Native Americans who were hostile toward the English.

Today, most tangible evidence of the colonists' relocation points to a group having peacefully settled and braved the harsh winter with the familiar Croatoan tribe around late 1587. More than a decade's worth of archaeological excavations at known Croatoan sites in North Carolina have unearthed thousands of artifacts of both Native American and English origin. The Native American objects, such as pottery and arrowheads, and English objects, including bits of sword, drawing slate, rings, and glass, have been found about four to six feet underground in the same layers of soil, indicating contemporaneousness.

This evidence suggests the Croatoans and the colonists might have lived alongside one another, or that the tribe plundered the settlement at Roanoke. Yet at these dig sites archaeologists have also identified post holes of both the round (Native American) and square (English) varieties. These holes, used to construct dwellings, were separated from one another by just tens of feet. White claimed to have found solace in the idea that the colonists had traveled to Croatoan, remembering the allyship of Manteo during the series of English expeditions. White's personal belief was that the colonists relocated to Croatoan under no threat or duress. After all, some historical accounts claim the colonists agreed to carve their new location into a tree if they opted to move, and that they would have carved a cross over the location if they were threatened.

Additional clues from the era support the idea that the Roanoke colonists cohabitated with one or more Native American tribes, including writings from the soon-to-be-established settlement at Jamestown, Virginia. In 1701, an English explorer named John Lawson claimed to have encountered Native Americans with blue-gray eyes living near Croatoan Island. Not only was this trait indicative of European descent, but these Native Americans also told stories of their ancestors who could speak perfect English. This ultimately suggests at least some of the Roanoke colonists lived well and built families with their native counterparts.

However, not all of the colonists may have met a happy end. One legend suggests that in 1607, Powhatan warriors killed many of the surviving Roanoke colonists, as well as their Native American allies, for fear that the Roanoke and Jamestown colonists would converge and pose a security threat. The few survivors of this attack were rumored to have traveled south along the Chowan River, which would accord with the story carved into the back of Louis E. Hammond's Dare Stone.

If the Roanoke colonists did split into multiple groups, it is highly likely that each group encountered different circumstances, potentially leading them to meet different fates. How many groups they divided themselves into, how many directions they traveled in, and whether they all departed Roanoke Island at the same time will likely remain a mystery, but that has not prevented individuals from making educated guesses. Some think the largest group went north toward the Chesapeake and that they were the first to leave the island. The rationale behind this idea was that a smaller contingent could wait at Roanoke for White's return, eventually guiding him to the new northern colony. If this was the plan, something presumably happened to cause the smaller contingent to abort their mission before White arrived.

As for White, he was unfortunately never able to test the hypothesis that his fellow colonists had moved to Croatoan to live with the local native population. He tried making the trip to Croatoan on several occasions, but storms ultimately prevented him from ever reaching the island. He returned home to England that fall and died three years later in 1593. In 1607, Jamestown was established by the London Company, finally becoming the first permanent English settlement in North America—a title the Roanoke settlement once thought it had claimed. It was only after Jamestown was up and running that search parties for Roanoke survivors started in earnest.

Interestingly, from the time of the colony's disappearance to the establishment of Jamestown, and for the two centuries that followed, the Roanoke colonists were never really considered lost. Again, the prevailing belief at the time—with much confidence—was that the colonists had assimilated with one or more Native American tribes. What, then, is the origin of the "lost" colonists story? Why are today's grade school students taught to be mystified by a community of over one hundred people up and disappearing?

The story of the Roanoke colony began to shift in popular discourse in the 1830s, around the time when US President Andrew Jackson ordered the mass migration of Native Americans from their ancestral homelands under the Indian Removal Act. During the Trail of Tears, numerous United States-Native American treaties were violated, and these historical events negatively shaped many Americans' perceptions of relations with tribal communities. US historians began referring to the Roanoke colonists as "lost" instead of acknowledging that they lived and had respectful relationships with Native Americans.

Today, this narrative shift is not widely known. The first accepted use of the term "lost colony" occurs in a magazine story titled *Virginia Dare; or, the Lost Colony*, published by author Eliza Lanesford Cushing in 1837. Even now, most retellings of the Roanoke colony's story place immense emphasis on its "mysterious" disappearance. Another typical area of emphasis is the birth of Virginia Dare, despite a complete lack of knowledge about her life. These snippets of the colony's story were used in some circles to fuel white nationalist sentiments in the nineteenth and twentieth centuries.

As scientific tools become more advanced and as historians develop more complete pictures of the past, it would seem natural to suspect that the next puzzle piece in the Roanoke story could be discovered on any given day. Unfortunately, the remains of the colony on Roanoke Island may now be permanently submerged in the Atlantic Ocean thanks to four hundred years' worth of coastal erosion and sea level rise, both of which are only increasing in severity.

To make matters worse, historians aren't completely sure where on Roanoke Island the colonists initially settled. White and his counterparts kept poor records, and the records that do remain contain multitudes of conflicting information. For example, White's notes claim that the 1587 settlement was located on the north end of the island, but sworn testimony from a Spaniard (who passed the settlement on ship) suggests the settlement was closer to the midpoint. The latter assertion may be supported by the discovery of a well and cannon near the island's bay.

Nonetheless, archaeological studies are ongoing, attempting to add more clarity to the colonists' oft-repeated story. Genetic studies have been pursued to determine whether Native Americans who still live in the vicinity of the colonists' suspected final destinations have English ancestors. These studies are plagued by the difficulty of finding a genetic control: DNA from a Roanoke colonist or their known descendant to which DNA samples from the study can be compared. After all, if we knew where to find the bones of the Roanoke colonists from which to glean control DNA, we wouldn't need to conduct such genetic studies in the first place.

For now, students would do well to read their history textbooks with a critical eye when it comes to their lessons on the "lost colony." There is no harm in fostering student interest in history using curious tales of the past, as long as important facts—or at least strong consensus amongst historians—are not left on the cutting room floor for the sake of intrigue. Perhaps more interesting than the colony's somewhat exaggerated disappearance is how the story of its migration evolved in accordance with America's social and cultural fabric. Now *that* would be a true lesson in how our understanding of history is shaped by the interpretations of those telling the tale.

Chapter 5

Salem Witch Trials

National Treasure: Edge of History teaches us that in recent years, Riley Poole has become a successful podcaster, which is honestly *so* on-brand based on our character analysis's suggestion that he craves positive attention. If I were to hazard a guess using his personal interests and expertise, Riley's podcast niche could be discussing archaeological finds and their present-day monetary values. From a podcaster's perspective, this would literally be the definition of "niche," and I do suspect Riley would harbor a secret grudge against bigwig podcasters covering more mainstream topics. For example, I believe he'd be quite peeved by the sheer popularity of true crime.

True crime and treasure hunting are remarkably similar, and yet one is far more beloved than the other. Both start with a "what": a treasure, an artifact; a murder, a scam. Both rely on a distinctly human fascination with that which is not easily fathomable. But true crime's fascination is rooted in the morbid and macabre, and as a genre it goes further by answering the "what" with a "why." In other words, everyone can understand how cool it is to discover a treasure that redefines history for all mankind, but they can't understand *why* a young woman would murder her entire family with thirty swings of an axe.

The same can be said for many legends of American and world history. Even in cases where plenty of historical details are recorded and little is left to the present-day imagination, the psyches of those involved continue to provide intrigue. Such is the case for the Salem witch trials, which some might argue represent one of the oldest cases of popularized true crime. In this story, there are seemingly infinite perspectives worth questioning—so many "whys" to explore. There is, of course, the question of *why* the accused behaved in ways that were deemed cursed. But equally, if not more, interesting is the question of *why* the accusers chose to become some of the earliest villains in American history.

The final "why" worth considering is *why* society at the time allowed the Salem witch trials to happen at all. And it is this query that leads to a fascinating discourse about how the trials—or the way they were conducted—flew in the face of the legal structures available during the era in question. Even today, the legacy of the Salem witch trials lives on, as the events that unfolded are both remembered and invoked as a dangerous example of what happens when paranoia and injustice converge in frightening ways.

Why Riley Would Care: Given the impact of the Salem witch trials on the modern American justice system, Riley could learn a thing or two to help him steer clear of prison during future treasure hunts.

HUNT DOWN THAT HISTORY

Our story begins across the pond, centuries before the Salem witch trials induced their trademark terror. Fear of witchcraft was rampant in Europe by the 1300s, and this fear persisted throughout the continent well into the 1600s. As you might expect based on this timeline, colonists of the New World packed their witchcraft paranoia alongside their physical belongings as they traveled overseas to the Massachusetts Bay Colony, where our tale will ultimately take place.

But to get there, we must first understand how the conversation surrounding witchcraft evolved, and how certain historical institutions contributed to widespread hysteria over the practice. In the olden times, popular discourse suggested that witches pledged their allegiance to the Devil and were subsequently afforded powers that could harm those of the mortal realm. Said witches needed to be stopped at all costs, at least according to various religious establishments across Europe.

The written connection between witchcraft and religious heresy in Europe was a major catalyst for the persecution of suspected witches. In 1484, Pope Innocent VIII issued a papal bull called *Summis*

Desiderantes Affectibus, which formally declared that witches should be convicted. A few years later, in 1487, the publication of a German text known as the *Malleus Maleficarum*, or *Hammer of Witches*, added more fuel to the anti-witchcraft fire, becoming Europe's best-selling book (outperformed only by the Bible) for more than a century.

The *Malleus Maleficarum* was significant for numerous reasons, such as its (sexist, of course) declaration that women were more likely to be witches than men and its framework for how to identify those capable of witchcraft. The *Compendium Maleficarum* (1608) took things one step further, summarizing what witchcraft purportedly looked like in practice so aspiring witch hunters could begin rooting out the evildoers among them.

Unsurprisingly, American witch hunts were predated by those in Europe. Three-quarters of all European witch hunts took place in Belgium, France, Germany, Italy, Luxembourg, the Netherlands, and Switzerland. Southwestern Germany witnessed the highest number overall, occurring with the greatest frequency between the years 1561 and 1670. During this time, much effort was dedicated to sniffing out new witches as opposed to simply prosecuting those who were already suspected of the illicit practice; this is how the term "hunt" came to be.

In these situations, accused witches were often observers of whatever Christian denomination was the minority religion where they lived. In other words, Protestants were accused in locations that predominantly practiced Catholicism, and Catholics were accused in Protestant-heavy communities. Demographically, many of the accused were elderly women living in small villages; their accusers were typically religious figures who traveled into rural areas seeking converts to Christianity. When missionaries encountered non-Christian practices with which they were unfamiliar, they quickly assumed those practices were evidence of the occult.

Midwives made up another commonly accused group. Because they were invariably present when mothers gave birth to stillborn children, rumors circulated that midwives sacrificed children to Satan. Midwifery wasn't the only unsafe occupation, however. Brewers of alcoholic beverages were also suspected because their intoxicating libations were thought to make people more susceptible to the Devil's influence. More often than not, accusers were related to those they accused. In other words, blood was certainly not thicker than water in these early days, as family members commonly threw one another under the bus.

While it remains unclear exactly how many people were accused of witchcraft in each European witch-hunting hotspot, it is generally accepted that, in total, around 110,000 people underwent trials. Of that number, between forty thousand and sixty thousand were ultimately found guilty and executed as punishment for their perceived crimes. And just as this so-called "European witch craze" was wrapping up, across the Atlantic Ocean, America's very own Salem witch trials were just getting started.

Per the Witchcraft Act of 1604, the practice of witchcraft in America was considered a felony, for which punishment could range from a year of prison time (for a minor offense) to death (if an individual was found guilty on two separate occasions). In the Massachusetts Bay Colony, the setting of our story, the Body of Liberties (1641) was the first legal code approved in the entire New England region, and it cited biblical precedent as the reason why the practice of witchcraft was one of the highest possible crimes in the land.

The Massachusetts Bay Colony was dominated by Puritan beliefs, which, among other things, asserted that individuals could never be completely confident their actions were acceptable to God. As a result, fears that the Devil would lure Puritans astray were rampant. The combination of this religious context and a strained social environment brewed the exact conditions necessary for the Salem witch trials to take shape.

Heightened tensions in Salem Village, located in present-day Danvers, Massachusetts, could be attributed to numerous factors. King William's War, a conflict between England and France on American soil, had sent refugees fleeing New York, Nova Scotia, and Quebec into Essex County, Massachusetts. This influx of unfamiliar new neighbors strained Salem's resources, and the situation contributed to a growing sentiment of lack of control within the colony, especially as England continuously sought to impose new rules.

Some of those rules were on the topic of religion, though the religious makeup of the Massachusetts Bay Colony was undergoing a robust transformation. Although it was established as a strictly Puritan colony in 1630, Quakers and Christians were moving in at a rapid rate, adding to social strains. To further complicate matters, the region contended with a smallpox epidemic, severe storms, and contentious relations with local Native American tribes. Relations with neighboring colonists were equally poor, considering the growing hostility between Salem Village and the nearby community of Salem Town.

Salem Town, which benefited from a thriving port economy, sat about ten miles away from the inland Salem Village, and the question of how much the two communities should be connected was controversial, especially from the perspectives of two influential families running the show in the village. The Porter family had strong ties to Salem Town and wanted to maintain the communities' close relationship, while the Putnams, a less wealthy family, advocated for more separation. Cue the infighting.

Community drama also derived from the appointment of Samuel Parris as minister of the church at Salem Village, a move facilitated by the Putnam family. Parris was a businessman in search of an apparently drastic career pivot, and he was the definition of "underqualified" for a religious role. Soon after beginning his new job, Parris demanded a raise and sought ownership of the entire parsonage. Naturally, members of the congregation balked at these unusual demands—which were almost as unusual (and disliked) as his extremely orthodox interpretation of the Puritan belief system. This added considerably to the strain in Salem, and it was only a matter of time before something—or someone—snapped.

Prior to the Salem witch trials, remarkably few people had been executed for witchcraft in the English colonies. Based on England's legal custom, convictions for crimes could only be achieved with incontrovertible proof of the accusation's veracity. In practice, this often meant at least two witnesses needed to testify, and tangible evidence needed to be presented. Oh, and to further simplify or complicate matters (depending on your worldview), the accused needed to *confess*. What was about to occur in Salem in the late-seventeenth century would ultimately call into question the efficacy of this system.

At long last, this brings us to the infamous trials, which began in earnest in 1692 when a group of girls living in Salem Village accused numerous women in their community of practicing witchcraft. Two girls in particular, nine-year-old Elizabeth "Betty" Parris and eleven-year-old Abigail Williams, Minister Samuel Parris's daughter and niece, respectively, were the first to make these allegations. Betty and Abigail began exhibiting out-of-character behaviors, such as contorting their bodies, screaming violently, making strange noises, throwing objects, and complaining of biting and pinching sensations. William Griggs, the doctor serving Salem Village, examined the girls and declared that their "fits" were the result of bewitchment.

Other local girls, including twelve-year-old Ann Putnam Jr., began experiencing similar afflictions. All told, about ten girls and young women, whose ages ranged from nine to nineteen, claimed they had been bewitched following their behavioral fits. Once the community agreed that witchcraft was to blame, attention turned to identifying *who* was responsible for the girls' plights.

Various homemade methods were tested in a desperate attempt to identify the local witches; an unusual example was the baking of "witch cakes," crafted using the urine of the bewitched youth. Minister Parris declared these methods blasphemous from a religious perspective (though I like to think he found them blasphemous from a commonsense perspective too).

By the end of February, a month after the apparent mass bewitchment, three women were accused by the girls as having been the source of their afflictions. Tituba, an enslaved Barbadian woman of the Parris family, Sarah Good, an unhoused woman, and Sarah Osborn, an impoverished and elderly woman, were quickly arrested. Notably, neither Good nor Osborn was a regular churchgoer, which certainly contributed to the suspicions cast their way by frantic community members. The three accused women shared the trait of being considered "lesser" members of society.

During a public trial that began on March 1, the women were interrogated under the supervision of magistrates Jonathan Corwin and John Hathorne. Among the spectators of the show (because that's what it turned into) were the young accusers, who continued to exhibit their apparent "symptoms" from the audience. Good and Osborn maintained their innocence, but facing merciless pressure, Tituba ultimately confessed to practicing witchcraft. She recounted vivid stories of her interactions with the Devil's animal proxies, shared a tale about how a man from Boston coaxed her to sign Satan's book, and swore that other villagers were witches too. Today, it is widely believed Tituba fabricated her confession and blanket accusation attempting to avoid conviction.

Whatever Tituba's rationale, the result of her action was straightforward: mass hysteria spread not just throughout Salem Village, but throughout the entire Massachusetts Bay Colony. Increasingly more people were accused of witchcraft, a phenomenon fueled by unrest and general animosity, and accusations were no longer confined to outcasts and other less respected members of society. Upstanding members of the community and regular churchgoers were immune no more.

This was abundantly apparent in the patterns of the girl accusers. As they gained more attention, and as they watched the chaos grow, their accusations became progressively bolder. They began targeting the likes of Martha Corey and Rebecca Nurse, women who were so greatly respected in the community that fellow villagers reached a simple conclusion: if these two could be witches, *anyone* could be a witch!

Ultimately, the demographics of Salem's accused varied considerably, with the youngest being four-year-old Dorothy Good, daughter of Sarah Good (one of the first three women to be accused). In the end, many of the accusers would turn out to be Putnam family members, and many of the accused were known enemies of the powerful family. Whether or not villagers deemed this suspicious is unclear, but every accused individual was forced to await a formal trial.

During the earliest of the Salem witch trials, some of the accused took a page out of Tituba's book, issuing their own confessions and then proceeding to point a finger at others in the community. The result was what seemed like an exponential increase in the number of accused witches by the day. Soon, the local justice system was overflowing with cases it simply did not have the capacity to handle.

Enter William Phips, the new governor of Massachusetts who found himself operating his colony under an equally new charter issued by England. On May 27, Governor Phips established a Court of Oyer and Terminer, which would be given the sole responsibility of hearing the cases of accused witches in Essex, Middlesex, and Suffolk Counties. Seven judges presided over the court, including one of the magistrates responsible for conducting the first Salem witch trial, John Hathorne. Another of the judges was Lieutenant Governor William Stoughton, who essentially served as head judge.

That was the good news. The bad news was that no one had yet found the time to establish laws under the new Massachusetts Bay

Colony charter, and as a result, the Court of Oyer and Terminer had the distinct pleasure of creating its own rules regarding what would qualify as evidence in the trials it oversaw. Based on English precedent, courts were generally supposed to question the accused and accuser separately, supplementing these testimonies with solid evidence. These parameters were swiftly thrown out the proverbial window, as the Court of Oyer and Terminer elected to follow the exact *opposite* terms during the Salem witch trials that followed.

The court that convened was far from orderly in its proceedings, with uncontrolled accusations being launched from every corner of the room and hysteria migrating from the streets into the chambers. Loose, "causal" evidence—such as prior conflicts, ownership of perceived tools of witchcraft, impressive strength, and certain birthmarks—was considered permissible. The accused were required to defend *themselves*, and while they desperately pleaded their cases, their accusers watched from the audience while continuing their displays of "fits." Somehow, these literal performances taking place in the peanut gallery were seen as further proof that the person on trial was still actively afflicting their victim.

To make matters worse, some of the judges had exactly zero legal training but were still asked to render judgement, leading to a predictable trend in outcomes. In general, individuals who were on trial and stood by their innocence were punished by the court. On the contrary, those who confessed to witchcraft, or who confessed and named other local witches, were not disciplined owing to the Puritan belief that God's punishment would suffice.

The court's (negative) impact on the community would become a thing of legend. The first trial overseen by the brand new, supremely underqualified, and wildly unprepared Court of Oyer and Terminer was that of Bridget Bishop, an older woman who fell into the "village outcast" category. Bridget Bishop had initially been accused of witchcraft and found innocent twelve years prior, but her luck had since run out. She became the court's first conviction on June 2 and was hanged for her apparent crime on June 10.

She was the first of many Salem "witches" to meet their ends at the gallows. One day per month was designated for guilty witches to be hanged, resulting in five executions on July 19 (including Rebecca Nurse and Sarah Good), five on August 19 (including the village's former minister, George Burroughs), and eight on September 22. At the time, it was strongly believed that a true witch would be incapable of adeptly reciting the Lord's Prayer, which Burroughs did flawlessly as he stood at the gallows. Naturally, this prompted uneasiness amongst some onlookers, who became skeptical of his guilt.

All told, fourteen of the nineteen individuals hanged in Salem Village for witchcraft were women. For centuries, it was believed these executions occurred on top of Gallows Hill, located near the west edge of the community. It wasn't until 2016 that historians amended their supposition, agreeing that the events' real setting was Proctor's Ledge at the base of the hill. This new interpretation is based on analysis of eyewitness accounts provided by villagers who lived nearby and said they could view the public hangings from their porches.

Without question, the victims of the Salem witch trials—both the acquitted and convicted—suffered in innumerable ways. Giles Corey, the eighty-year-old husband of Martha Corey (who herself was seventy-two years old when she was hanged on September 22), refused to enter a plea to the court when he was arraigned. As punishment, he was pressed to death under the weight of heavy stones.

All told, somewhere between 144 and 185 men, women, and children were accused of witchcraft across the region, indicative of the hysteria having spread rampantly—even to Boston. Colonists in Andover and Salem were so terrified that they resorted to killing two dogs that were thought to have been bewitched in some way. At least five accused witches died while awaiting trial in jail.

Like the trend in Salem Village, 75 percent of accused witches across the Massachusetts Bay Colony were women. Fingers were typically pointed only at men when they were known friends, family members, or defenders of accused women, and the practice of witchcraft was widely believed to be passed through families to children. Everyone seemed to agree with the prevailing sentiment that women were far more likely to be witches because of the biblical story of Eve succumbing to temptation. Men were seen as more mature from both spiritual and intellectual perspectives (a wild generalization, if you ask me), so *of course* they were unlikely to be witches (according to most colonists).

With so many witchcraft allegations rampant throughout the colony, why does history remember the case of Salem Village specifically? Salem's trials were unique in frequency and quantity, resulting in many hangings over the span of only a few short months. By comparison, witch trials in nearby Connecticut occurred over several decades and resulted in only eleven hangings in total.

Even so, the executions associated with the Salem witch trials ceased about as quickly as they started. By September 1692, less than a year after the frenzy's onset, public sentiment regarding the trials took a sharp turn, and churchgoers began balking at the ongoing spectacle as their fellow parishioners were increasingly accused. The villagers didn't stop believing witches existed, but they did stop believing in the court's ability to accurately pinpoint who the witches were. However, everyday community members weren't the first to question the trials' overall efficacy.

After Bridget Bishop's execution—the village's first guilty witchcraft verdict punished by hanging—Governor Phips consulted with some of the colony's ministers, such as Cotton Mather, to better understand their perspectives on the trials. Some of these ministers responded to the governor's inquiry by expressing concern over the Court of Oyer and Terminer's practices.

Specifically, Mather called into question the court's allowance of spectral evidence during trials. Spectral evidence, in short, consisted of stories about the accused witch projecting themself into the dreams of their victims to inflict pain or torture. While clearly unverifiable, such spectral evidence was frequently the nail in the coffin of the accused, becoming a key to securing a guilty verdict from the Court of Oyer and Terminer. That's probably why the court elected to ignore the ministers' concerns.

Cotton Mather's involvement at this stage was somewhat dubious, as some purport he cast doubt on the trials, while other accounts suggest his actions supported them. Regardless, Cotton's father and the president of Harvard College, Increase Mather, would eventually echo the troubled sentiments of his son (and his son's fellow ministers) about spectral evidence. By October, Increase Mather vocally asserted that the evidence used to convict accused witches needed to be just as high-quality as the evidence presented in any other court case.

Riley's Favorite Fact (Probably): Spectral evidence, or the unproveable claim that an accused witch invaded their victim's dreams, was considered ironclad evidence of witchcraft at the height of the Salem witch trials.

Soon after, on October 29, Governor Phips abolished the Court of Oyer and Terminer, partially in response to the public's growing dissatisfaction with its efforts, and partially because his wife had just been questioned in association with witchcraft. His order to do away with the court prevented further arrests of potential witches and resulted in the release of many of the accused who were still jailed and awaiting trial.

But witchcraft was still a crime; the colony just needed a better system for properly adjudicating cases. That's why Governor Phips replaced the Court of Oyer and Terminer with the Superior Court of Judicature, which would continue to hear and provide judgment on cases of witchcraft until early 1693. Fortunately, the Superior Court of Judicature would not accept spectral evidence—or any testimony related to dreams or visions—when trying these cases, and the outcome of this small change was stark. Of fifty-six total cases heard by the new court, only three resulted in a guilty verdict. And by May 1693, the tide had turned completely, with Governor Phips releasing—and fully pardoning—anyone remaining in jail on charges of witchcraft.

But too much had already happened; too much irreversible pain had been inflicted. It didn't take long for Salem Village, and indeed the Massachusetts Bay Colony as a whole, to look back on the events of 1692 with distaste and regret. The colony's court system began issuing public apologies for the Salem witch trials in January 1697, and in 1702 it deemed the full suite of trials to have been unlawful. Samuel Sewell, a judge from the Court of Oyer and Terminer, and Ann Putnam Jr., one of the girls who partook in the mass accusations, ultimately issued apologies in 1697 and 1706, respectively.

Formal apologies were an important first step but could not be the only step in mitigating the immense damage that had been done. In 1711, Massachusetts issued legislation attempting to restore the credibility of those who had been executed because of the irresponsibly conducted court proceedings. While this could be seen as having little real effect on these local figures, a more tangible outcome was Massachusetts's issuance of financial restitution to their heirs.

And for more than two centuries, that was the end of the story. It wasn't until 1957 that the state of Massachusetts issued its own formal apology for the events. In 2011, ten more accused witches were officially exonerated. Only one convicted and long-deceased woman, Elizabeth Johnson Jr., had yet to have her name cleared in the public record. Following a passionate campaign conducted by an eighth-grade civics class, Elizabeth Johnson Jr. was finally pardoned in July 2022.

LISTEN TO RILEY

There are many angles from which to examine the legendary case of the Salem witch trials that could—or even should—result in curiosity. One such curiosity involves the social and power structures of the era. Considering how women and girls were given very little voice or authority during this time in American history, it is genuinely astonishing that a group of girls and young women were effectively running the show during the Salem witch trials. As accusers, their voices were not only being heard, but so much credence was given to their allegations that the girls effectively determined the fates of their helpless community members.

This apparent reversal of gender-based power structures could make for an interesting thesis, especially when adding in other dynamics such as age (the accusers were invariably young) and social class (most of them belonged to one of the village's most powerful families). Observers would be justified in wondering how the preexisting social tensions in and around Salem Village affected the community's unyielding belief in the accusations of a group of girls who, by all accounts, should have wielded less power than they ultimately did.

Another longstanding intrigue related to the case at hand is the reason why the girls' fits began in the first place. While the witch trials were conducted under unfair conditions and highlighted unreliable evidence, it was at least true that the "afflicted" girls were behaving strangely. But was this a matter of behavioral challenges—of "acting out"—or could there have been another reason?

For years, people have sought to assign a scientific explanation to the strange actions collectively described as "fits" that were common amongst the accusers. A study published in the journal *Science* in 1976 was the first to attribute the fits to ergot, a type of fungus found in rye, wheat, and cereals that is a precursor to the drug lysergic acid diethylamide, or LSD. According to toxicologists, the consumption of ergot can result in many symptoms consistent with the girls' fits, such as delusions and muscle spasms.

However, the ergot theory has been revisited over time and has gained little support from the historical and scientific communities, which have noted that ergotism was a real challenge in the Middle Ages—not the 1690s, when farmers would be skilled at identifying contaminated products. Alternative scientific or medical explanations have been posed, including combinations of asthma, encephalitis, Lyme disease, epilepsy, and psychosis. However, these conditions would fail to explain why so many girls shared the same symptoms in rapid succession. Indeed, girls falling "ill" to fits one by one would imply disease transmission or exposure to the same infectious agent—if an illness was at play at all.

Perhaps unsurprisingly, most historical observers have pinned the girls' tandem behaviors on vindictiveness. Consider how the girls grew increasingly bold in their accusations once they learned they were being taken seriously: their initial targets were social outcasts, but over time the group of victims expanded to include respected members of society. The trend of accusers from the Putnam family pointing fingers at their known enemies—especially those tied to the rival Porter family—has done much to support this theory in the court of public opinion.

If this was indeed the case, perhaps the girls took inspiration from 1600s-era pop culture to inform their antics. Some have speculated that the girls were familiar with Cotton Mather's book *Memorable Providences, Relating to Witchcraft and Possessions* (1689), which includes the story of a Bostonian girl who, in 1688, exhibited markedly similar symptoms as the Salem girls and was considered by her community to have been bewitched.

While the behavior of the accusers will undoubtedly provide debate fodder for years to come, equally interesting to scrutinize is the behavior of the Salem Village community writ large. After all, the community perpetuated the witch craze, ensured the trials were conducted in hostile environments, and turned out in large numbers for the public hangings of those who were convicted. Many believe their actions were the result of tense social conditions; local and regional politics combined with church drama, uncontrollable children, and religious stringency created a perfect storm that allowed the Salem witch trials to flourish. Mass hysteria was certainly the result if it wasn't already the cause in a nasty feedback loop.

Riley's Next Hunt: Forget what caused the Salem girls' behavior; let's talk about why the villagers were so quick to believe them! Given his proclivity for conspiracies, Riley might suspect a seventeenth century blackmail situation, and he'd be the perfect person to research any damning information the girls might have collected about their neighbors.

Despite the numerous perspectives from which we can examine the Salem witch trials today—removed from the events by centuries, gawking at them wide-eyed from the comfort of our couches—their impact on the Salem community persisted for years. Of course, the trials and the social setting surrounding them were made famous by Arthur Miller in *The Crucible* (1953), which sought to analogize the Salem-based happenings of 1692 to McCarthyism. The trials are still referenced allegorically in response to bigoted, extremist, racist, or otherwise hatred-based situations in which marginalized groups are persecuted.

If you visit Salem, Massachusetts, today, you'll experience a Halloween-themed destination whose overall vibe can best be described as "commercial witch." Perhaps a new curiosity associated with the witch trials, then, is the ethics of the town having turned its past horrors into a booming tourism sector characterized by witch-themed stores, restaurants, museums, and other attractions. Is it within the community's rights to transform its trauma into something from which it can benefit, or does the community run the risk of making a mockery of—or worse, exploiting—its ancestors? The true answer probably lies somewhere in between.

But if modern-day Salem is the trials' commercial legacy, their legal legacy might be equally consequential. Scholars largely agree that during the Salem witch trials, the accused were denied rights that should have been afforded to them under English common law—especially since their colony had not yet established its own laws under its new charter. The trials, therefore, made a salient mark on the eventual legal system of the United States, which would ultimately guarantee that defendants have the right to legal representation, to cross-examine their accuser, and to be believed innocent until proven guilty.

Most interesting, however, is the US legal system's determination that hearsay shall not be permitted in court, preventing rumors and gossip—today's version of spectral evidence, perhaps—from being entered into court proceedings. Indeed, when the Bill of Rights was ratified in 1791, it would go on to protect individual freedoms that could not be denied by the federal government. These were the exact types of rights denied to Salem's accused in 1692—and we would do well to ensure they are not denied again.

Chapter 6

Blackbeard the Pirate

One thing that has remained generally true since the advent of pop culture as we know it is that it's possible to tell how relevant something or someone is by simply counting the number of times they show up in mainstream media. This is perhaps most obvious in the case of celebrities. When a starlet breaks onto the scene, suddenly they seem to be in every major film, commercial, and social media meme. The same is true for figures mired in of-the-moment scandal. In the end, all press is good press, they say.

But I don't believe those situations would do much to impress Riley Poole. That's because, if you're a living, breathing human with any amount of influence or reach (thanks to the entertainment industry or even the social media sphere), you can absolutely play a role in your own perpetual relevance. You can choose to create online content every day or elect to spend time with eye-catching people or even put yourself in scandalous situations (do it for the 'gram). Instead, what would intrigue Riley is how figures from *history* remain relevant—including in pop culture—for decades or even centuries after they have left this mortal plane.

Think about it. Whatever those individuals did in life must have been sufficiently legendary for their mystique to persist far beyond the lifetimes of even the people who knew them. At some point I've been told that everyone dies twice: once when your body ceases to function, and once more when your name is spoken aloud for the final time. By this token, some will live forever.

One of those seemingly eternal historical figures is the infamous pirate colloquially known as Blackbeard, whose longstanding recognition need not rely on living, breathing humans uttering his name due to the sheer number of times he appears in various forms of pop culture. My first introduction to Blackbeard, for instance, was not in school, but rather an episode of the *Scooby-Doo!* franchise. (If I learned anything during my youth, it's that you know you've made it as a celebrity—historical or otherwise—when your persona is co-opted into a *Scooby-Doo!* character.)

The celebrity of Blackbeard, however, has been preserved in mediums spanning far beyond children's cartoons. He is the namesake of the film *Blackbeard the Pirate* (1952) and was thrust into the modern limelight with a feature appearance in *Pirates of the Caribbean: On Stranger Tides* (2011). Moments in pop culture have certainly maintained Blackbeard's mystique and crafted his careful legend, but have you ever stopped to consider how much of it is true? It turns out that films and television may be responsible for shaping a legacy that is very wrong, not just for Blackbeard, but for pirates in general.

> **Why Riley Would Care:** Blackbeard boasts the type of persistent legacy that Riley probably longs to achieve in his own life, and he wouldn't balk at that legacy including rumored but mysteriously unconfirmed riches, either.

HUNT DOWN THAT HISTORY

It probably goes without saying, but for the record, pirates are individuals who rob or commandeer ships. They've sailed the high seas for as long as maritime travel has existed, and they haven't always been unwelcome. The New World was colonized with the help of legalized piracy, also known as privateering, whereby ruling parties would grant ship captains permission (in the form of "letters of marque") to raid ships belonging to other nations—always specifying *which* nations' ships were "allowed" to be targeted. The plunder acquired from a privateering raid was meant to be presented before an Admiralty Court of the home nation, but in reality, privateers often bent or skirted these rules to maximize personal profits.

In 1562, a French naval officer by the name of Jean Ribault established an outpost for privateers on present-day Parris Island, South

Carolina—one of the earliest settlements on the American East Coast. The outpost was named Charlesfort, and the intent was for French privateers to use the island as a home base from which to attack passing Spanish ships. For more than a century, New World piracy was all the rage. But by the end of the 1600s, the European monarchs' goodwill toward pirates was quickly depleting; England, having successfully established its colonies, was specifically eager to crack down on pirates whose activities were now causing the monarchy's checkbook to suffer.

By this time, pirates were operating as far north as Massachusetts and as far south as the Caribbean islands and Central America. Ironically, the English colonists in America interacted frequently with pirates, and not always in bad or unwanted ways. Sure, *occasionally* the pirates stole from the colonists, and that certainly wasn't great, but oftentimes pirates served as willing trade partners. And it wasn't just ordinary people who traded with them; governors did too. Governors valued these relationships so much that some vocally supported pirates in the early stages of English skepticism.

Then there were the colonists who actually *admired* pirates for balking at a ruling class that was increasingly seen as corrupt. Taken as a group, pirates were known to be shockingly egalitarian, or even democratic. Captains established their own codes of conduct by which their crews were required to abide, and spoils from raids were shared by everyone aboard a ship.

Contrary to popular belief, pirates did not spend their entire lives sailing the high seas. Ships docked and crews came ashore for days on end, bringing their riches with them. After all, what good is money confined to a ship where there's nothing to buy? Docking was also necessary to facilitate repairs and to visit families, because yes, many pirates had those. In fact, the British National Archives is the proud home of a petition signed by forty-eight wives requesting that British royalty pardon their pirate husbands; the wives were eager to have their seafaring husbands' assistance caring for their families.

The British crackdown on pirates took effect in earnest in 1713, when proclamations were released haranguing piracy as a practice. These proclamations were the first step in converting public opinion about pirates from one of neutrality (or even outright positivity) to one of fear and disgust. As a result of souring colonist perceptions, pirates could no longer safely return home, and left with few alternatives, they began attacking the colonies with greater frequency in lieu of their previously common practice of cooperation.

By the time the Revolutionary War broke out, pirates had become rather scarce. But that didn't stop the Continental Congress from reinvigorating the practice of privateering by hiring fifty-five thousand sailors to attack ships sailed by British forces. These privateers ultimately commandeered or destroyed around six hundred British ships and looted $18 million in assets.

Thanks to their quintessential role in the colonization of the New World, pirates became engrained in the history of early America. Consider how the College of William and Mary in Williamsburg, Virginia, was established, in part, with the help of a monetary donation by English pirates seeking a pardon. Another notable example of American piracy is that of Sam "Black Sam" Bellamy, the richest pirate known to date who operated out of Massachusetts and captured numerous large ships. The wreckage of Bellamy's final vessel, *Whydah*, was only recovered in 1984, a monumental moment in advancing our understanding of the "Golden Age of Piracy."

The Golden Age of Piracy took place between the late 1600s and the mid-1720s, an era characterized by more than five thousand pirates wreaking havoc on the high seas. Those who operated in the Caribbean and the southeastern coast of the eventual United States during this time would become some of the most famous—and infamous—pirates in all of world history, owing mostly to their vast success. These pirates played interference with the economies of three great empires, each in their heyday of expansion. During this time, Great Britain and other powers existed in a constant state of fear that pirates surrounding their shiny, new colonies would burn or blockade fledgling cities.

In the latter years of this golden age, pirates in the New World commonly made their home base in Nassau, Bahamas, following Queen Anne's War (also known as the War of Spanish Succession, which lasted from 1702 until 1713). On this island sat a true stronghold of a fort, and pirates regularly stocked it with supplies. From this central location, pirates could venture out to Florida and the Caribbean islands to perpetrate quick raids.

Much of what we know—or think we know—about pirates from this era is derived from a single book, *A General History of the Robberies and Murders of the Most Notorious Pyrates*, published under the name

Captain Charles Johnson (likely a pseudonym) in 1724. The text is replete with detailed, accurate accounts of pirate activities . . . written alongside complete and utter fabrications. The trick is somehow determining which is which.

Importantly, *A General History* relays biographies of many famous pirates while introducing pirate concepts that maintain a stranglehold on modern-day pop culture. For example, it is believed this book was the first to assign the name Jolly Roger to a pirate flag emblazoned with a skull and crossbones. The book originated our belief of pirates burying treasure, missing legs, and wearing eyepatches. *A General History* was so influential that it ultimately inspired Robert Louis Stevenson's *Treasure Island* (1883) and J. M. Barrie's *Peter Pan* (1904). It was also *A General History* that first informed a rapt audience that Blackbeard, a pirate with fourteen wives, was notoriously vicious and bloodthirsty.

Blackbeard's pirate tenure coincided with the English crackdown. Not much is known about his early life, and even his real name is up for debate. Most believe his name was either Edward Thatch or Edward Teach (the latter option originating from an article in the *Boston News-Letter*), and he may have grown up in England, or Jamaica, or North Carolina, or Philadelphia. Given that these possible locations are quite dissimilar geographically, it's pretty fair to say we don't really know anything about his origins whatsoever, though we feel minorly confident that he was born sometime around the year 1680 (give or take). Honestly, the basics of Blackbeard make for a pretty compelling mystery all on their own.

Blackbeard's pirating career likely began quite legally. He was probably a privateer during Queen Anne's War and became a bona fide, unauthorized pirate sometime following the war's conclusion. After all, a great many privateers opted for piracy in this era, as it was a skill they had perfected in the preceding decade. (Privateers seemed to understand the adage "dress for the career you want.")

Blackbeard's fearsome reputation might be a thing of persistent legend, but that's because he carefully curated a terrifying image for himself during his maritime exploits. According to *A General History* (and, notably, no other corroborating source), Blackbeard was said to wrap slow-burning matches in his long, black facial hair, causing smoke to billow out around his head. He worked under the assumption that if the crew of his target ship perceived him as intimidating and ruthless, they would put up less resistance to his raids. This is also why he supposedly holstered three guns to his chest and put on displays of great strength.

During raids, Blackbeard apparently collected books and other commodities in addition to seizing entire ships. One of his telltale strategies was to approach unsuspecting vessels at the break of dawn, capitalizing on the element of surprise. Despite these cunning tactics and contrary to our modern conception of the figure, no historical records indicate that he ever killed anyone aboard a ship he was plundering (until his eventual demise, but we're getting ahead of ourselves).

Now that we understand his persona and modus operandi, we can begin to examine Blackbeard's geographic range, which will ultimately lead us to his rise and fall. Blackbeard probably came onto the illegal piracy scene in 1713 and was one of the pirates to use the fort at Nassau as his home base. Many suspect he was pirating in 1715 when a Spanish fleet departing Cuba wrecked on the east coast of Florida due to an unforeseen hurricane; when a large cohort of British pirates came out of the woodwork to pillage the wreckage, Blackbeard may have been among their ranks.

The first incontrovertible historical record of Blackbeard dates to late 1716, when he was working under Benjamin Hornigold, an established pirate in the Caribbean. At this time, Blackbeard piloted a sloop (a common flavor of pirate ship) replete with a ninety-person crew and eight cannons. Hornigold was said to have been kicked off his own ship, *Marianne*, sometime earlier that year, at which point he restarted his career with the support of Blackbeard and any remaining crew members that maintained their loyalty to him.

It wasn't until August 1717 that Blackbeard first commanded a ship all on his own. Stede Bonnet, the son of a wealthy family in Barbados, decided to try his untrained hand at pirating for some unknown reason, and he failed epically. Bonnet lost his ship, *Revenge*, to Blackbeard. Aboard the *Revenge*, Blackbeard regularly sailed around the Chesapeake Bay, Philadelphia, and New York by October 1717, successfully taking command of no fewer than fifteen ships in the process. His primary targets were merchants.

Things progressed quickly for Blackbeard, who, along with Hornigold and Bonnet, returned to the eastern Caribbean in late fall of 1717 and encountered *La Concorde* off the coast of Martinique. *La*

Concorde was a French vessel based out of the Loire River—a hub of the country's slave trade. The ship had previously completed slave transport expeditions between Africa and the Caribbean without incident in 1713 and 1715. This involved the ship's captain purchasing enslaved Africans from the west coast of the continent, transporting them across the Atlantic Ocean via a route known as the Middle Passage, and selling them as sugar cane laborers in Guadeloupe, Haiti, or Martinique. On the ship's return to France, it carried a supply of sugar.

La Concorde's luck—and, by association, that of its owner René Montaudoin—was about to change on its third trip to the Caribbean. On November 17, 1717, *La Concorde* had been transporting 516 enslaved Africans and twenty pounds of gold dust. By the time the ship encountered Blackbeard's pirate crew, it was just one hundred miles shy of the Martinique coast and had already suffered mightily en route, with sixty-one enslaved people and sixteen crew members perishing during the journey.

Primary sources suggest Blackbeard and company were piloting two sloops—one outfitted with twelve cannons and 120 personnel, and the other carrying eight cannons and thirty personnel—when they stumbled upon *La Concorde*. The French ship didn't put up much of a fight, as most of the remaining crew members were plagued by scurvy or dysentery, so Blackbeard easily took command. The ship was sailed to the Grenadines, where the French crewmen and enslaved Africans were mercifully sent ashore while the pirates conducted a thorough search of the vessel.

Some of the Frenchmen elected to join Blackbeard's crew of their own volition, but a handful—including a captain, doctors, carpenters, and a chef—were forced. *La Concorde* was Blackbeard's new flagship, and he left the smaller pirate sloop and most of the enslaved Africans to the French, who renamed their new, smaller vessel the *Mauvaise Rencontre* (*Bad Encounter*). It is perhaps interesting that Blackbeard did not welcome some of the enslaved men onto his crew, as he was known to host many Black crewmen throughout his pirating journey. While aboard pirate ships, Africans were typically not enslaved, making piracy a somewhat attractive alternative for many at the time.

In any case, the French weren't the only ones in need of some creative renaming; Blackbeard swapped out the name *La Concorde* for *Queen Anne's Revenge*. It remains unclear why he chose this moniker for his flagship, though around the time of Blackbeard's operations, Queen Anne had passed away and been replaced by the wildly unpopular German King George I. To further his fearsome image, Blackbeard's additional stylistic modifications included a flag featuring both a blood-soaked heart and a skeleton figure bearing an hourglass and a spear.

Queen Anne's Revenge was truly the perfect pirate ship. It had all the ideal qualities: big, fast, and built to carry a ton of cannons. After departing the Grenadines with his prize, Blackbeard is believed to have sailed north, attacking ships near Antigua, Nevis, St. Lucia, and St. Vincent. By the end of 1717 (yes, we're still in the year 1717; I told you things heated up quickly), he reached Puerto Rico en route to Hispaniola (present-day Dominican Republic). The guy got around.

It was about this time that Blackbeard learned King George I had offered to pardon any pirates—and would allow them to keep their pirated goods—if they surrendered to a British governor by September 1718. Whether or not Blackbeard was immediately intrigued by the opportunity, he still had nearly a year to decide if he wanted to hang up his holster.

Perhaps that's why he continued in his pirating ways as 1718 commenced, even though we don't know exactly where he went early in the year. Some evidence, for example, suggests he may have been pillaging near Veracruz, Mexico. But by April, Blackbeard turned up near the islands off the coast of Honduras, captured several ships in Central America, and somehow had very little to show for his efforts. He moved along in the spring, heading back to familiar stomping grounds on the southeastern coast of America.

In May 1718, *Queen Anne's Revenge* and Blackbeard's three tailing sloops pulled up in Charleston, South Carolina. Here, his activities have gone down in history because of how audacious they turned out to be. In an unprecedented move, Blackbeard instructed his four ships to blockade the entire port of Charleston for close to a week. If a ship tried to enter or leave the port (which was honestly pretty foolish), he commandeered it and stole its cargo, which mostly amounted to pitch, tar, and rice. On one occasion when Blackbeard took a ship called the *Crowley*, its unfortunate crew and passengers became prisoners.

In exchange for his prisoners, Blackbeard requested a ransom of medicine, and once it was delivered, he made good on his promise to free the hostages. While it is largely thought that Blackbeard was at his pirating height around this time—with a crew of between three hundred and four hundred men and a fleet of several ships—his demand for medicine might indicate he and his men weren't doing as well (at least healthwise) as an onlooker might have believed.

After releasing the prisoners and, frankly, Charleston as a whole, Blackbeard's fleet turned its attention toward North Carolina. It seemed that Blackbeard was indeed interested in taking King George I up on his offer: pledge allegiance to the monarchy and solemnly swear to never pirate again, and he'd be guaranteed a pardon without loss of his previously stolen wealth. North Carolina would be his destination for making his bargain.

Doing so wasn't as simple as he might have hoped. Blackbeard and his fleet attempted to navigate into Old Topsail Inlet (present-day Beaufort Inlet) in North Carolina, but he immediately encountered trouble due to the port's shallow waters. *Queen Anne's Revenge* and a sloop were grounded, causing the two ships to be hastily abandoned. Because of the later testimony of David Herriot, captain of the grounded sloop, many have posited Blackbeard intentionally grounded half his fleet because his crew had grown too large and unmanageable. Detractors of this theory propose a much simpler solution: Blackbeard abandoned the two ships simply to make the best out of a bad situation.

Regardless of the situation's true cause, Blackbeard left most of his fellow pirates near the grounding site and then departed for Bath, North Carolina, with a substantially smaller crew and his remaining spoils. While in Bath, Blackbeard took the oath of loyalty to the crown and stayed put for some time as a local. During this period, he supposedly married Mary Ormond, a young woman from the town.

You might think that a formerly notorious pirate living amongst everyday citizens would make townspeople and local leaders queasy, but Blackbeard and his former crew had something to offer not only to Bath, but also to North Carolina Governor Charles Eden. As individuals with combat training, the pirates could lend a hand defending the colony if and when skirmishes occurred. As a result, Blackbeard wasn't the only one pardoned; so was his entire remaining crew. The governor would go so far as to grant Blackbeard the legal title to the sloop he sailed in on.

Blackbeard would soon move on from Bath to semiretire on

Ocracoke Island, part of North Carolina's famed Outer Banks. These barrier islands served as outposts for many pirates because of their shallow, somewhat secluded inlets, and this is where Blackbeard parked his remaining ship, *Adventure*. But the retired pirate must have grown restless, as officials from the nearby Virginia and South Carolina colonies began accusing him of conducting ongoing ambushes. In 1718, both colonies issued their own authorizations to have Blackbeard's ship raided, aiming to capture his crew.

But if Blackbeard was balking at the oath of nonpiracy he had taken, wouldn't the governor of North Carolina have been obligated to put a stop to his illicit activities? It turns out that Governor Eden had much more to gain by looking the other way. That's because Eden and the colonists of North Carolina benefited greatly from any raids Blackbeard conducted at sea, since he routinely sold his stolen goods to them for much less than the going market rates. Governor Eden even took a healthy commission from his BPFF (best pirate friend forever).

> **Riley's Favorite Fact (Probably):** Blackbeard was a skilled negotiator, striking a covert deal with North Carolina's governor to continue raiding unsuspecting ships even after swearing under oath that he'd given up piracy for good.

The scheme worked well for some time. One of Blackbeard's last successful raids occurred in August 1718, when he targeted and seized the *Rose Emelye*, a French ship he located in the waters surrounding Bermuda. Blackbeard collected the *Rose Emelye*, sent its French crew back to Europe on a smaller, accompanying ship, and earned 180 barrels of sugar and hundreds of bags of cocoa as his prize. For appearances (probably), he claimed to Governor Eden that he had simply found the ship abandoned at sea, which technically gave Blackbeard full salvage rights to the ship and its cargo.

Little did Blackbeard know that his good fortune was about to dry up. The events that would soon unfold were said to have been inspired by nearby governors—and particularly Governor Alexander Spotswood of Virginia—learning about the true events surrounding the *Rose Emelye* raid. At the time, Governor Spotswood was already in hot water as the subject of numerous investigations, so without batting an eye he ordered an attack on Blackbeard, despite lacking the authority to do so. He claimed he was simply responding to sailors' pleas for help combating the rogue pirate.

Governor Spotswood's decision would ultimately cause Blackbeard to meet an untimely end. On November 22, 1718, Spotswood's funding sent Royal Navy Lieutenant Robert Maynard with small, cannonless sloops to Ocracoke Inlet, where Blackbeard's ship was stationed. It was hoped that by piloting smaller, stealthier ships in the inlet's shallow waters, Maynard would be able to use Blackbeard's favorite tactic, the element of surprise, against him. This, however, came at the cost of Maynard's crew needing to rely on personal weapons and hand-to-hand combat to take down their villain.

But the best laid plans of mice and men often go awry, and Maynard almost immediately *lost* the element of surprise when his ships still managed to run aground. To shake them loose, many heavy objects were thrown overboard. Maynard and Blackbeard would end up conversing from the decks of their respective ships, at which time Maynard threatened his adversary, who, in turn, began launching cannonballs. Maynard's two ships, the *Jane* and the *Ranger*, withstood heavy fire, causing significant damage and casualties. In need of a quick resolution, Maynard instructed the crew of the *Jane* to make their way below deck in the hopes that Blackbeard would believe the ship was abandoned.

Blackbeard took the bait. As soon as he and his crew boarded the *Jane*, Maynard and *his* crew spilled out of the ship's bowels, attacking the unsuspecting pirates. Their close-contact battle was swift and perilous. It is believed that around ten sailors from the Royal Navy and ten pirates died in combat, with more than twenty sailors suffering injuries. Blackbeard himself was stabbed twenty-five times and shot five more, resulting in imminent death. In a vicious, symbolic gesture, he was decapitated, and his lifeless body was thrown overboard.

On its way back to Virginia, Maynard's ship sported Blackbeard's head hanging from the bowsprit, while fourteen pirate prisoners were carried onboard. When Maynard finally returned home in January 1719, Governor Spotswood fitted Blackbeard's head on a spike, which was strategically placed on the bank of the James River as a warning to all pirates. Local legend claims that part of his skull was eventually coated in silver and used as a punch bowl at a tavern in Williamsburg.

The fall of Blackbeard is thought by many to represent the end of East Coast piracy, although smuggling and other illegal sea-based activities would continue to create tension in the lead-up to the American Revolution.

LISTEN TO RILEY

The events surrounding Blackbeard's death are fairly well understood. Most popular intrigue surrounding the famous figure centers on that which pirates tend to be known for to this day: treasure. Like many, Blackbeard was said to have possessed a vast treasure, with some people guessing his successes at sea would have led him to amass a fortune valued at tens or hundreds of millions of dollars. This assertion is supported by—you guessed it—*A General History*. The book claimed that the night before Maynard's fateful attack, Blackbeard promised his crew that "no-body but himself and the Devil, knew where [his treasure] was, and the longest liver should take all."

Those who believe in Blackbeard's legendary treasure are quick to point out that when his flagship, *Queen Anne's Revenge*, wrecked at Old Topsail Inlet, its sinking was a slow one. This would have given Blackbeard plenty of time to offload valuable treasure from the vessel. As a result, treasure hunters have theorized several locations where hypothetical riches could be hidden, starting with one of the caves surrounding Ocracoke Island. Others have suggested the treasure was placed around Plum Point (Blackbeard's home in Bath) or a nearby structure where the pirate worked on his ship hulls. Searches of this former property have turned up only remnants of the house's foundation.

Another theory purports that since Blackbeard had a synergistic relationship with Governor Eden, he may have asked the political figure for assistance hiding treasure at his gubernatorial home, Archbell Point. Some people believe Blackbeard had near-full reign of the governor's compound, allowing him to smuggle materials on and off the property when he was giving Governor Eden his share of any raid spoils. This would have offered Blackbeard ample opportunities to use the grounds for treasure-stashing purposes.

Still others have hypothesized that given the substantial amount of time Blackbeard spent pirating throughout the Caribbean, he may have hidden his wealth on one of the region's many islands. This would widen the search zone exponentially. Regardless, since the wreck of *Queen Anne's Revenge* had been lost to history for centuries, it was hoped that if and when the ship was recovered, it would reveal clues regarding whether a treasure ever existed or where it might be located . . . perhaps even on the sunken ship itself.

It wasn't until 1996, when the wreckage of *Queen Anne's Revenge* was finally found, that historians would begin testing this widespread belief. The remnants of the ship were identified twenty-five feet underwater and less than two miles from the shoreline at Beaufort Inlet by a private research firm, which first noticed a slew of cannons and anchors on the seafloor. Once the site was marked, artifacts kept revealing themselves, with one of the larger ones being a bronze bell dated 1705.

The wreck was identified as *Queen Anne's Revenge* once and for all in 2011. Formal identification involved a process of cross-referencing artifacts at the site with maps and documents dating back to the 1700s; these records shared accounts of the ship's grounding, the distance the wreckage seemed to displace from the point of impact, and of course the characteristics of the ship itself.

Evidence supporting the identification included not only the wreck's location and size (since it was uncommon for large ships to try navigating such shallow channels), but also the fact that some of the cannons were loaded with scrap metal (a typical pirate practice). Another smoking gun (pun intended) was the recovery of restraints consistent with a ship that had once carried enslaved people, as well as measurement markings characteristic of old French vessels.

> **Riley's Next Hunt:** Blackbeard came, saw, and conquered a lot of ships in his illustrious pirating career, so why did he specifically choose *Queen Anne's Revenge* as his flagship? Historians will point to the vessel's high-quality specs, but Riley would probably suspect the pirate of having other, more secretive reasons.

At the time of this writing, *Queen Anne's Revenge* is the second oldest shipwreck ever found in North Carolina waters, and it remains the property of the state. Exploration of the wreckage began in 1997 under the guidance of the North Carolina Department of Natural and

Cultural Resources's Underwater Archaeology Branch, and efforts to understand the historical site have implemented mapping techniques, remote sensing, and more.

The artifacts recovered from the site are helping historians understand the early 1700s by providing insight into ship technology of the era, details about the slave trade, hints about what seafaring life was like, as well as factoids about piracy itself. For example, the wreckage has already allowed historians to determine that Blackbeard's crew likely hunted, since the remains of wild boar, deer, and turkey were found onboard.

Other small items that have been recovered include cannon balls, a pewter platter, fragments of pottery, tools, gold specks, lead shot, glass beads, copper alloy pins, plates, bowls, and coins. Over four hundred thousand artifacts have been surfaced, with the eventual goal of creating a complete catalogue and then displaying the collection in a museum. But in the meantime, scientists at East Carolina University's Greenville campus use a special conservation laboratory to keep the artifacts safe while using X-ray imaging to visualize what lies beneath corrosion and marine growth that clings to each new item found at the underwater archaeological site.

To the dismay of many hopeful treasure hunters, no "treasure" in the pop culture sense of the word was found aboard the *Queen Anne's Revenge*, and that's likely because Blackbeard's treasure never actually existed. Although he remains one of the most famous pirates in history, Blackbeard wasn't a terribly successful pirate if we're using material wealth as a quantitative proxy. But the wreck of his ship offers a different kind of treasure: one that will allow us to continue learning about his lifetime for many years to come.

After all, there's plenty left to discover about the life and times of this infamous figure. For instance, in 2015, historian and genealogist Baylus Brooks pieced together the family tree of a man named Edward Thache, a former resident of Spanish Town, Jamaica. Brooks believes Thache, a captain and, by all accounts, a high-class man, was Blackbeard's father. This assertion is consistent with the story told by an Englishman who visited Jamaica in 1739 and claimed to have met people on the island who were relatives of Blackbeard.

Another key discovery Brooks made was a 1706 document written by Edward Thache's son, who bore the same name as his father. This document gifted the Thache estate to Lucretia, the younger Thache's stepmother. This property transfer had been drafted aboard a Royal Navy ship named *Windsor* when it was docked at a Jamaican port, implying that if the author was indeed Blackbeard, his origins trace back to the Royal Navy.

Based on his research, Brooks believes Blackbeard's family once lived in Bristol, England, departing for Jamaica during Blackbeard's youth in the hopes of capitalizing on slave labor to gain wealth. At some point, presumably in early adulthood, Blackbeard boarded a merchant ship to return to England, where he joined the Royal Navy. Given basic pirate history, it wouldn't be terribly shocking if a stint of privateering later led him to his more well-known life of illegal piracy. And while it is unclear whether Brooks's theory is correct, his findings underscore the fact that there is still much to learn about Blackbeard and his fellow pirates, a reality that will facilitate their persistent legacy for generations to come.

Chapter 7

Corps
of
Discovery

When I think about pivotal moments in the history of the United States, my brain immediately travels back to the year 1776 and the moment our Founding Fathers put pen to paper on a truly treasonous document. Would this be every American's first thought? I'm really not sure, given that my perspective is obviously biased. Perhaps others would point to the ratification of the United States Constitution, the initial reading of the Emancipation Proclamation, or the civil rights movement of the mid-1900s. Each of these events represents an incontrovertibly pivotal moment.

Another interpretation of the same prompt might involve an oft-revisited story found in textbooks on early American history. As a fledgling country, the United States expanded rapidly following its establishment thanks to the seizure of Native American lands and acquisitions from other countries that had previously done the same. Reading the journal entries of early American explorers remains a fascinating exercise when considering that every creature they saw, every land formation they traversed, and every civilization they encountered was a brand-new experience. Their journals are firsthand accounts of history as it was literally being made.

Without question, the most famous stories of America's westward expansion derive from a journey spearheaded by two men: Meriwether Lewis and William Clark. Their travels were significant for the innumerable discoveries they enabled, but also because of the microcosm of social conditions they represented. In fact, the most interesting and significant element of the Lewis and Clark expedition (in my humble opinion) seems to be the one detail left on the cutting room floor when textbooks are printed: this expedition witnessed the first instance of a woman and an African American participating in American democracy, as well as the first-ever American vote west of the Mississippi River.

> **Why Riley Would Care:** Not only did Riley's ancestor track the Corps of Discovery in real time, but the Corps's mission cemented Lewis and Clark's legacy in American history and pretty much guaranteed them a book deal—something Riley could certainly appreciate.

HUNT DOWN THAT HISTORY

To better understand this monumental moment in US history, we must first meet the protagonists of our story. Meriwether Lewis—who will turn out to be the tale's tragic hero—was born in Virginia in August 1774. He was raised in Georgia, returned to Virginia for school, and graduated from college in 1793. As a member of Virginia's state militia, Lewis was tapped to serve as a captain in the US Army, but his tenure was short-lived. President Thomas Jefferson, whose Monticello estate was near Lewis's birthplace and who therefore had known Lewis since his childhood, invited the young man to be his personal secretary. Some would say Lewis was in the right place at the right time; others would say he was the beneficiary of great privilege, but the end result was President Jefferson becoming his mentor.

It makes sense then that when Jefferson was looking for someone to lead the expedition of the century across the American plains, he turned to his protégé. The mission the president had in mind was simple in theory but daunting in scope: conduct an exploratory journey across the lands west of the Mississippi River. These lands represented great promise and hope, having been recent acquisitions under the auspices of the Louisiana Purchase.

In 1803, the Louisiana Purchase had made official France's sale of its Louisiana Territory to the United States for $15 million. For context, the size of present-day Louisiana pales in comparison to the area covered by the eponymous purchase, which spanned 827,000 square miles. The reasons for the acquisition were numerous and included Jefferson's concerns that if the United States didn't take control of the land west of the Mississippi River quickly, Great Britain would beat the young country to it. He was so adamant about the United States expanding westward that he had been ruminating over ideas for an exploratory expedition prior to the purchase becoming official.

Indeed, President Jefferson had implored numerous esteemed men to pursue such a trek for several years prior to what would eventually become the Lewis and Clark expedition. These initial conversations might have contributed to his eventual choice of Lewis as expedition lead, because the young man had volunteered to take part in one of Jefferson's early schemes. While none of these initial voyages formally took shape, some of Jefferson's trusted colleagues conducted basic scouting that, alongside publications detailing other nations' westward explorations, would end up informing the initial steps of Lewis and Clark's route.

All of this is to say that it's highly likely President Jefferson would have pursued an American expedition even if the Louisiana Purchase had not panned out. Doing so, however, would have required obtaining formal permission from France, as any such journey would have necessitated substantial travel through French territory. But the Louisiana Purchase made this contingency obsolete, and Jefferson ultimately asked Congress for a measly $2,500 to fund the mission. After all, now that the United States owned the land, they should probably figure out what it contained.

To some extent, the expedition was an exercise in known unknowns. Jefferson sought information describing the land's terrain, ecology, and local Native American residents. Regarding these tribes, he wanted to learn about their cultures while establishing some amount of comradery. He knew doing so would help minimize conflict and potentially win over valuable trade partners.

In the natural resources category, the president was keen to discover previously unknown or seemingly rare species of animals; in fact, he genuinely believed the expedition would reveal living, breathing wooly mammoths and giant ground sloths. He also hoped his explorers would bring home maps to help future settlers and merchants navigate the mysterious terrain. Naturally, this would include details on geographic formations like mountains, waterways, and their resources.

This type of information would potentially allow Jefferson to achieve his greatest goal: to chart a water-based route from the eastern

United States to the Pacific Ocean, a theorized throughway known as the Northwest Passage. In essence, Jefferson was searching for early American MapQuest directions that could facilitate ease of global trade. He thought he would find an ideal route by closely tracking the flow of the Missouri and Columbia Rivers.

Meriwether Lewis, on board with leading the expedition at hand, had substantial prep work to do. Jefferson's demands for the journey required a more than rudimentary understanding of various scientific disciplines, so he sent his expedition captain to the American Philosophical Society in Philadelphia for academic boot camp. Lewis would end up pursuing crash courses in astronomy, botany, medicine, and zoology, among other subjects. Perhaps realizing the journey would be best led as a team, he selected his friend, William Clark, to be his cocaptain.

Lewis and Clark's friendship had begun several years earlier. In 1795, the two met when a twenty-one-year-old Lewis, who was in the US Army, allegedly challenged someone in his unit to a duel. This was clearly a problem, so Lewis was transferred to a different unit whose commander was none other than William Clark. Clark was just a bit older than Lewis, born in Virginia in 1770 and raised in Kentucky. Like Lewis, Clark had served in his state's militia before joining the national armed forces. The two made a charismatic, complementary pair, which may be why history texts remember them so fondly: Lewis is perpetually portrayed as a brooding academic sort, while Clark is depicted as a poorly educated but practical backwoods-type character.

With the two-man leadership team established, preparations became increasingly tactical. Lewis was responsible for gathering munitions and the keelboat that would be the expedition's home away from home for the duration of its water-based journey. He acquired these key supplies in Pittsburgh, while also sourcing everything from wayfinding instruments and camping supplies to clothing, medicine, and books. He compiled a massive stockpile of weaponry consisting of rifles, muskets, tomahawks, and knives, alongside two hundred pounds of gunpowder and four hundred pounds of lead for bullets. Also considered to be critical supplies were beads, mirrors, tobacco, cloth, and other items the expeditioners could offer as gifts to the Native American tribes they encountered.

Clark had his own groundwork to lay, and I would think his principal preparatory task was daunting. After all, how easy would it have been to solicit willing volunteers to journey into the geographic unknown for an equally unknown period of time? It was Clark's responsibility to recruit the expedition's crew, and he specifically targeted men who had few attachments (read: unmarried) and possessed strong survival skills. The willing group he amassed comprised translators, experienced sailors, and former US Army soldiers. Lewis would ultimately sail his shiny, new keelboat loaded with supplies down the Ohio River to collect Clark and his freshly formed team.

The expedition, known as the Corps of Discovery, launched on May 14, 1803, outside of St. Louis, Missouri, heading upstream on the Missouri River. The cohort counted forty-five men, including Clark's enslaved servant, York, as well as one nonhuman passenger, Lewis's Newfoundland dog, Seaman. The principal keelboat, flanked by smaller boats, traveled at a painstaking rate of approximately fifteen miles per day, though progress was hindered by various environmental factors, such as unexpectedly strong river currents.

Before long the expedition encountered its first Native American tribe, the Yankton Sioux. Throughout the trek, the group would end up meeting around fifty distinct tribes, including the Shoshone and Blackfeet. Lewis and Clark had established a standard protocol for managing initial contact with each community. First, they presented the local chief or tribal leader with a Jefferson Indian Peace Medal, an engraved coin. Second, they communicated that the United States owned the tribe's land and offered military protection if the tribe agreed to a peaceful relationship. Overall, the expedition's exchanges with Native Americans were met with varying degrees of acceptance. While some tribes were more than happy to establish trade relations, others were understandably skeptical.

> **Riley's Favorite Fact (Probably):** In what sounds like an extremely humbling experience, Meriwether Lewis survived unfriendly encounters with a rattlesnake, wolverine, bison, and grizzly bear all in a single day.

Writings about the travelers' encounters with novel animal species are similarly fascinating, and many accounts—including reactions to the animals—can be read in the expedition's official journals. For instance, in the fall of 1804, the explorers first laid eyes on prairie dogs, pronghorns, coyotes, and jack rabbits while passing time in modern-day South Dakota. They allegedly spent an entire day trying to capture a prairie dog, and they ultimately succeeded after resorting to flooding the poor creature's holes. They sent the living prairie dog back to President Jefferson (alongside many other specimens of flora and fauna).

Other accounts are equally humorous. For example, the explorers were said to have been intrigued by jack rabbits' impossibly long and expressive ears. They also thought a pronghorn was a type of deer, and they stuffed two to send to Jefferson for examination. Later in their journey, Lewis recounted in his journal a belief that "the entire animal kingdom has conspired against me," referring to sequential near-death experiences he suffered at the proverbial hands of a rattlesnake, wolverine, bison, and grizzly bear . . . all in the same day.

The expedition was forced to contend with challenging weather conditions on numerous occasions. The crew's first winter, for instance, was spent at Fort Mandan, a makeshift community they had constructed alongside the Mandan tribal village in present-day North Dakota. For five months, the explorers camped out while planning their onward route with geographic intel from the local Native Americans and nearby French-Canadian traders. They also spent time crafting tools that could be swapped with their native neighbors in exchange for food; at this time of year, that primarily consisted of corn, melons, and beans.

It was during this critical winter that Lewis and Clark first made the acquaintance of a French-Canadian man named Toussaint Charbonneau. Through Charbonneau, the two met one of the most famous Native American figures in United States history: Sacagawea, a young Shoshone woman. Sacagawea's story is both sobering and intriguing, as she was kidnapped by a rival tribe at age twelve and subsequently sold to Charbonneau, who would make her his wife.

Lewis and Clark hired Charbonneau as an interpreter, but Sacagawea was the real key to their communications success. A true asset, she translated conversations with Shoshone communities encountered on the expedition while simultaneously providing support services that we would probably call diplomatic relations today. Sacagawea brought her infant child along for the expedition, and this combination of a mother and child presented a friendly, peaceful image to tribes. She would end up being the only woman member of the expedition team.

By the time spring of 1805 approached, some members of the

Corps of Discovery were sent back east to St. Louis, tasked with the transportation of innumerable flora and fauna samples, maps, and other reports that conveyed the team's progress. It is said that from the moment President Jefferson received this substantive update, he began corresponding with his scientific colleagues to discuss and interpret the expedition's early findings.

The remaining crew members continued westward, immediately finding difficulty navigating the unfamiliar river. At one point, the river forked, necessitating quick thinking and analytical decision-making to determine which branch marked the correct way forward. They aimed to continue along the Missouri River and predicted correctly that the southern branch was their intended route based on the presence of waterfalls; during their time at Fort Mandan, the native communities had advised them to look for this geographic feature to mark their way. Later, they would encounter a three-pronged fork in the river, which they took the pleasure of naming. The most obvious westerly route—the route they opted to take—was dubbed the Jefferson River, while the other two were named Madison and Gallatin for the secretary of state and secretary of the treasury, respectively.

When the team neared the Continental Divide, they happened upon the ancestral lands of Sacagawea's Shoshone people. Serendipitously, Sacagawea came face-to-face with both her childhood friend and her brother, Cameahwait, the latter of whom had risen in the ranks to become the tribe's chief. This built-in positive relationship between the Corps of Discovery and the Shoshone was a massive reason for the success of the latter portion of the trek west. This would be the most challenging part of the journey, made possible only by trading with the Shoshone for horses. Additionally, Shoshone guides were instrumental in the explorers' ability to cross the Bitterroot Mountains without incurring any fatalities (suffering only frostbite, hunger, and dehydration instead).

After reaching the other side of the mountain range, the adventurers regained their health in present-day Idaho with the help of the Nez Perce tribe, whose members provided the weary travelers with sustenance in the form of salmon, roots, and berries. The Nez Perce also agreed to temporarily care for the expedition's horses while the group completed their final push westward, intending to collect the horses once more on the return journey.

Via the Columbia River, Lewis, Clark, and their team reached the

Pacific Ocean in November 1805, an event that marked the end of their sight-unseen journey. However, they knew they would be unable to return home until winter passed, so the group considered options for potential campsites and put the decision to a vote. The vote ultimately resulted in the establishment of their camp at Fort Clatsop in Oregon, but that's probably the least interesting thing about it. Both Sacagawea and York were active participants in this vote, representing a landmark moment for women, Native Americans, and African Americans in the history of the country—it was the first time individuals from any of these demographic groups participated in American democracy.

If the explorers recognized the importance of the moment, we have no evidence of it, and their attention soon turned to surviving the harsh winter, which subjected them to poor weather, insect pests, and illness. While the group departed Fort Clatsop on March 23, 1806, it waited a bit longer—until late spring, once the snow had melted—to complete the treacherous Bitterroot Mountain portion of the return trip.

In July 1806, Lewis and Clark split their crew into two groups, with Lewis's cohort veering north on the familiar Missouri River and Clark's cohort (which included Sacagawea), heading south on the as-yet-unexplored Yellowstone River. It was during this split-contingent period that Lewis and his crew became perpetrators of the only known violent encounter of the entire expedition: when two Blackfeet men were caught trying to steal weapons and horses, the expeditioners killed the offenders at a location now known as Two Medicine Fight Site. Soon after, Lewis also suffered an accidental gunshot wound to his buttocks while on a hunting excursion; the responsible party from his own crew claimed he believed Lewis to be an elk.

The overarching lack of violence during the expedition's lengthy duration is both shocking and impressive given the sheer number of new contacts made with tribes as well as encounters with equally unfamiliar animals. It turns out that this mostly peaceful journey was somewhat fortuitous. The Spanish, with settlements in the southwest, feared the United States was encroaching on their territory. As a result, they sent their own soldiers, as well as a group of Native American allies, to intercept and detain the Lewis and Clark expedition, but their search party never caught up with the adventurers.

On August 12, 1806, Lewis's and Clark's separate parties reconvened where the Missouri and Yellowstone Rivers converge in North Dakota.

Just a few days later they reached the location where they had first welcomed Charbonneau and Sacagawea to their team, and the two translators departed for home. The final leg of the return route was a comparatively short foray downstream along the Missouri River. After traversing eight thousand miles, the Corps of Discovery concluded its voyage in St. Louis on September 23. Remarkably, only one member of the team—a young man who suffered from a suspected case of appendicitis—succumbed to illness or injury throughout the entirety of the trek.

But Lewis and Clark's storied journey didn't truly end in St. Louis, because that autumn the two had an audience with President Jefferson in Washington, D.C., to recap the expedition. They reported being unable to identify a Northwest Passage; the Rocky Mountains were the real nail in the coffin of this theorized (and idealized) route. However, Lewis and Clark successfully proved that land-based travel was certainly possible to connect the eastern United States to the Pacific Ocean. Plus, the quality and quantity of knowledge generated from the expedition— the creation of maps and the identification of 122 and 178 animal and plant species, respectively—was truly invaluable, as were the positive relationships established with Native American tribes.

As a reward for their efforts, Lewis and Clark both received double the compensation they were initially promised when signing onto the journey. If that wasn't enough, they were also granted 1,600 acres of land. The members of their expedition team—minus Sacagawea and York, unsurprisingly—also benefited from financial compensation. Lewis was given a fancy new title, governor of the Louisiana Territory. Not to be outdone, Clark was dubbed brigadier general of militia for the Louisiana Territory and federal Indian agent. Clark would later go on to serve as the governor of the Missouri Territory until it gained statehood.

During the expedition, Clark developed a strong bond with Sacagawea and her son. He provided the son, Jean Baptiste Charbonneau, with an education in St. Louis, and in August 1813, following Sacagawea's death a year prior, Clark became her children's legal guardian. At the time, Jean Baptiste and his sister Lisette were aged ten and one, respectively. Clark lived a full life until his death in 1838 at the age of sixty-eight. On the contrary, Lewis's postexpedition story was an altogether more tragic and mysterious one.

LISTEN TO RILEY

Meriwether Lewis was known to suffer throughout his life from what we would now recognize as depression. For example, when he celebrated his thirty-first birthday in 1805 during his history-making expedition, Lewis wrote in his journal that he felt so unaccomplished that he feared he was wasting his life. He also understandably exhibited a great deal of anxiety about the Corps's logistics, such as making sure the group reached certain landmarks before the weather became unseasonable or contemplating how they would acquire horses for the mountainous portion of their trek.

Upon his return, these mental health challenges were exacerbated by several factors. For one thing, during his tenure as governor, Lewis nearly lost his job over accusations of mismanaging government funds, but he wasn't great at managing his personal finances either. He suffered from alcoholism and never got married, something that historians believe bothered him greatly based on what he shared in written correspondence.

In October 1809, Lewis chose to venture from St. Louis to Washington, D.C., hoping that upon his arrival, he would be able to allay any concerns and resolve any problems related to his gubernatorial finances. During this trip, Lewis allegedly attempted suicide on two separate occasions, and he was ultimately found dead at a rest stop in Tennessee along a woodland trail known as the Natchez Trace. His body bore gunshot wounds in the head and chest.

The circumstances surrounding Lewis's passing remain somewhat mysterious. The scene of the "crime," which some believe the situation to be, was an inn known as Grinder's Stand. The innkeeper's wife, Priscilla Knight Grinder, testified that Lewis was behaving strangely on the evening of the incident, pacing fervently and speaking loudly to himself. She was so perturbed by his actions that when she heard two gunshots in the night and found an injured Lewis pleading for help at her door, she was too scared to open up and provide help. When Lewis's servants later found him in his cabin, he was still conscious but in such bad condition that he purportedly asked his servants to kill him mercifully. As they did not comply with his desperate wishes, Lewis succumbed to his injuries within a matter of hours.

Today, most historians agree that Lewis died by suicide, citing his previous attempts and broader mental health challenges. His acquaintances agreed, as he had apparently given several of them instructions regarding how to divide and dispose of his possessions in the event of his demise. He also drafted a will during his final, yet incomplete, journey to Washington.

Even so, many hobbyists believe the legendary Meriwether Lewis was murdered, introducing a natural question: why would someone want the famous explorer dead? Theories in this regard range from the somewhat plausible to the fancifully imaginative (to put it kindly). On the former end of the spectrum, some have pointed out that the Natchez Trace was frequented by dangerous individuals, so Lewis could have been an unfortunate or even indiscriminate casualty of nefarious dealings on the trail. On the creative end of the spectrum, some have suggested that the innkeeper, Robert Grinder, murdered Lewis for his money or that an aggrieved military general assassinated him because he knew about the general's traitorous actions. And although Lewis's acquaintances favored the suicide theory, the man's own family suspected he had been murdered by his servant, John Pernier.

Present-day locals living in the area where Lewis died are some of the strongest advocates for the belief that the explorer was murdered. Whether for these reasons or others, some of Lewis's descendants have requested his body be exhumed to permit further investigation using modern methods. For instance, if gunpowder residue could be detected on Lewis's remains, or if his skull could be inspected for characteristic fracture patterns, investigators could determine whether he had been shot at close range (supporting the suicide verdict) or from a distance (indicating murder).

Perhaps some of the speculation and intrigue surrounding Lewis and his untimely end can be traced back to his expedition and the related responsibilities he still carried at the time of his death. Consider how Lewis had been traveling with his expedition journals when he died, and how one of William Clark's initial reactions to hearing about Lewis's passing was to worry about what would become of the Corps's substantive writings.

On that fateful day in October 1809, Lewis had been toting the journals because he was supposedly preparing their contents for publication—something that was long overdue and a problem of his own making. More than two years earlier, in April 1807, Lewis had traveled to Philadelphia to get the publication ball rolling in earnest. He knew the urgency with which the journals needed to be shared with the public for fear that other expedition members might beat him to the punch (you could say he worried about being "scooped").

While in Philadelphia, Lewis secured John Conrad as a publisher. He found a naturalist, Frederick Pursh, who agreed to sketch all the plant specimens the expedition had found and described. He sought Alexander Wilson, an ornithologist, to draw his team's many bird discoveries. But there was one thing Lewis didn't do during his time in Philadelphia—or frankly at any point thereafter. He didn't actually write the book.

It is not far-fetched to believe the combination of Lewis's mental illness, alcoholism, and professional challenges created an insurmountable roadblock preventing his progress on the written portions of the publication. But his delay did not go unnoticed, including by his most important advocate. President Jefferson frequently asked for status updates; his letters became increasingly vexed in tone, probably aided by the fact that Lewis systematically ignored them. I think we can all agree that ignoring a series of personal inquiries from the president of the United States is a categorically bold move. In any case, upon Lewis's death, the journals in his possession were returned to Jefferson.

The collection of journals that came from the Lewis and Clark expedition is robust. The men wrote about every experience, discovery, and encounter that happened along their journey. In terms of tangible materials, eighteen red books of notes are associated in some way with the expedition, though packets of loose notes and other crewmembers' writings are also considered part of the complete collection today. However, it wasn't always so easy to define the bounds of this "collection."

Lewis and Clark's official expedition journals were finally published for the first time in 1814, but this publication represented a somewhat hasty, definitely abridged version of their notes and failed to include almost all their scientific observations. The scientific data were added in 1893 when a new edition was released; this updated version included content from thirty packages of notes not considered in the first installment. You might therefore be wondering why so many sets of notes were associated with the expedition records; surely these men who wrote so prolifically were at least somewhat organized in their journaling efforts that spanned multiple years. Right?

Wrong. It turns out that when the expedition returned to St.

Louis and the analysis of its discoveries began in earnest, myriad pages were torn loose from the journals to share with scientists from various disciplines for closer examination. It was Jefferson himself who successfully tracked down all the journals and loose pages (or so he thought), a process that took until 1818, at which point he sent them to the American Philosophical Society to be housed more permanently (and less destructively).

Fast forward to the early 1900s. Five previously unknown and unaccounted for journals of William Clark, as well as some of his miscellaneous maps and letters, were recovered from his granddaughter and donated to the Missouri Historical Society. Subsequently, the journal that kept track of Lewis and Clark's pre-expedition preparations was found and given to the American Philosophical Society. Clark's field notes and maps were sent to Yale University, and the journals of some of the Corps's less-famous members have been collected and dispatched to various archives in Illinois and Wisconsin. Today, what is overwhelmingly seen as the definitive, complete account of the expedition was published by University of Nebraska Press in thirteen volumes that were released from 1983 to 2001.

The seemingly constant revelation of new documents derived from the expedition's official records throughout the twentieth century has led many hobbyists to ponder whether additional records are just waiting to be discovered. On the contrary, some believe these discoveries are evidence that still-missing records will be lost forever, likely destroyed in the last two centuries. A related theory, this one supported by some historians, says that Lewis's writings—particularly his daily accounts—are incomplete.

> **Riley's Next Hunt:** Historians might believe the Corps of Discovery's expedition journals represent a complete collection, but Riley would naturally disagree. Riley and Ben are the perfect candidates to recover a long-missing, secret-revealing journal belonging to Meriwether Lewis.

When considering Lewis's authenticated writings, many days of journaling are missing between September 19 and November 11, 1803. He also wrote very little from May 14, 1804, to April 7, 1805; between August 26, 1805, and January 1, 1806; and from August 12, 1806, until the expedition's conclusion. Historians have counted that his missing entries amount to over four hundred days' worth of content. That's some serious writer's block, if I do say so myself.

While the final lapse in writing can likely be attributed to the recovery from his accidental gunshot injury, it is far more difficult to rationalize the preceding gaps. As President Jefferson's right-hand man in planning the expedition, Lewis certainly grasped how important complete record-keeping was to the value of the journey. So it's not surprising that Lewis kept diligent, elaborate records in the days leading up to the expedition during the planning process. Then why did he all but cease journaling during the bulk of his travels, especially in the winters when he would theoretically have much less daily work to do? Or at the very beginning of the expedition, when Lewis would have been more likely to take seriously Jefferson's demand for thorough notes?

Some suspect that Lewis may have kept field notes—effectively unpolished drafts—that he meant to transcribe into the expedition's official journals but, for whatever reason, never did. By this theory, it is supposed that said field notes were lost over time. Others believe entire journals were lost, citing that one of the expedition's smaller boats accidentally overturned in May 1805, leading to a loss of material goods. At minimum, we know for certain that this unfortunate incident was the catalyst for replicates of the expedition's records to be made.

Yet another possible explanation is that William Clark was a meticulous—some might even say religious—record keeper, so Lewis may not have felt the need to duplicate his colead's efforts. All things considered, the most likely reason for Lewis's "missing" writings is that the two captains split the responsibilities of day-to-day journaling, with Clark taking on most of the task. This rationale would mean Lewis's writings are complete, albeit sparse. That said, certain trends exist in the notes Lewis did elect to take. As the expedition's naturalist, he kept most records of animals, plants, minerals, geological features, and astronomical phenomena.

In the end, there may actually be very few mysteries surrounding Meriwether Lewis, who, in retrospect, could be the epitome of a fraught leader facing many of the same personal and professional challenges as the rest of us. His just happened to take place two centuries ago when society was far less sympathetic.

Chapter 8

Mecklenburg Declaration of Independence

The Declaration of Independence is an iconic element of United States history. Indeed, one could argue that the Declaration is the reason that United States history exists at all. The Declaration was written in the months of June and July 1776, approved by the Second Continental Congress on July 4 of the same year, and signed beginning that August. Even centuries later, the original document is maintained using careful protective conditions under the watchful eyes of conservators at the US National Archives and Records Administration. (I like to think that contrary to popular belief, Riley and Ben have enormous respect for those conservators' work.)

But while most people understand the historical significance of the document, few are taught that strange stories have surrounded the Declaration of Independence since its creation. One such story is that of the Beale ciphers. In 1885, a pamphlet published three ciphers that purported to describe the whereabouts, contents, and owners of a priceless treasure hidden in Virginia by a man named Thomas J. Beale. As the tale goes, Beale had found the treasure out west about sixty-five years prior and brought it back to the East Coast to be reconcealed.

With time, one of the three ciphers, seeming to be a modified book cipher, was decoded. Book ciphers—like the one Riley and team found on the back of the Declaration—utilize a single edition of a book or other ubiquitous document as a "key text" to translate a series of three-digit numeric codes into letters. When the first of the three Beale ciphers was cracked, it required none other than the Declaration of Independence as its corresponding key text. But don't get too excited: the other two ciphers were never unraveled, and today, most experts agree Beale's codes were a hoax perpetrated to sell the very pamphlets that told their story.

The curious case of the Beale ciphers—and their relationship with the Declaration of Independence—is well-known in the community of legend seekers and treasure hunters. A lesser-known historical enigma with close and arguably more scandalous ties to the Declaration is that of the Mecklenburg Declaration, known colloquially in some circles as the Meck Dec. Chances are you've never heard of this piece of oft-forgotten history, unless, of course, you happened to grow up (or currently live) in North Carolina, where an entire state holiday is dedicated to this very document that may or may not have even existed. And yet oddly enough, the case of the Mecklenburg Declaration isn't the only odd historical mystery tied to the state's Mecklenburg County.

> **Why Riley Would Care:** Thomas Jefferson, the golden child of the Founding Fathers, being accused of plagiarizing his most famous text is the kind of historical scandal Riley could get behind (and maybe even champion).

HUNT DOWN THAT HISTORY

The beginning of this history lesson is brief and to the point: the Mecklenburg Declaration was allegedly a document, written in 1775, that served as the first call for the thirteen American colonies to sever ties with Great Britain and become their own nation. I'm sure you can do the math, but if this allegation is true, the Mecklenburg Declaration preexisted the Declaration of Independence by a whole year, effectively altering our conceptualization of American history as we know it.

No one would feel the need to examine this alternative reality for quite some time, because no claims about the Mecklenburg Declaration's purported existence were asserted until the nineteenth century. In April 1819, more than forty years after the drafting dates of both declarations, the first light was shed on the Meck Dec story. An article by Dr. Joseph McKnitt Alexander was published in the *Raleigh Register, and North-Carolina Gazette*, the state of North Carolina's largest newspaper, and claimed that the famed Declaration of Independence wasn't quite what it seemed.

You see, as Great Britain began tightening its grip on the colonies like someone in a toxic long-distance relationship—through new provisions like the Stamp Act (1765), Townshend Duties (1766), and Tea Act (1773)—residents across the American colonies began pulling back. Pertinent to our discussion, the new taxes and regulations imposed by the British ruling class were going over *especially* poorly in North Carolina, a colony of immigrants from Pennsylvania, Maryland, and Virginia who were mostly Scotch-Irish by descent, Presbyterian by religion, and farmers by trade.

According to Dr. Alexander, North Carolina residents had just caught wind of the Battles of Lexington and Concord having launched the American Revolutionary War a month earlier. Colonel Thomas Polk, commander of Mecklenburg County's militia, called together a meeting of representatives on May 19, 1775, in the county's biggest city, Charlotte. He hoped to discuss how North Carolinians would respond to Great Britain's passive aggression *and* active aggression alike. Whatever the convening decided would ultimately serve as the common position for all colonists in Mecklenburg County. During this meeting, the representatives decided to draft five resolutions to opt out of British rule; in other words, Mecklenburg County was breaking up with the king.

Dr. Alexander went on to claim the resolutions were signed by more than twenty-five men from the county and read publicly from the steps of the local courthouse by Colonel Polk on May 20. Though not dubbed with the moniker until many years later, these resolutions purportedly made up the mysterious Mecklenburg Declaration, which some have determined to be the first American declaration of independence.

Observers might find themselves wondering where the controversy lies. After all, in his 1819 newspaper article, Dr. Alexander shared that his own father, John McKnitt Alexander, was present at the very meeting where the Mecklenburg Declaration was drafted. The elder Alexander had even served in the very important role of meeting clerk. Moreover, the newspaper article contained the Mecklenburg Declaration's text, which not only avowed the county's independence, but also labeled Great Britian as an enemy to North Carolina, to the colonies as a collective, *and* to human rights. Scathing. In support of its strong views, the Mecklenburg Declaration referenced the death of American colonists at Lexington, which the signatories viewed as wholly unacceptable.

Dr. Alexander's article made even more assertions, including that a well-known local figure named James Jack, who would later become a military captain during the Revolutionary War, traveled on horseback to bring the Mecklenburg Declaration to the Second Continental Congress, which was convening in Philadelphia. Jack was purportedly dismissed by North Carolina's delegates—Richard Caswell, William Hooper, and Joseph Hewes—who did not believe the colonists were yet in a mindset to accept a formal call for independence. At the time, rumor had it that reconciliation with Great Britain was on the table. Jack's return trip to Charlotte, particularly his passage through Salem, North Carolina, on July 7, 1775, was documented in real time by those living in the town.

As soon as it shot off the press, Dr. Alexander's article came under intense scrutiny, but it wasn't because the Meck Dec tale would have called into question America's choice of Independence Day. At the time, the real controversy was over the fact that if Dr. Alexander's story was correct and he included the real verbiage of this lost text in his article, the Mecklenburg Declaration's contents and language were extremely, almost *suspiciously* similar to those of the Declaration of Independence—both its draft and final versions penned by Founding Father Thomas Jefferson.

Several key phrases are either identically or nearly identically replicated when comparing the two documents, and we aren't talking about run-of-the-mill, common phrases. For example, both texts use the line "dissolve the political bands which have connected," which doesn't tend to roll off the tongue of ordinary folks in everyday conversation. Similarly, the phrases "free and independent" and "are, and of right ought to be" appear verbatim in both. While the Declaration of Independence reads "absolved from all allegiance to the British Crown," Dr. Alexander's Meck Dec retelling uses the strikingly similar "absolve ourselves from all allegiance to the British Crown." Where the Declaration of Independence states "pledge to each other our lives, our fortunes, and our sacred honor," the Mecklenburg Declaration uses the same words while also pledging "our mutual cooperation."

What can this all mean? Well, most obviously, if the Mecklenburg Declaration was real and its timeline matched Dr. Alexander's assertions, North Carolina was actually the first colony to declare its independence from Great Britain, and this monumental event would have happened well before the Second Continental Congress put ink to parchment to declare the same. Perhaps even more interestingly (and more scandalously), if the Mecklenburg Declaration's text was recorded accurately by Dr. Alexander, it would suggest that the Declaration of Independence we all know and love—and give Thomas Jefferson credit for—was probably inspired by, with parts potentially copied from, the Meck Dec.

> **Riley's Favorite Fact (Probably):** If the Mecklenburg Declaration was real, then at least part of North Carolina declared itself independent more than a year before the rest of the American colonies.

It's at this point that the astute (and perhaps confused) reader may propose an overly logical question. Certainly, a document as important to history as this Mecklenburg Declaration would be preserved and could be consulted for its timestamp and overall veracity. After all, Dr. Alexander must have copied its text from *somewhere*, right? Inconveniently for the sake of history—and deliciously convenient for the sake of legend—Dr. Alexander asserted that the original document burned in a fire that claimed his father's house in 1800. By the time Dr. Alexander published his newspaper article nearly two decades later, most eyewitnesses who had purportedly been involved in developing the Meck Dec had already passed away.

You may therefore be wondering how exactly Dr. Alexander was able to rewrite the text of the Meck Dec into his now infamous article. Sometime after the housefire, the elder Alexander supposedly rewrote the Meck Dec from a combination of his memory and his surviving notes from the meeting that produced the document to begin with. In fact, Dr. Alexander himself was said to have resurfaced his father's old papers from the time of the original drafting, aiding his retelling of the drafting meeting.

Such mysterious circumstances—and the allegations of plagiarism they so naturally connote—invoked immediate suspicion amongst some of the most important people in the land: the American Founding Fathers. John Adams, for instance, learned the Mecklenburg Declaration story when Dr. Alexander's article was republished by the *Essex Register* on June 5, 1819. (The article had enough shock value that it was reprinted by newspapers across the fledgling country; it was basically nineteenth century clickbait.) On July 15, Adams wrote to his friend Reverend William Bentley to share his surprise that Thomas Jefferson had directly copied so many elements of the Meck Dec into the Declaration of Independence. By all accounts, it seemed that Adams believed Dr. Alexander's story.

Just like any author passionate about defending their work, Thomas Jefferson wasted no time lambasting Dr. Alexander's claim. Essentially, Jefferson said what we're all thinking: why would a document of such importance be kept secret for so long, and why choose this random moment to reveal its existence? He criticized the convenient assertion that not only did a fire swallow up the original document, but no eyewitnesses were alive to tell the tale of its writing. Jefferson staunchly claimed he would refuse to believe the Meck Dec existed unless he saw real, original proof of it.

For those keeping track, this is a direct rebuttal of the theory that Jefferson had already seen the original and copied parts of it when drafting the Declaration of Independence. After all, he was the principal author of the document now displayed at the National Archives in Washington, D.C. Many historians believe that, like all people writing their own works, Jefferson took inspiration from both historical figures and contemporaries, such as John Locke and George Mason, respectively.

John Adams would end up sharing his concerns with Thomas Jefferson after learning the story of the Mecklenburg Declaration, and the two corresponded via letter. For his part, Jefferson assured Adams that his Declaration of Independence was completely original, and whether because Jefferson's correspondence was incredibly convincing or because the two were acquaintances, Adams was swayed into believing his fellow founder.

However, this exchange between Adams and Jefferson wasn't revealed to the public until it was published in 1829, after Jefferson died. The letters' publication is what first prompted widespread public skepticism (as opposed to quiet skepticism amongst the defensive Founding Fathers) about the Meck Dec's authenticity. The state of North Carolina's response to the publicized letters was to issue a formal investigation into the mysterious Mecklenburg Declaration. The state sought to determine without a shadow of a doubt whether this controversial document ever existed at all.

In 1829, the North Carolina General Assembly established a committee to take on this daunting investigative task. Senator Nathaniel Macon busied himself identifying, tracking down, and interviewing any eyewitnesses who were still alive. Even if the drafting committee was mostly deceased, perhaps he could find surviving individuals who had attended the alleged public reading of the document from the courthouse steps. He searched as far as Georgia and Tennessee for witnesses.

The results of the investigation were published just two years later in 1831. The thirty-two-page report included the testimonies of veterans of the Revolutionary War, ministers from Presbyterian churches, and others who were overwhelmingly deemed credible in the eyes of government and community members alike. Their accounts confirmed a prevailing belief that a document declaring independence was, in fact, drafted, signed, and publicly read, but the investigation could not determine conclusively when these events happened. Perhaps most interestingly, Captain James Jack, who was an elderly man at the time of the investigation, confirmed that he rode all the way to Pennsylvania to deliver the Mecklenburg Declaration to the Continental Congress.

And that was that. Like any entertaining legend, the formal investigation surrounding the Meck Dec leaves just enough room for continued speculation that onlookers can shape the results to fit their existing beliefs. Those who think the Meck Dec story was a hoax at worst, or a misinterpretation at best, point to the investigators' inability to craft a conclusive timeline. Those who believe the document was real underscore the firsthand testimonies themselves. In any case, North Carolina began celebrating the Mecklenburg Declaration's anniversary on May 20, 1825, and the controversy over its existence has prevailed ever since.

LISTEN TO RILEY

In the case of the locally famous and otherwise forgotten Mecklenburg Declaration, one mystery reigns supreme: was it real? Historians have scoured the archives for decades attempting to find a suitable answer to this question, but the question itself isn't quite so simple. If the Mecklenburg Declaration never existed, why say it did? If it did exist as Dr. Alexander recounted, Thomas Jefferson's skeptical criticisms remain. Perhaps the true answer, then, is less black-and-white. Perhaps the story of the Mecklenburg Declaration has been tainted, fused with other legends—both fact and fiction—from early North Carolina history.

In 1838, archivist Peter Force uncovered an abbreviated and previously forgotten list of resolves from Mecklenburg County that when written, sought to overturn and create replacements for colonial laws instated by Great Britain. The list was found in the June 1775 issue of a local Southern newspaper. Force had discovered—or rediscovered, rather—the Mecklenburg Resolves.

Written on May 31, 1775, the Mecklenburg Resolves comprised a set of statements that rejected British laws but were a few steps short of formally declaring independence. While the resolves purported to share the opinions and reflect the will of North Carolina's residents, they did encourage other colonies to follow suit and take steps toward self-governance. Among other things, the Mecklenburg Resolves's guidance allowed Colonel Polk and Dr. Joseph Kennedy to acquire gunpowder and other weaponry. Perhaps inspired by the earliest Revolutionary War battles, the thought was that if the county sought to govern itself, it would also need to defend itself.

The goal of the resolves was to put in place a rudimentary system of rules until North Carolina's leadership decided those rules were no longer relevant or until Great Britain got its act together and stopped treating the colonies unfairly. In other words, the Mecklenburg Resolves established a temporary government until Great Britain stepped up to the plate (or walked away with its tail between its legs; whichever came first).

If you think the Mecklenburg Resolves sound eerily similar to the Mecklenburg Declaration, you wouldn't be the only one. The first suggestion that the two documents might be one and the same came from Charles Phillips, a University of North Carolina – Chapel Hill professor, in 1853. It wouldn't be until even later—in 1907—that historian William Henry Hoyt expanded on Phillips's theory in *The Mecklenburg Declaration of Independence: A Study of Evidence Showing That the Alleged Declaration of Mecklenburg County, North Carolina, on May 20th, 1775, Is Spurious*. While its title could definitely use some workshopping, this text is widely considered the most complete refutation of the existence of the Mecklenburg Declaration as Dr. Alexander envisioned it.

But even if the Mecklenburg Declaration was a misremembrance of the Mecklenburg Resolves, does it really matter? Wouldn't the resolves be just as damaging to our understanding of history, given that they were still written a year before the Declaration of Independence? The truth isn't as simple as that, since the resolves came short of formally declaring independence. Nonetheless, Hoyt believed their strong wording, which surely would have been considered treasonous at the time, could have led onlookers to erroneously believe that independence had, in fact, been declared.

This is why many Meck Dec skeptics feel strongly that the Mecklenburg Resolves are what Dr. Alexander, Captain Jack, and the other witnesses who were part of the 1829 investigation were remembering in their various writings and testimonials. The fact that the documents were supposedly written in the same month of the same year, taken alongside their markedly similar themes, would have made anyone do a double take. It would hardly be surprising if elderly folks (like the investigation's subjects) misremembered minor details from an event that happened in the distant past.

Still, some have argued that the eleven-day difference in purported signing dates of the two documents is a significant length of time, so surely they are distinct. But even this discrepancy has a possible historical explanation. The Gregorian calendar was adopted by Great Britain in 1752, but it's very possible that this change in convention wouldn't have reached remote, rural Charlotte by 1775. As a result, Charlotte residents may have still been using the Julian calendar, which was exactly *eleven days* behind the Gregorian one. By this token, the declaration and resolves could have been the same document originating on the exact same date, but what that date was would have depended on who you were asking.

But questions remain. If the documents were the same, why did Dr. Alexander's retelling of the story include text that differed so substantially from that of the resolves, and perhaps more importantly, how did the text of the Declaration of Independence get dragged into this mess? Hoyt's hypothesis was that after John McKnitt Alexander experienced his house fire in 1800, he realized that all his papers related to the drafting of the resolves were lost. Knowing their significance, he set out to rewrite as many notes as he could remember, ranging from early discussions and planning to the final text itself. Perhaps he recalled the words as having been stronger, more assertive than they actually were. According to Hoyt, from these notes, either the elder Alexander or someone else wrote the Mecklenburg Declaration, borrowing language from the Declaration of Independence to fill in the blanks.

Despite Hoyt's extensive thesis, plenty of Meck Dec enthusiasts still reject his claims, and they have their own answers to the questions raised by the contemporaneous timelines of their beloved document and the Mecklenburg Resolves. Some have suggested that the Mecklenburg Declaration was in fact written *after* the Declaration of Independence, and that it was meant to meld the Declaration of Independence with the Mecklenburg Resolves to create a uniquely North Carolinian text.

Another assertion is that the Meck Dec avowed independence but didn't actually succeed in creating a replacement government and bylaws for Mecklenburg County, and so the Mecklenburg Resolves were written to fill that void. Some who favor the Meck Dec's existence suggest that after it was written, a committee was selected to improve its coherence and robustness, and the resulting document was the Mecklenburg Resolves. By this iteration, it is unclear whether Captain Jack transported the Mecklenburg Declaration, the Mecklenburg Resolves, or both to Philadelphia.

All in all, most historians today agree that the Mecklenburg Declaration is a misremembrance; to put it bluntly, the document that Dr. Alexander transcribed into the newspaper was fake. These historians take Thomas Jefferson's questions of skepticism one step further: If the Mecklenburg Resolves were on the record of the local government, why wasn't the Meck Dec? If North Carolina's governor was upset about the resolves (which was well-documented to be the case), wouldn't he have been even angrier about the Meck Dec, whose assertions were stronger (and wouldn't this displeasure have been noted somewhere)? And perhaps most damningly, why would the North Carolina colonists declare independence with the Mecklenburg Declaration, only to walk it back with the resolves less than two weeks later?

Yet old habits (and traditions) die hard. The state of North Carolina still celebrates the Mecklenburg Declaration every year on May 20, the date it was supposedly signed. Mecklenburg County observes "Meck Dec Day," which is a regional holiday at which four former US presidents have spoken. But visitors to the state and county need not wait until May 20 to see evidence of the Meck Dec's persistent cultural relevance; they need only examine some of the state's common symbology and local lore.

For starters, May 20 is emblazoned on the state's official flag, but this design choice was not made until the time of the vote for North Carolina to secede from the Union and join the Confederacy at the start of the Civil War. At the time, many North Carolina residents were uncomfortable with secession, so the state's leadership opted to tie the Meck Dec to their cause in an effort to alter public sentiment. By this token, May 20, the date North Carolina supposedly declared *its* independence, could be analogized to the secession since the Confederacy was attempting to do the same. (It also didn't hurt that their vote to secede was held on May 20, 1861.) Later, in 1893, the date of the Meck Dec's signing was also added to North Carolina's state seal.

The legend of the Meck Dec, and the controversy that follows it, has also earned this likely fictitious document a place in the historical archives. The papers accumulated by Dr. Alexander as he rifled through his father's effects and wrote his newspaper article are now filed away at the University of North Carolina – Chapel Hill. And perhaps this makes sense. Regardless of the Meck Dec's real origins, it is incontrovertibly true that North Carolina was on the leading edge of America's independence. On April 12, 1776, North Carolina passed the Halifax Resolves, which allowed the colony's delegates to advocate and ultimately vote for independence from British rule. It was the first colony to come to this agreement.

But as I alluded to at the beginning of this chapter, the tale of the Mecklenburg Declaration is not the only curious historical case to come out of quiet, unassuming Mecklenburg County. One need only fast forward a handful of decades from the time of the Meck Dec to uncover yet another bizarre historical mystery that still grips the county's residents to this day. Although these two mysteries share only a geographic location in common, I would be remiss if I didn't briefly expound upon this second strange occurrence.

That strange occurrence is a person, and that person has a name: Peter Stewart Ney. A schoolteacher, Ney claimed to have been born in Scotland when he immigrated to the United States in 1818. To those he encountered, he shared his interest in the goings-on of the military, demonstrated his talent at wielding a sword, and spoke at length about his involvement in the Napoleonic wars (especially after an evening of drinking). When not in the bar or classroom, Ney spent a substantial amount of time at Davidson College, located in Mecklenburg County, where he was commissioned to design the college seal in 1840. During his time on campus, he perused the library's collection of texts on French history. We know this because he took the liberty of scrawling notes in the books' margins correcting their accounts.

Even when he was alive, Ney was seen as a somewhat enigmatic figure, and it has long been believed that his self-told origin story and real-life personality didn't quite match up. Perhaps it would be unsurprising to learn, then, that many people believed Ney was actually Marshal Michel Ney, Napoleon's right-hand man who had allegedly been executed by firing squad in 1815.

Conspiracy theorists had long toyed with the idea that Michel Ney never actually died that fateful day, compiling their own evidence and assertions as to how he survived the stunt. They point to the unusual circumstances surrounding the execution, such as an abrupt change in location, or the fact that the firing squad tasked with executing Ney comprised his own faithful men. Plus, his family did not attend his funeral, and after his death, his wife didn't seem aggrieved. Taken together, these realities have led some to purport that the blood visibly spilled during the execution was dye squirted from a prop animal bladder. In other words, the execution was fake.

By this theory, Michel Ney escaped France and sailed across the Atlantic Ocean to the United States as Peter Stewart Ney. His first stop was in South Carolina, but while there he may have been outed as Michel Ney based on his striking physical resemblance to the well-known French military man. He then moved throughout the Carolinas before finally settling in Mecklenburg County. This story accords with what little we do know about Peter Stewart Ney, as his time in Mecklenburg County was, in fact, predated by time spent traveling throughout the region.

Circumstantial evidence also exists to support the conspiracy theory that Michel Ney and Peter Stewart Ney were one and the same. For instance, the name of Michel Ney's father was Peter, and his mother's maiden name was Stewart. Another example relates to the Davidson College seal, designed by Peter Stewart, which is reminiscent of a medal that Napolean had bestowed upon his decorated marshal. Plus, Peter Stewart Ney purportedly disagreed so vehemently with a pictorial representation of Michel Ney in a Davidson College book that he actually drew his own version in the pages of the text.

> **Riley's Next Hunt:** What if Peter Stewart Ney scrawled a clue to the whereabouts of the original Meck Dec into one of Davidson College's library books? Riley and crew could feasibly kill two Mecklenburg County mysteries with one stone.

Yet perhaps the prevailing reason for believing Peter Stewart Ney and Michel Ney were the same man is because Peter Stewart said as much himself. During his final days in 1846, when an ailing Peter Stewart Ney was being cared for, war scars were observed across his entire body, *and* he called out for his wife—but Ney was not married. It's said that he admitted to being Michel Ney with his dying breath.

Today, many believe all the similarities between Peter Stewart Ney and Michel Ney are purely coincidence, and that tales from his deathbed are exaggerated myths. One of the most vocal disapprovers of the Ney conspiracy theory was none other than William Henry Hoyt of anti-Meck Dec fame. It turns out that Hoyt had a thing for myth-busting local legends, because he also spent time investigating Peter Stewart Ney and concluded that Michel Ney did not, in fact, escape the firing squad back in France.

Peter Stewart Ney's body is buried at Third Creek Presbyterian Church in Cleveland, North Carolina, under a marker that (probably erroneously) claims he fought under Napoleon. On numerous occasions, the body has been exhumed for study with modern techniques in an attempt to definitely prove whether or not this Ney was *the* Ney. Most recently, in 2023, researchers extracted DNA from Peter Stewart Ney's flute—part of Davidson College's collection—and used genetic analysis to confirm that Peter Stewart Ney's hair color, eye color, and skin tone were notably different than those of Michel Ney, seemingly laying the controversy to rest.

Even so, Peter Stewart Ney remains the subject of lingering intrigue in North Carolina, and his legacy lives on in the seal of Davidson College. After all, the seal is emblazoned with a fascinating motto, *Alenda Lux Ubi Orta Libertas*, which translates to "Let knowledge be cherished where liberty has arisen." Is it a coincidence that this motto is a reference to the Mecklenburg Declaration of Independence? I can't help but notice how, in Mecklenburg County, North Carolina, we're left with multiple instances of two things in history that may—or may not—have actually been one and the same.

Chapter 9

The Headless Horseman

Some of the most persistent legends that have permeated civilizations are those containing mysterious figures or events that we can't quite explain. This lack of understanding—when reality lies somewhere just beyond the grasp of human comprehension—is tantalizing enough to tempt the imaginations of both the learned and the naïve. That's probably why stories about the paranormal, cryptids, and unidentified aerial phenomena are some of the most intriguing to the collective hivemind that is society.

Ghost stories, in particular, are so naturally integrated into the human subconscious that they have held a rightful position in civilization for centuries, if not millennia. It is no surprise that they have spawned an entire genre of pop culture—from books to movies to reality television series—that capitalizes on one important fact. At present, scientists cannot examine or test theories related to what exists beyond the plane of our existence using the scientific method and its socially acceptable tools. As long as this remains true, any story—fictional or otherwise—purporting to illuminate a reality beyond our human senses reaches an impasse: it is neither true nor false until some new method is devised to poke and prod it.

But the veracity of ghost stories is neither here nor there, and frankly whether you believe in or scoff at the paranormal is of little relevance. For what it's worth, even as a person of science, I (and probably Riley too) can recognize that things do occasionally happen—observables are measured—that defy our conventional understanding of the world around us. And I have also had enough experiences in my life—I have broken enough shoelaces, as Riley would say—for my mindset to be affected at least minimally by superstition. To what these mysterious occurrences can be attributed I am not prepared to say. Yet I *am* prepared to admit that they make me think twice before making certain decisions or arriving at certain conclusions.

Personally, the ghost stories that strike the most impactful chord are the ones that seem *just* real enough. If and when science catches up one day and proves said stories entirely true, I wouldn't be especially surprised. In my experience, these eerie tales have one quality in common: they consist of a curious mix of incontrovertible fact and unconfirmable legend. Somehow, they blur the lines so effectively that onlookers are forced to wonder where the reality stops and the tall tale begins. And in American history, there is no greater example of this whimsical weaving of fact and fiction than *The Legend of Sleepy Hollow*.

> **Why Riley Would Care:** Riley would appreciate the headless horseman's starring role in the first American ghost story, which helped insert the paranormal—a subgenre of legends and mysteries—into mainstream conversation.

HUNT DOWN THAT HISTORY

On first glance, it feels like a bit of a farce to be writing a section about history when considering a tale the world knows is a very popular work of fiction. *The Legend of Sleepy Hollow*, while adapted into many formats and interpreted in many ways over time, was written by American author Washington Irving in 1820. But it did not originate as its own unique text. The tale was part of a broader collection, *The Sketch Book of Geoffrey Crayon, Gent.*, which itself was published in serial installments between 1819 and 1820.

Irving's *Sleepy Hollow* shares with the other installments of *The Sketch Book* an overall tone that meshes satire with fictional stories and narrative facts. It comprises numerous short stories and essays, six of which are meant to provide exposition and commentary about life in nineteenth century America. While the complete collection is well-known amongst the literary community, no story within it is quite as famous as *The Legend of Sleepy Hollow*, which is largely considered the first ghost story in the United States (and by some accounts, one of the first short stories of *any* genre in the country's history).

But to truly understand the history of *Sleepy Hollow* (because substantial history does, in fact, underpin this fictional story), it is important to get the narrative gist of Irving's most popular work. The tale is set in Sleepy Hollow, or Tarrytown, New York, and centers on the arrival of the community's new schoolteacher, Ichabod Crane. Crane is personally fascinated by the ghost stories centered in Sleepy Hollow, and coincidentally he becomes the victim of one such local legend. After romantically pursuing one of the town's wealthiest young women, Katrina van Tassel, Crane is relentlessly chased by a headless horseman, who pummels Crane with a pumpkin (though Crane believes the projectile is the equestrian's severed head).

By the end of the story, it is somewhat implied that the headless horseman figure was actually a disguised Brom Bones, the man who had been courting van Tassel prior to Crane's arrival in town. But ultimately, it's up to the reader to decide whether Crane suffered a dark fate—which the story's townspeople assume—or skipped town of his own volition following the harrowing incident.

Stylistically, *Sleepy Hollow* is written as a retelling of the history of an early American town; it's as if the narrator, named Diedrich Knickerbocker, is sharing something that truly happened in the past. In line with the other compositions found within *The Sketch Book*, some critics have asserted *Sleepy Hollow* is meant to satirize the culture—especially that of the wealthy elite—in communities established by Dutch settlers.

But what casual readers and even many Halloween-time enthusiasts of *Sleepy Hollow* often fail to realize is that the story deeply integrates real American history from the Revolutionary War and how it was experienced by the Tarrytown community. In a sense, *Sleepy Hollow* might be not just the earliest example of an American ghost story, but also an early iteration of the "historical fiction" genre that has become so popular in multimedia today. And it is because of this seamless integration of true local history into a synthetic plot that *Sleepy Hollow* provides readers with a nagging feeling that the tale can't be so easily written off as simply a silly ghost story. If you ask me, that's why it became an instant classic.

The historical roots of *Sleepy Hollow* are derived from the life of a German, or Hessian, mercenary who fought on American soil during the

Revolutionary War. By the time October 1776 rolled around, George Washington, commander of the Continental Army, had encountered many setbacks on the battlefield. Most recently, these setbacks included taking an L at the Battles of Long Island and Harlem Heights in New York. Following these crushing defeats, Washington and his army scurried back to his well-stocked military base in White Plains, located less than ten miles from Tarrytown, a very real, very "sleepy" community of Dutch descent.

But the reprieve from battle did not last long. On October 28, Washington's army, still settled at White Plains, suffered an attack by British forces under the command of William Howe (the namesake of *National Treasure* villain Ian Howe). The battle was a substantive one, involving more than ten thousand men in total when summing the number of Americans, British, and Britain's Hessian helpers. For a while, Washington's army stood its ground, holding off the British from a local landmark known as Chatterton Hill.

But when British Colonel Johann Gottlieb Rall sent a contingent of Hessian horsemen ahead of his troops to punch through the right flank of the American lines, the situation devolved into chaos. All told, more than four hundred American, British, and Hessian soldiers ended up dead or wounded by the time October 28 drew to a close. While exact estimates vary, it's largely agreed that both sides of the battle suffered approximately equal numbers of casualties.

With a name derived from *Hesse-Kassel*, their place of origin in Germany, the Hessians were significant contributors to the British cause throughout the Revolutionary War. Thousands of Hessians were sent (often by German princes) to America as formal reinforcements for the British, but they also helped the British forces level up their military prowess.

The Hessians' vicious reputation preceded them. In the Battle of Long Island, for example, rumor had it that these mercenaries were particularly adept at using their bayonets to pin American soldiers to trees. With the Hessians' help, the British scored victories at White Plains (forcing Washington and his army to flee to New Jersey) and later at Fort Washington. But they were met with defeat on December 26 during the Battle of Trenton, which is where Colonel Rall and the Hessians under his command were ultimately captured.

White Plains's proximity to Tarrytown wasn't the only important factor that eventually connected Revolutionary War history to Irving's *Sleepy Hollow*. In the days that followed the Battle of White Plains, one Hessian artilleryman was said to have been decapitated by an American cannonball. In fact, local accounts suggest the decapitated Hessian, or "headless Hessian" as he would later be called, was quickly buried in the cemetery of Old Dutch Church, the church serving Tarrytown's constituents. This moment was documented by Major General William Heath in his journal on November 1, 1776.

> **Riley's Favorite Fact (Probably):** The headless horseman is real! (Sort of.) The character is based on the true story of a Hessian soldier who was decapitated in battle during the Revolutionary War.

These moments in history were clear points of inspiration for Irving's *Sleepy Hollow* story, but the author was also motivated by his personal experiences living in Tarrytown and the broader Hudson River Valley. The youngest of eleven children, Irving was born in 1783, and based on my personal read on his life, he quickly exhibited the relatable trait of career indecisiveness. As a young adult, he was a prolific writer of essays, and one of his most famous texts, *A History of New York . . . by Diedrich Knickerbocker* (1809) (yes, the same narrator as the one in *Sleepy Hollow*), gained renown for its humorous criticism of the New York-based Dutch. Yet Irving wasn't *just* a writer, as he was also bitten by the travel bug and somehow still found time to certify as a lawyer.

Irving would end up doing some work as a lobbyist in Washington, D.C., and serving the government as a US envoy to Spain. Throughout these numerous and diverse career pivots, he continued to write from both sides of the Atlantic Ocean. He must have been more skilled as a writer than any of his other professions, though, and I base this bold judgment on how he has been remembered throughout time, as well as how he was viewed by his literary contemporaries.

In his author capacity, Irving met President Martin Van Buren and engaged in substantial correspondence with Charles Dickens, who later admitted to being inspired by Irving's writings when *A Christmas Carol* (1843) was penned. Other renowned writers of the time, such as Edgar Allan Poe, were said to greatly respect Irving's expertise and seek out his literary stamp of approval. In other words, Irving had substantial street cred in the soon-to-be-legendary-writers club.

However, these numerous accolades and shameless name-drops, while impressive, are hardly relevant to our understanding of *The Legend of Sleepy Hollow*. What matters most for our purposes is the fact that, in 1798, Washington Irving was a teenage boy sent to live with his friend James Kirke Paulding in Tarrytown—his first introduction to the tiny community where he would later spend the end of his life. At the time of his initial move, Irving's hometown of New York City was plagued by an outbreak of yellow fever; his relocation was arranged to safeguard his health. Who would have known his teenage experience of Tarrytown would impact him so deeply? (I guess that's why they call them "formative years.")

Interestingly, yellow fever may have still been on the brain (metaphorically speaking) when Irving eventually authored *Sleepy Hollow*. In its exposition, the story describes its eponymous town as having "contagion in the very air . . . it breathed forth an atmosphere of dreams and fancies infecting all the land." And while this is meant to set the stage for Ichabod Crane's arrival, giving the town an aura of drowsiness and calm, some critics have noted the almost clinical language could be reminiscent of the epidemic conditions that colored Irving's early years.

Many have also credited Irving's youth spent in and around Tarrytown with launching his imagination and creativity. Indeed, the town's brief yet rich history seems to have been engrained in the man's constitution, as he readily referenced real Tarrytown landmarks, such as Old Dutch Church, in his writings. In *Sleepy Hollow*, he even went so far as to name his fictional characters after actual families who had lived in the town for generations. The family name van Tassel was both very real and very local, and there was a military colonel named Ichabod B. Crane who served forty-five years during Irving's lifetime (though there is no reason to believe the two ever met). It's probably fortunate that defamation lawsuits weren't a thing back in Irving's time.

Some have predicted it was during his youth that Irving first learned the story of the headless Hessian soldier who met his grisly fate during the American Revolution and was subsequently buried nearby. I like to imagine myself as an impressionable teenager hearing this story and finding it so gripping that I would peruse every inch of the cemetery in search of evidence supporting its veracity. Perhaps Irving was somewhat like me, but instead of descending upon the local graveyard, he opted to put pen to paper and mix his personal fascination with Revolutionary War history and his own imagination to craft *Sleepy Hollow*.

While local history was clearly a factor in the crafting of Irving's short story, many have asserted he probably took inspiration from prominent literary sources as well. One such influence might have been *The Chase* (1796), written by Sir Walter Scott. Irving first made Scott's acquaintance when the former was a young man traveling in England lobbying on behalf of his brother Peter's shipping company. The two apparently shared mutual admiration before having ever met each other, with Scott appreciating Irving's most well-known text at the time (*History of New York*). During his business travels in 1817, Irving arranged to meet with Scott in Edinburgh. The introduction went so well that Irving spent several days with his new friend and his family.

Irving saw Scott as a mentor figure, and many people believe their short but impactful time together helped set Irving's sights on becoming a serious writer. After all, up until that point, writing was just one of his many professional pursuits. It would be logical, then, to assume Irving took a few cues from *The Chase* when writing *Sleepy Hollow*, since the two stories share some common attributes, including supernatural undertones.

Scott published *The Chase* at the age of twenty-five within the longer text, *The Chase, and William and Helen*. The story, which is thought to be based on Norse-origin mythology, is itself a translation of a well-known German tale, "The Wild Huntsman," originally written by Gottfried Bürger. In general, the story centers on a game hunter who suffers a twisted fate: *he* is destined to be hunted for all eternity as a punishment for his wrongdoings in life.

LISTEN TO RILEY

While the *Sleepy Hollow* legend is mythical in nature, it is nowhere near the first story to be written about a headless figure. In fact, local legends about headless *horsemen*, in particular, date all the way back to the Middle Ages. Even in these early iterations, the figure is portrayed as a supernatural entity that haunts the living. It is commonly agreed that the figure is seeking revenge, which manifests physically in a search for a replacement head.

Historians and anthropologists have claimed that headless horsemen are symbols of retribution, plaguing people who feel "haunted" by something from their past. This is why, for instance, new versions of headless horseman legends have frequently been tied temporally to wars, postwar periods, and other events characterized by extreme loss.

One of the most famous headless horseman tales can be traced to the 1300s. "Sir Gawain and the Green Knight," a text that I was rudely tasked with reading over the summer in preparation for my high school AP European History class, is a British poem that includes well-known characters from Arthurian legend. As the story goes, a giant green knight rides his horse into Camelot to issue a challenge to the men of King Arthur's court. They are invited to behead the mysterious green knight, but only on the seemingly superfluous condition that they meet back up with their victim one year later for a rematch. At that time, the green knight would be able to return the beheading attempt.

Only one of King Arthur's knights, Sir Gawain, accepts the task, presumably understanding that if he successfully beheads his challenger, his challenger will not physically be able to seek redemption a year later. After beheading the mysterious figure, Sir Gawain is dismayed when the green knight retrieves his decapitated head and rides away on his steed, taunting Sir Gawain as he departs. The tale is ultimately one about dignity, as Sir Gawain grapples with the mortal commitment he has made.

But "Sir Gawain and the Green Knight," despite being one of the earliest written headless horseman tales and thus the inspiration for many later ones, may not be entirely original itself. Some believe the story is derived from an Irish myth called "Bricriu's Feast," which was ultimately recorded in the eleventh century text, *The Book of the Dun Cow*. This version focuses on a group of men who take part in a series of challenges to win a feast, and one of their challenges involves attacking a giant with an axe. And you guessed it—the giant is permitted to return the favor. As the tale goes, the giant's head is chopped off numerous times and recovered after each incidence.

If "Sir Gawain and the Green Knight" isn't the first historical headless horseman text that comes to mind, perhaps an even more common one can be traced to Jacob and Wilhelm Grimm, better known as literary duo the Brothers Grimm, in the 1600s. It turns out that the Brothers Grimm added not one, but two headless horseman stories to their collections. Both iterations derive from the depths of German folklore and generally presume that people who commit crimes punishable by decapitation will remain headless in spirit form after death.

The brothers' first headless horseman is found within the pages of "Hans Jagendteufel." In it, a woman collecting acorns in eastern German woodlands is approached by a spooky, gray-cloaked equestrian lacking a head. His horse is also gray. The startling figure warns the woman that she should not take things that do not belong to her—a reference to the acorns—or else she will be condemned to a fate like his in the afterlife.

The second headless horseman story retold by the Brothers Grimm is, interestingly, a version of the same story that Sir Walter Scott would later translate in *The Chase*. According to the brothers' iteration, a German man makes a pact with God to continue hunting for all of eternity, transforming him into the Wild Huntsman, a dark figure who hunts with a trusty pack of vicious black dogs. Legend has it that marksmen who hear the Wild Huntsman's horn blaring should refrain from hunting in the days to follow. Like a mothman or other omen-like figure, some believe the Wild Huntsman's sound portends bad things to come.

At this point, we've logged headless horseman stories from several destinations across Europe—England, Ireland, and Germany—so it's probably unsurprising that Scotland also has its own version to share. Scotland's Ewan the Headless ups the ante by riding a headless *horse*. People across rural Scotland have claimed to witness Ewan the Headless for centuries, and he is widely believed to be the ghost of Eoghan a'Chinn Big (also known as Ewan Maclaine), the son of a wealthy Scottish clan chief.

According to local lore, Ewan sought to forcefully take his father's land on the Isle of Mull, so in 1538, the two engaged in a duel that ultimately cost Ewan his head. The legend further suggests that Ewan's horse galloped a great distance carrying its rider's decapitated body, stopping only once it grew tired. If a member of the Maclaine clan spots the apparition, a death in the family is imminent.

With so many stories having weaved their way into cultural heritage, it can be hard to determine where the beginning of the headless horseman myth truly lies. However, there is one legend most commonly assigned as the original specter: the Irish Celtic Dullahan, which translates to "dark man." It is both the most robust and most malignant form of the story, whereby the Dullahan, a mounted rider who carries his head, serves as a grim reaper type of figure.

Celtic mythology purports that the Dullahan is a physical manifestation of a fertility god named Crom Dubh, who could be appeased only with blood sacrifices obtained via decapitation. Crom Dubh may be further derived from an even earlier Irish god, Cromm Crúaich, with origins somewhere between the 800s and 1100s. In any case, sacrifices to Crom Dubh were required on an annual basis to ensure that both women and land (one and the same, apparently) would be fertile. Furthermore, an ancient text called the *Metrical Dindshenchas* seems to suggest that a common Irish practice included sacrificing the firstborn child in exchange for a bountiful harvest.

Of course, widespread worship of Crom Dubh, and ritual completion of all associated practices, ceased once the Irish embraced Christianity. At this time, Crom Dubh was banished from the country—an action supposedly taken by Saint Patrick—when the worshipping stone used to make sacrifices was smashed to bits. The fact that sacrifices were no longer welcome was further underscored by the celebration of a *new* stone, the Killycluggin Stone, which is currently housed at the Cavan County Museum to commemorate Christianity's foray into Ireland.

But the story doesn't end here. Legend has it the Dullahan is a modern, vengeful form of Crom Dubh who is peeved that the Irish rejected him. He's also ticked off because he no longer receives blood sacrifices, so to fill the void he rides around towns declaring the names of those who will soon die. Naturally, he carries his head, which sports a decaying face, under one arm, and he is even said to wield a whip made of human spine.

The Dullahan is known to ride in style. Occasionally people have reported seeing him guiding a massive, macabre, black coach pulled by a caravan of headless horses. If the coach arrives at your porch and you answer the door, you'll be doused in blood. Even worse, if you hear him calling your name, he's serving double duty as the grim reaper and has come to claim your life.

Riley's Next Hunt: *National Treasure* doesn't deal in the supernatural as a rule, but that wouldn't necessarily stop Riley from trying to convince Ben of the importance of headless specters. Their ability to connect geographically and temporally disparate cultures (like the Templar treasure does) might be Riley's most compelling argument.

And with that, would you believe it if I said there are still *more* variations of the headless horseman legend? We've covered the most historically significant ones, but it's worth noting that Scandinavian countries, India, and even Texas all have local versions of a headless horseback rider. In pop culture, Marvel Comics's Ghost Rider is thought to be an updated, modern version of the headless horseman, since it is essentially a cursed figure bound to Earth riding some version of a steed.

In the end, it's worth asking just how much of Washington Irving's inspiration for *Sleepy Hollow* came from his own mind, his fascination with Tarrytown, and his literary muses compared to the vast collection of European headless horseman tales that existed even during his lifetime. Irving's parents were originally from Cornwall, England, a location that is quite Celtic in both heritage and culture. Irving would end up drafting *The Legend of Sleepy Hollow* while he was traveling abroad in that very country. While it's impossible to say how much he was influenced by Europe's early ghost stories, it would probably be naïve to think they played no role in his writing.

Today, *Sleepy Hollow* is considered quintessentially American. Just as the United States is a melting pot of ethnicities, *Sleepy Hollow* could be said to combine stories from numerous cultures while simultaneously mixing in a substantial amount of American history and New York landmarks. Irving's *Sleepy Hollow* story has stood the test of time, having had such an impact on its namesake community that North Tarrytown formally changed its name to Sleepy Hollow in 1996. It is now a tourist destination that hosts hundreds of thousands of visitors annually. These guests certainly venture to the quiet town throughout the year, but their numbers increase substantially during the autumn months, as *Sleepy Hollow* remains a fan-favorite tale around Halloween.

The influence of *Sleepy Hollow* persists beyond the tourism sector as well. Tarrytown's high school mascot is the headless horseman, and the mascot rides around on a horse at homecoming football games. And because legends aren't fun unless just a *little* belief persists, local lore suggests the headless horseman still haunts the Sleepy Hollow cemetery to this day. The ghostly rider ties up his horse in the graveyard, sneaking into the night in pursuit of his lost head.

Unless you frequent Sleepy Hollow as a local or visitor, the headless horseman myth likely lives in your mind rent free thanks to various forms of pop culture and multimedia. Nowadays, the headless horseman is a common figure in storytelling for the masses because of the malleability the character provides. His description, existence, and motivation are just vague enough in our collective imagination that any story can be projected onto him. He is a figure that is easily summoned to portray or symbolize vengeance—a concept that will forever be relatable to people from all walks of life.

Chapter 10

Blair House

We all know the feeling of being fascinated by a house. Whether it's hidden at the end of a long, tree-lined driveway, surrounded by a rusty wrought-iron fence, or marked with one too many "no trespassing" signs, a mysterious, off-limits abode is a concept so familiar that it's been baked into cinematic and television plots for decades. (In fact, the concept is such a common, unifying experience that this won't even be the only time we discuss it in the course of this book.) Houses made famous in pop culture are often haunted or capable of affecting their occupants in malignant ways. Occasionally homes are memorialized for less sinister reasons, like bearing witness to great moments in history.

Sometimes, it's the people inside a house who are the real subject of intrigue. Maybe the owners have never set foot on the property, so no one seems to know who they are. Perhaps the occupants are famous, yet elusive. Or better yet—maybe they're hiding something. There are innumerable reasons why houses—small and large, simple and elaborate—are the physical and metaphorical foundation of so many local legends spanning the United States and even the world.

Think back to the town where you grew up. Now think of that one house that all the local kids knew not to approach. It's the house you willingly skipped when trick-or-treating. And when your frisbee accidentally landed in this house's backyard, you invariably chose to sacrifice your toy rather than ring the doorbell to retrieve it. It's the house you drove to at 11:11 p.m. the first night you had your license, just to see if the resident apparition—probably a young woman in white—would appear at this agreed-upon time (kindly obeying either daylight saving time or standard time, whatever was appropriate).

One thing I've observed about these mysterious houses is that regardless of their age, location, or general layout, they're always well-known to locals—and maybe even some visitors too. That's why it's so shocking to learn that a mysterious house sits right at the center of the nation's capital—in one of the most heavily trafficked tourist locations—and comparatively few people know of its existence. Even fewer know its story. The Blair House has served an integral yet quiet role in the US government and broader American history right under the noses of D.C. locals and visitors alike. But those who know its intriguing story would likely agree that the colloquialism "if walls could talk" could have been invented to describe this very home.

> **Why Riley Would Care:** Riley would love nothing more than to be a fly on the wall in rooms where important decisions are made by world leaders. What better way to fuel (or even confirm) his favorite conspiracy theories and urban legends?

HUNT DOWN THAT HISTORY

The Blair House is a Federal-style townhome located in the heart of Washington, D.C. Despite its importance and mystery, its address is no secret: 1651 Pennsylvania Avenue Northwest (in case you'd like to pass by on your next visit to the city). Yes, this is the same Pennsylvania Avenue made famous as the location of another, significantly more renowned house that just so happens to serve as Blair House's mansion-like next-door neighbor. That's right: Blair House sits across from the White House on Lafayette Square.

Constructed in 1824 as one of the first homes on the square, Blair House was built as the residence of Dr. Joseph Lovell, who, six years earlier, had become the first surgeon general of the United States Army. Though his portrait still hangs on a wall in the home today, Dr. Lovell would not necessarily be considered Blair House's most influential former inhabitant. Following the doctor's passing in 1836, the house was purchased by its namesake, Francis Preston Blair, for $6,500. (Excuse me while I go mourn the loss of times when houses were affordable.)

A year after the exchange, the Blair family, which included Francis

Preston, his wife Eliza, and their three children, moved into their new home. The family had initially relocated to Washington from Frankfort, Kentucky, seven years prior thanks to a job opportunity Blair simply couldn't refuse. He was personally invited by President Andrew Jackson to make the move in service of rejuvenating a local, failing D.C. newspaper, the *Globe*. President Jackson had been following Blair's journalistic successes in Kentucky from afar, growing particularly impressed by the writer's editorials that heavily praised Jackson and his decisions.

It was a no-brainer for the president to recruit this Upland South editor to Washington, D.C., as the commander-in-chief sought to transform the *Globe* into a news outlet that was adamantly friendly toward his administration. Jackson effectively tasked Blair with translating his writing prowess to the country's biggest political stage, and the president's faith in Blair was immediately rewarded. Things at the *Globe* turned around quickly, which led Blair and a counterpart, John C. Rives, to collaboratively establish the *Congressional Globe* in 1834. The *Congressional Globe*'s mission was to publish the proceedings of the United States's legislative branch, and it still does so today under the name *Congressional Record*, a moniker it formally adopted in 1873.

Given the personal invitation that brought Blair to D.C. in the first place, it probably isn't surprising to learn that he became highly influential in Washington's political scene. For Blair, who started as a humble editor, the metaphorical ladder sat in front of him for the climbing, and he would ultimately become the most trusted member of President Jackson's informal advisory committee. This committee, known by most skeptics as the kitchen cabinet, was established because the president's real cabinet proved wildly ineffective almost as soon as Jackson took office in 1829. Such futility was rooted in a persistent dispute between Vice President John C. Calhoun and Secretary of State Martin Van Buren.

But the president needed to collect perspectives and insight from somewhere, and thus the kitchen cabinet was born, remaining active until President Jackson was finally able to request the resignation of his problematic, real cabinet members in 1831. Once the Jackson Administration ended, Blair's insight would remain highly sought after by subsequent presidents, including eighth President Martin Van Buren, sixteenth President Abraham Lincoln, and eighteenth President

Ulysses S. Grant. Furthermore, Francis Preston Blair and his two sons, Montgomery and Frank, were instrumental in establishing the Republican Party and helping Abraham Lincoln win the presidency.

Blair House remained in the family for quite some time. After assuming occupancy in 1855, Montgomery Blair undertook the home's first major expansion by adding the third and fourth floors. But expansion soon took on a different meaning for the home, as it slowly transformed from a single-family abode into a veritable complex. For example, consider the adjacent Lee House, which was initially constructed by Francis Preston Blair in 1859 for his daughter Elizabeth and her husband, Admiral Samuel Phillips Lee. Over time, Lee House would be swallowed up by the Blair House compound. As the years wore on, Blair House would eventually consist of four connected townhomes, with the final two pieces of the structure built in 1860.

By the early 1900s, the very existence of the notable home was threatened by political goings-on in Washington, D.C. Congress had proposed a bill to revitalize the capital city at the expense of many historic structures, including not only Blair House, but also Decatur House, Saint John's Church, and several other beloved landmarks. Preventing this massive project and thereby saving these historic sites was going to require a fight.

Fortunately, Blair family members were up to the challenge. The original Blairs' descendants, who lived in the home at the time, staunchly, verbally opposed Congress's proposal. They wrote letters to the Senate and the local newspaper to express their disapproval over the suggested demolition of what was both a family home and a site that had witnessed important historical events. Gist Blair and his wife, Laura Lawson Ellis, took up sole occupancy of Blair House around 1912 and dedicated significant time to recording and sharing the home's history. They believed making this history known would serve to protect the structure as the threat of destruction loomed.

You could say that saving Blair House became somewhat of a pet project for Gist. He would end up hosting President Franklin Delano Roosevelt at the house for dinner early in his administration, presumably attempting to gain the most influential possible advocate for his cause. It's unclear how quickly or how fulsomely President Roosevelt supported Gist's plans, but Blair ultimately landed his ally. Roosevelt would soon become a supporter of historic preservation writ large, influencing Secretary of the Interior Harold Ickes to authorize the Historic American Building Survey. This survey was the first attempt to formally catalogue historic structures in the United States.

And just like that, the first domino had fallen. Shortly after, the National Park Service began the process of determining which sites around the country should receive historic designation. By a cruel twist of fate, and likely to the great dismay and frustration of Gist Blair, the Blair House was initially deemed not important enough to warrant preservation by the federal government.

At the time, it was suggested that Blair House would merit historic status only if it was acquired by the US government and transformed into a museum that captured the essence of Washington, D.C., in the era spanning the Jackson and Lincoln Administrations. But Gist wasn't eager to concede. By sheer persistence at the conclusion of a decades-long, family-fought battle, in 1939, Blair House was commemorated with a plaque that would eventually become the template for national historical site markers with which we are familiar today.

While the very existence of Blair House was likely much more obvious in its early years, especially as Lafayette Square was under initial development, the four-townhome complex blends in with its surroundings in a much more crowded and modern Washington, D.C. Nowadays, Blair House might be better known by a different name: the President's Guest House. It functions as an official diplomatic residence for high-ranking dignitaries, their families, and delegations from other nations.

On average, the house plays home to one or two dignitaries every month. Once you know it, it's hard to forget (and equally strange to ponder): some of the world's most influential leaders and diplomats are regularly eating, sleeping, and meeting just a few hundred yards away from one of the most visited tourist hotspots in the nation's capital.

But if that surprises you, consider this: before Blair House took on its present-day role, the president's formal visitors would frequently spend their first night on American soil *in* the White House. I'll bet you never thought of the White House as an inn before, but it did serve that sort of purpose (it was a fancy inn, but still). The reason for this five-star hospitality was really a matter of logistical convenience; as any D.C. tourist knows all too well, the city's lodging options book up shockingly fast. That said, if a dignitary was spending additional nights in town, they would usually find space at a local hotel or at their home embassy for the remainder of their visit.

Clearly, the need for a Presidential Guest House was not always clear. But in early 1942, the US government considered a plan to rent Blair House as a space to accommodate an increasingly large number of domestic and foreign visitors who sought meetings with President Franklin Delano Roosevelt during World War II. These visitors included everyone from the Joint Chiefs of Staff to presidential advisers to politicians and other VIPs. Gist Blair's second cousin Percy Blair was instrumental in having Blair House considered the ideal location for receiving these diplomatic visitors. It is believed Percy was inspired by his curatorial work at the Anderson House on Massachusetts Avenue, which the State Department sometimes borrowed for its own diplomatic convenings.

That same year, President Roosevelt pulled the trigger and made things official. Per his authorization, the State Department was instructed to purchase Blair House for $150,000. Also acquired in the deal were the Blair family's furnishings, porcelain, silver, rugs, portraits, and other collections, which still make up about one-third of the Blair House's aesthetic.

Rumor has it the straw that broke President Roosevelt's back—what finally convinced him to sign off on the house's purchase—was a visit from Prime Minister Winston Churchill of the United Kingdom. As the story goes, while spending his promised evening in the White House, Churchill sought to wake up the president in the middle of the night to continue their shop talk. First Lady Eleanor Roosevelt was understandably *displeased* when she encountered her guest in the halls at an ungodly hour.

Once it became a diplomatic guesthouse, Blair House's first official visitor, Peruvian President Manuel Prado Ugarteche, arrived in spring 1942. But the State Department didn't formally take over the home and its operations until February of 1943, following the passing of Gist Blair's wife, who was the house's last civilian resident. At one point in 1943, diplomatic receiving needs exceeded the capacity of the home, prompting the adjacent Lee House to be subsumed into the compound. As previously stated, two additional townhomes known simply as 700 and 704 Jackson Place were purchased between 1969 and 1970 to complete the expansion of the government-owned property.

Blair House's guestbook is as lengthy as it is impressive and diverse, with temporary inhabitants coming from a wide range of countries, political leanings, and public perceptions. The residence's famous faces have included Queen Elizabeth II and Margaret Thatcher of Great Britain, Justin Trudeau of Canada, Emmanuel Macron of France, Nelson Mandela of South Africa, and Vladmir Putin of Russia, just to name a few. It's hard not to wonder what sorts of world-changing discussions—or even *decisions*—may have taken shape within these walls.

Part of the reason for the home's striking guest list is because the site also doubles as a stand-in hotel for the incoming US president in the day or days before their inauguration, after which they move into the White House. Recent exceptions to this otherwise common formality include President Bill Clinton, who opted to stay at the Hay-Adams Hotel prior to his inauguration. President Barack Obama hoped to spend a few *extra* days at Blair House—he wanted to move to Washington, D.C., a little early because his daughters were set to start school—but unfortunately the Blair House team could not accommodate this request because Australian Prime Minister John Howard was already visiting. In the event of a former president's death, the individual's surviving family members will also briefly stay at Blair House to receive US and foreign dignitaries who wish to extend their condolences.

The day-to-day operations of Blair House are managed by the Office of the Chief of Protocol at the State Department. While the four townhomes that make up the complex appear distinct from the outside, they are connected within, creating a vast 60,600 square foot living and service space divided into 120 rooms. Included in the list of chambers are fourteen guest bedrooms, thirty-five bathrooms, three formal dining rooms, and two conference rooms, with additional accommodations ranging from a fully staffed kitchen and hair salon to a fitness center, laundry facility, and more. While it's hard to imagine, especially when observing the complex from the street, Blair House's square footage is actually quite a bit greater than that of the White House.

When a foreign dignitary is in residence at Blair House, several special actions are taken. First and foremost, the flag from the dignitary's home country is flown outside of the complex. Inside, the house's staff is prepared to serve the visitor and their delegation, with even the most minor details prearranged. For example, the staff tries to predict or glean information regarding what sorts of foods—including culturally specific dishes—the guests might like while visiting. Before the official visit takes place, the dignitary's advance team—staff assigned to scope out sites and plan logistics relevant to an impending visit—is permitted to stop by and even haul in equipment, if needed.

Just before a guest arrives, the First Lady typically sends a seasonal bouquet of flowers to Blair House's principal guest room. The staff may also tailor or adjust the house's art, furniture, and décor prior to arrival, with special attention paid to displaying items from the house's collection that come from the dignitary's home country. Whenever the space requires a little refreshing, redecorating, or even historical upkeep, the nonprofit Blair House Restoration Fund facilitates the job.

To get better acquainted with the massive-in-size yet little-known Blair House, let's review a few of the space's most famous or notable rooms (because if we examined every room in the house, we'd probably find ourselves on an FBI watch list *and* wouldn't have space for the remaining chapters in this book). The first is the Lincoln Room, the former office of Francis Preston Blair. The room earned its nickname because it was frequently used by President Lincoln to engage in off-the-record conversations with Montgomery Blair, who was a member of the president's cabinet and served as US postmaster general.

Another key chamber within the complex is the library, which houses more than fifteen hundred books detailing the histories and cultures of myriad nations. In fact, when dignitaries visit Blair House, they often bring a book from their home country to add to the growing collection. The library is a space in which many presidents-elect have practiced their inauguration addresses. Nearby, the Lee Dining Room hosted President Harry S. Truman's cabinet meetings, while the Truman Study is fairly self-explanatory in both name and function.

Given the age, location, and intergenerational story of Blair House, it is perhaps obvious that many notable moments in American history have taken place within its confines or on its grounds—moments that occurred both before and after the house's formal acquisition by the US government. For instance, in 1850, the drawing room doubled as a wedding venue for General William Tecumseh Sherman and Ellen Ewing. The high-profile nature of this wedding derived from the fact that the father of the bride, Thomas Ewing, had held several significant political positions, including US senator from Ohio, secretary of the treasury, and secretary of the interior.

Thomas Ewing would end up raising Sherman, an orphan who later joined the Union Army during the Civil War. Sherman gained notoriety during wartime based on his highly publicized—and highly destructive—campaigns throughout the South, which leveled cities such as Atlanta. Naturally, when Sherman and Ellen Ewing tied the knot at Blair House, the guest list was one for the ages and included the likes of President Zachary Taylor, Secretary of State Daniel Webster, and Senator Henry Clay.

Perhaps the idea of holding the wedding in Blair House's drawing room came from a smaller wedding hosted there seven years earlier, when Francis Preston Blair's daughter Elizabeth married Samuel Phillips Lee. In the following century, Lynda Bird Johnson (daughter of thirty-sixth President Lyndon B. Johnson) married Charles Robb at the White House, and the couple chose to spend their wedding night at Blair House to avoid the prying eyes of the media.

In 1861, during the earliest days of the Civil War, Blair House was the site of yet another historically significant moment—one that is often missing from modern-day textbooks. Francis Preston Blair and his son, Montgomery, invited none other than Robert E. Lee for a meeting at their home. As the small group took their seats in the Lincoln Room, the elder Blair proceeded to offer Lee the position of commander of the Union Army, at the request of President Lincoln, of course. Lee, a military colonel at the time, politely declined the offer. His home state, Virginia, was just days away from following in the footsteps of Alabama, Florida, Georgia, Louisiana, Mississippi, South Carolina, and Texas by seceding from the Union, so he resigned his military position entirely. Two days after his meeting at Blair House, Lee took over as commander of the Confederate Army of Northern Virginia.

> **Riley's Favorite Fact (Probably):** At the onset of the Civil War, Robert E. Lee visited Blair House, where he was offered (and declined) the role of commander of the Union Army.

Despite its lengthy history of hosting notable names, Blair House has largely remained out of the news and, as a result, out of the public's collective consciousness—so much so that few Americans even know it exists. One notable exception to this "out of the news" ethos occurred in 1981, when the *Washington Post* published an article that accused

President Jimmy Carter of installing surveillance devices in the home. President Carter's anger over the claim led him to demand a public apology, but it was later revealed that Russian Premier Leonid Brezhnev and his delegation had similar suspicions when they met with President Richard Nixon in 1973. Perhaps unsurprisingly, the Russian delegation meticulously examined the guest rooms for listening devices.

One of the reasons Blair House's relative anonymity remains most astonishing, in my opinion, is that the complex has brought together major world leaders in not-so-secret convenings. Consider, for example, that the house was the venue of choice for President Obama's bipartisan meetings on healthcare policy with members of the United States Congress in 2010. Just two years later, Blair House hosted a summit of G8 countries' foreign ministers. Cultural exchanges with foreign diplomats and luncheons for foreign ambassadors following US presidential inaugurations are also held here. Recently, Blair House was a blip in the 2021 news cycle when Vice President Kamala Harris moved in while the typical vice-presidential residence, the Naval Observatory, underwent a few months' worth of renovations.

LISTEN TO RILEY

If convenings of world leaders represent one of my reasons for being confused about people's general lack of Blair House awareness, the other big one would be the fact that Blair House was effectively the White House for an entire presidency. And if you're scratching your head because you took at least one—if not multiple—years of US history in school and never heard such a thing, you're certainly not alone. History classes scarcely mention the time Blair House was known colloquially (to those who *did* know it existed) as the "Truman White House."

The rationale for this decision was simple: the real White House was in pretty bad infrastructural shape by the time President Harry S. Truman took office in 1945. Pretty soon, an inspection of the full structure revealed serious concerns, including significant damage to the first family's living quarters as well as the oft-utilized State Dining Room. By mid-1948, the US government had little choice but to approve and then get moving on some hardcore renovations, which would ultimately last four years. During the full renovation period, President Truman and his family lived at Blair House.

The most dramatic political event to occur during President Truman's time residing at Blair House wasn't a policy decision, speech, or public function. It was the moment President Truman was the subject—and then survivor—of an assassination attempt on November 1, 1950, around 2:00 p.m. local time. And while I suspect some history textbooks memorialize this famous assassination plot (though mine unacceptably did not), I wonder if they remember to include Blair House as the scene of the crime. So for all the students of history whose education on the Truman assassination attempt was entirely or partially lacking, here's a Blair House-centric summary.

Two assailants collaboratively planned and executed the plot. Oscar Collazo and Griselio Torresola were sympathetic to the cause of Puerto Rico's independence, and they believed assassinating the president of the United States would draw both national and international attention to their cause. Their scheme was hatched just two weeks before they carried it out, traveling from New York to Washington, D.C., to take advantage of what they believed would be much less security—both in quantity and efficacy—at Blair House compared with the White House.

Collazo and Torresola's plan was to walk right up to Blair House's front door (or as close as they could get to it from the street) and fire a series of bullets through the home in the hopes of striking the president. What they didn't know was that at the time of their attack, President Truman was partaking in an afternoon snooze in an upstairs bedroom.

The assailants were probably correct in their assumption that it would be logistically easier to fire a weapon from the street at Blair House compared to the White House, the latter of which is set much further off the surrounding roadways. But they were definitively wrong in their belief that security would be sparse. Torresola was killed almost immediately after the duo's first shots were fired, while Collazo was quickly wounded. White House police officer Leslie Coffelt, whose bullet killed Torresola, was himself hurt in the attack, and he later succumbed to his injuries.

President Truman, who was awakened by the commotion outside and had to be instructed to stay away from the windows, was eager to downplay the severity of the incident. He felt so strongly about keeping up appearances that he attended his previously scheduled engagement at Arlington National Cemetery later that very day. When questioned about the assassination attempt, he purported to be baffled by his attackers' motivations, citing that the Puerto Rico Federal Relations Act had been passed just months earlier. In other words, now that Puerto Rico was permitted to establish a local government and constitution, he failed to see a reason for Collazo and Torresola's frustrations that had turned unacceptably violent.

Collazo survived his injuries and was sentenced to death in 1952 as punishment for his role in the assassination attempt. However, President Truman himself commuted the sentence to life in prison one week before the execution was scheduled to take place. Later, in 1979, President Jimmy Carter followed the recommendations of high-ranking government officials and further commuted the life sentence, resulting in Collazo's release.

Despite the fortunate failure of the assassination attempt, the event did prompt changes to presidential security. For example, despite the very short distance between the two locations, the president would thereafter be transported between Blair House and the White House in a bulletproof vehicle. Prior to the plot, he could (and would) frequently stroll across the street from one site to the other.

It's a shame that President Truman's time at Blair House was historically tainted by such a terrible event—and one that had so little to do with his policies and overall presidential tenure. What else could the so-called Truman White House be remembered for? Well, for starters, it was during the Truman Administration—and therefore from the sanctuary of Blair House—that the United States began taking a more active role in foreign affairs post-World War II.

> **Riley's Next Hunt:** If any Washington, D.C., location is bound to harbor international secrets, it's Blair House. Riley would be enticed by secrets—and Ben by clues—that US presidents and their foreign dignitaries could have conceivably hidden within its walls.

Specifically, the Truman Doctrine and Marshall Plan asserted that the United States should support foreign countries working to prevent their own subjugation *and* provided billions of dollars in aid to sixteen war-torn European nations, respectively. Regardless of their long-term legacies, both the Truman Doctrine and Marshall Plan are important pieces of historical US foreign policy, and both were crafted in Blair

House's Lee Dining Room.

But what would the tale of a historic building be if not punctuated by that which launched our conversation to begin with: purported proof of the paranormal. Indeed, some people believe Blair House to be haunted, but not necessarily by the person you might expect. (You were guessing President Truman, right? Since he lived there for years?) The spirit that is said to walk the halls of Blair House is surprisingly that of President Woodrow Wilson, an apparition that President Truman attested to witnessing himself. According to legend, President Wilson's ghost is most frequently observed sitting in a rocking chair.

While we're at it, Blair House isn't the only location on Lafayette Square that hosts a presidential apparition. President Lincoln's spirit is believed to haunt the White House, with sightings of his spirit most frequently reported in the aptly named Lincoln Bedroom as well as the Yellow Oval Room. First Lady Grace Coolidge, Prime Minister Winston Churchill, and Queen Wilhelmina of the Netherlands are amongst the high-profile visitors who claimed to have set eyes on President Lincoln's ghost.

Those who are spiritually or paranormally inclined may chalk up this recurring ghost story to the fact that First Lady Mary Todd Lincoln was known to participate in séances in the White House's Red Room in the early 1860s, particularly following the death of her son Willie. Séances were a fairly common practice for Civil War-era families who sought comfort and closure as a remedy for their grief stemming from the loss of family members during battle. In fact, sightings of Willie's spirit would later be reported by White House staff members from the Grant Administration; this took place about a decade after the young man's passing.

One of the most unsettling apparitions rumored to call the White House home is that of President Andrew Jackson, who has not only been sighted on innumerable occasions, but has also been heard laughing eerily. Mary Todd Lincoln was just one White House resident who claimed to have heard President Jackson's cackle. Elsewhere on the property, President Thomas Jefferson is said to haunt the Yellow Oval Room by playing a violin, President John Tyler has been witnessed in the Blue Room, and President William Henry Harrison's ghost has inexplicably been reported in the attic. White House staff have described smelling wet laundry and lavender in the East Room, where Abigail Adams was known to hang clean washing, while Dolley Madison apparently prefers fresh air since she's been spotted outside in the Rose Garden.

Whether spirits strike your fancy or you're simply a fan of little-known United States history, the structures that line Lafayette Square have no shortage of stories to tell. But while one of these structures—the White House—gets all the popular attention, a somehow larger structure with just as much influence sits quietly across the street hosting the most significant political figures from around the world. Next time you're playing tourist in the nation's capital, be sure to spend an extra moment admiring the White House's neighbor: four unassuming townhomes that secretly join as one.

Chapter 11

Assassination of President Lincoln

Eleven chapters into this book, one thing should be abundantly clear: I envision Riley as being unyieldingly fascinated with how history is remembered and its stories told—especially in classrooms and their textbooks. By the transitive property, it's equally riveting to examine what history is actually taught to students, inherently shaping their future perspectives on quintessential topics like the rise and fall of governments and the conduct and outcomes of war. As we've discussed in the introductions to numerous chapters, there tends to be great variability in not just how these historical events are presented, but also which ones are communicated from the start.

This leads us to what is, contrary to an analogous story shared just one chapter ago, one of the most universally taught moments in American history. While the length of the story, the presence of a prologue or epilogue, and its lasting impact may vary, scarcely—or perhaps never—will you find a person who attended grade school in the United States and didn't learn about the assassination of President Abraham Lincoln.

Just as famous as President Lincoln's death is the name of the *infamous* man who perpetrated the crime: John Wilkes Booth. It really is a shame that history's greatest villains are remembered with as much, if not more, fervor than many of the world's most impactful heroes. But retelling the story of President Lincoln's assassination would truly be incomplete without understanding the motivations of the man behind the felony. Diving into these details lends insight into Booth's flawed rationale, sure, but it also helps paint a picture of life in America in the days following the Civil War's conclusion.

But what is maybe most interesting for our purposes is how a conspiracy spearheaded by one man and his followers has birthed innumerable conspiracies in the years and decades to follow. To this day, hypotheses—some more plausible than others—still float around online forums and popular history outlets regarding what became of John Wilkes Booth, why he "really" did what he did, and so much more. Since the event that inspired these conspiracy theories occurred more than 150 years ago, it's impossible to ignore the curious reality that so many people are unable or unwilling to accept broadly agreed interpretations of history.

> **Why Riley Would Care:** Although he couldn't have known it when authoring his debut book, Riley's second life-altering treasure hunt would eventually be launched by one of the many conspiracies surrounding President Lincoln's assassination.

HUNT DOWN THAT HISTORY

During his administration, President Abraham Lincoln was no stranger to death threats. In fact, he received a countless number of them, but that didn't stop him from regularly journeying outside the White House grounds on his own. For instance, when spending his presidential summers at a cottage in Washington's present-day Petworth neighborhood (a historic site now known as President Lincoln's Cottage), Lincoln regularly rode his horse to and from the White House each day. In the early 1860s, presidential security wasn't much of a thing—something Lincoln would ultimately and inadvertently have a role in changing.

As for history's most notorious villain, it's unclear exactly when John Wilkes Booth began his treasonous plotting against President Lincoln and the broader United States of America. However, we do know that his first meeting with two eventual coconspirators, his childhood friends Sam Arnold and Michael O'Laughlen, took place in Baltimore in September 1864. Booth grew up in Harford County, Maryland, and at the time of the event that forever etched his name in history books, he was a twenty-six-year-old original "nepo baby"—an actor from a prominent family of thespians.

As a stage performer, Booth got his big break in Richmond, Virginia, during the 1859–1860 theater season; this success ultimately scored him invitations to work at several well-known venues throughout the country. He traveled from New Orleans to Chicago to Boston and beyond, and by all accounts, he was quite popular with fans and fellow actors alike. It's worth considering whether Booth *could* have been remembered for his successful acting career if he had not ended up perpetrating one of the most reviled acts of treason in American history.

Booth, like many of his fellow citizens from Maryland, resonated with the sentiments of the South during the Civil War. After all, slavery was legal in Maryland, and when President Lincoln indicated his intent to free enslaved people throughout the Confederacy, Booth believed the president was infringing upon individual rights. The actor also took issue with many of the president's actions to prevent Washington, D.C., from falling into the hands of the Confederacy during the war. Furthermore, Booth was impressed by the Confederacy's general ethos, relating to the Southern states' self-proclaimed honorable nature and respect for history.

You might expect that Booth's passion was inspired by his immediate family, but that couldn't have been further from the truth. In fact, the rest of the Booth family, including his brother and fellow famous actor Edwin, sided staunchly with the Union. Edwin Booth had publicly supported President Lincoln during the 1864 election, while his grandfather Richard Booth was a member of the network that facilitated the Underground Railroad. So strong were the Booth family's convictions that it's said the only reason John Wilkes Booth failed to enlist in the Confederate Army was to appease his mother; she had already lost four children during her lifetime and couldn't bear to lose another. Even so, as the Civil War drew closer to its conclusion, Booth grew increasingly disappointed in his decision not to partake.

At some point between his meeting with Sam Arnold and Michael O'Laughlen and early the following year, John Wilkes Booth formulated a plan. And while the plan didn't call for a full-blown assassination of a sitting president, if successful, it would have made history books all the same. Booth initially sought to *kidnap* President Lincoln, transporting him to the South and holding him for ransom. In exchange for the president's freedom, Booth would demand the release of Confederate prisoners of war.

It was a bold strategy, and Booth intended to act it out on March 17, 1865. But things don't always work out as planned, and a change in President Lincoln's schedule on the date of the plot kept him from the location where Booth and his coconspirators sat waiting to carry out their ambush. While this fateful change of plans prevented President Lincoln's kidnapping, it sort of cost him his life.

That's because Booth ran out of time to attempt his kidnapping again. Confederate General Robert E. Lee surrendered to Union forces on April 9, ending the Civil War and prompting Booth to shift his plan from a kidnapping to an assassination. Many people suspect Booth turned to this drastic course of action after hearing the president's April 11th speech, which, among other things, shared the sentiment that African American men who had fought for the Union should be eligible to vote.

Compared to his kidnapping plot, Booth's assassination plan was rather complex (though two-thirds of it would ultimately fail). In addition to murdering President Lincoln, which we'll discuss momentarily, Booth also assigned two coconspirators to kill Vice President Andrew Johnson and Secretary of State William Seward at the same time on the same night. While other conspirators were therefore part of the plot, Booth devised the series of events on his own. He thought if he could create enough chaos in the nation's capital by assassinating three high-ranking men in the US government, the Confederacy could regroup and effectively reignite their war efforts. (Dude really couldn't take a loss.)

The irony of this complex plan was that Booth either didn't know or straight-up ignored the process for government succession. If all three murders had proceeded as planned, Senator Lafayette Sabine Foster of Connecticut would immediately have been tapped to serve as acting president until March 4, 1866, with Speaker of the House Schuyler Colfax sitting as next in line. A special election would have taken place in November 1865 to elect a new president who would have taken office the following year. In other words, while Washington would have certainly *felt* chaotic, the government would have continued operating without issue.

But all this is neither here nor there, as only one murder took place as a result of Booth's scheming—the murder he was personally in charge of carrying out. As a stage actor, Booth was a frequent performer at Ford's Theatre in Washington, D.C., so he was familiar with the venue's layout and staff, who were accustomed to seeing him around. He was also a friend of John T. Ford, the theater's owner, and since Booth was often on the road, he used the theater as a personal mailing address when he was in town.

On the morning of April 14, 1865, Booth visited Ford's Theatre to pick up his mail, and that's when he learned President Lincoln was scheduled to attend a performance of *Our American Cousin* on-site that evening. This was the opportunity Booth had been waiting for, and it was time to put his plan into action. At 8:00 p.m., he convened a final meeting with his remaining coconspirators at Herndon House, located a block away from the theater. Those coconspirators, whose contributions (and punishments) we will consider later in this chapter, included Lewis Powell, George Atzerodt, and David Herold.

President Lincoln, his wife, and their guests, Major Henry Rathbone and his fiancée Clara Harris, arrived at the theater that evening fashionably late (read: after the play had already begun). They were seated in a box overlooking stage left. In testimony following the events of the night, actress Jeannie Gourlay claimed she had spotted Booth in the theater's lobby during the show, but he had disappeared by the time she next glanced in his direction. She believed he used her scene—one characterized by dramatic and interesting dialogue—to make his way to the president's box. Strategically, Booth opted to proceed at a moment when the audience's attention was undoubtedly fixed on the stage.

It is thought that when Booth reached the outer door to the box, he presented his calling card to Charles Forbes, the president's messenger who had been positioned outside of the enclosed seating area. Again, Booth was a famous face, and at the time there was little reason to believe his presence was intended as anything other than a brief greeting between renowned figures. Upon entering, Booth locked himself in the small entryway between the hall and the box itself by barring the door shut behind him.

The time was around 10:15 p.m., with the show in its final act. Familiar with the dialogue of *Our American Cousin*, Booth opted to make his move during a comedic moment in the play—that night, the line in question was delivered by actor Harry Hawk and elicited uproarious laughter from the audience. The moments that immediately followed are well-known. Upon entering the interior section of the box, Booth fired a .44-caliber derringer pistol within inches of the president's head.

Later, several actors were quoted as saying they thought the shooting sound came from a back room, or that it was a gag added to the show. Some audience members thought it was part of the play.

As quickly as Booth entered the box, he sought to leave it—and did so in dramatic fashion. He climbed onto the railing, fighting Major Rathbone's attempts to apprehend him by slicing the man's arm with a dagger. The assassin jumped to the stage, catching the spur of his boot on a Treasury Guards flag hanging from the front of the box and therefore landing awkwardly. Most people agree he broke his leg in the process.

Upon reaching the stage, Booth emphatically declared to a stunned and confused audience, "*Sic semper Tyrannis*" ("Thus always to tyrants"), though some witnesses remembered his words as "the South shall be free" or, alternatively, "the South is avenged." Booth then exited stage right, fighting off orchestra conductor William Withers as he departed via the theater's back door and rode off on a waiting horse. We'll return to his movements shortly.

In the meantime, the crowd at Ford's Theatre was just beginning to understand what had transpired before their very eyes. In response to calls for any doctors who were present, physicians Charles Leale and Charles Sabin Taft quickly made their way up to the presidential box, examining President Lincoln's head wound and diagnosing the shot as fatal. As good Samaritans carried the president out of the theater and into the street, they were ushered into Peterson House, which sat directly opposite Ford's Theatre, by tenant Henry Safford. It was suspected that a bumpy carriage ride across six blocks of unpaved roads to the White House might have worsened President Lincoln's condition, and at this point onlookers hoped he could pass away peacefully surrounded by family.

Peterson House quickly turned into a command center for both the Lincoln family and the executive branch of the US government. First Lady Mary Todd Lincoln stayed in the home to visit with her husband, who never regained consciousness. She and her son Robert would spend most of the night in the front parlor given her extreme distress. Meanwhile, Secretary of War Edwin Stanton stationed himself in the boardinghouse to begin an investigation into the shooting. From the night of April 14 to the early morning of April 15, more than forty people wandered into and out of the house.

Outside on Tenth Street, citizens were understandably freaking out, with the panic originating with audience members emerging from Ford's Theatre. Rumors began circulating that the Confederacy had launched an attack on the nation's capital. All night long, people camped outside the boardinghouse waiting for news on the president's condition, and doctors would periodically emerge to share updates. They would soon learn that President Lincoln died at 7:22 a.m. on April 15, the morning following the attack. Merely hours later, Vice President Andrew Johnson took the oath of office to become the seventeenth president of the United States.

> **Riley's Favorite Fact (Probably):** President Lincoln wasn't the only intended victim in John Wilkes Booth's murderous plot. If all had gone as planned, Vice President Johnson and Secretary of State Seward would have shared a similar fate.

By then, assassin John Wilkes Booth was long gone. After departing Ford's Theatre, he rode his horse southeast into Maryland, crossing a bridge that was supposed to be closed so late at night (but the guard, who hadn't yet heard the news, made an exception and let him pass). After crossing the state line, Booth met up with David Herold, who had failed in his task of murdering Secretary of State Seward earlier that evening. It didn't take long for the US Army to begin its pursuit of Booth as one thousand Union soldiers were tasked with facilitating his capture.

It would take the pursuers a decent amount of time before finding success, because although Booth was injured (whether from his fall to the stage or from his horse falling and landing on his leg during the escape), he was pretty effective as a criminal on the run. First, he and Herold made a pitstop at Surratt's Tavern in Maryland, where they acquired guns, field glasses, and other supplies that had been stashed there previously. By 4:00 a.m. on April 15, they arrived on the doorstep of Dr. Samuel Mudd, telling the doctor that Booth's leg was broken from his horse's fall. They demanded that Mudd perform treatment quickly without sharing the reason for their haste. After immobilizing Booth's leg in a splint, Mudd invited the men to stay and rest in his home until midafternoon.

While Mudd initially claimed Booth and Herold were strangers to him, it was eventually determined that he had been part of Booth's original kidnapping plot. By some accounts, it wasn't until the afternoon on April 15 that Mudd learned via newspaper about the crime Booth had committed the night before. Based on this timeline of events, Mudd then asked the two men to leave his home, but he chose not to turn them over to the authorities.

Before long, a $100,000 reward was offered by the War Department on a publicly distributed "wanted" poster for well-known and uber-recognizable actor John Wilkes Booth. The assassin managed to remain officially missing for twelve days, during which time he covered about ninety miles of terrain with the help of plenty of individuals who were very much aware of his actions. For example, Confederate sympathizer Thomas A. Jones helped Booth and Herold hide near his Maryland home until they could safely boat across the Potomac River into Virginia. They spent a fair amount of time hiding in local pine thicket (where I personally like to think they suffered from ample poison ivy and mosquito bites).

By many accounts, during his time in hiding, Booth read every newspaper article he could get his hands on that attempted to tell the tale of his actions, and he was somehow shocked by the overwhelmingly negative public reaction to what he had done. What surprised him most was that many Southern or Southern-sympathizing cities condemned the assassination, yet these were the exact audiences Booth was sure would find his deed heroic.

On April 26, a few days shy of the two-week anniversary of the assassination, Booth and Herold were cornered by Union troops, who had been tipped off to the men's hiding place by someone who had helped them just days prior. Booth and Herold were laying low in a tobacco barn on the Virginia property of Richard Garrett; the family permitted the men to stay on their grounds because Booth and Herold claimed to be wounded Confederate soldiers. However, Garrett's son Jack observed his guests' strange behavior when Union soldiers were nearby, raising suspicions that the men were covert thieves.

Upon approaching the barn, Union troops declared they would set the structure ablaze if Booth and Herold, who had locked themselves inside, didn't emerge. Herold soon surrendered, but Booth refused. The assassin requested his pursuers back away from the barn door by a distance of one hundred yards, at which point he would exit and engage in combat with his pistol and knife. When his request was denied, he haggled, requesting a new distance of fifty yards. Each sequential request was swiftly refused.

Chaos quickly, and somewhat accidentally, ensued. One of the troops lit a rope on fire and stuffed it into a crack in the barn, causing some hay inside the structure to burn. As the fire spread, soldier Thomas "Boston" Corbett fired his weapon into the barn without explicit instructions to do so, and his shot severely wounded Booth, paralyzing him from the neck down. Corbett would later claim he had been spying on Booth through the barn's wall slats and shot him as a matter of defense. Despite exhaustive attempts to interrogate him as he lay dying, Booth couldn't really speak, which was a huge blow for investigators and really everyone who sought answers for his seemingly inexplicable crimes.

When Booth's paralyzed body was dragged from the building, he was said to have whispered, "Tell mother, I die for my country." Booth did not succumb to his injuries for several hours, passing away around 7:00 a.m. Theatrical until the bitter end, his last words were "useless, useless," uttered dramatically as he stared at his hands.

At this point, the nation was still coming to terms with the violent death of its president. While it would be more pleasant to say the country's reaction to President Lincoln's assassination was universally scornful, that (unfortunately) would be rather untrue. In fact, the national response was very mixed, with some people expressing deep sadness and others celebrating the president's untimely demise. (If Booth had escaped capture long enough to see some of the heinous *positive* reactions to his crime, perhaps he would have believed his actions hadn't been as "useless" as they seemed.)

First Lady Mary Todd Lincoln was adamant that she didn't want a flashy funeral for her husband, but as so many women's assertions both were and are, her desire was cast aside. Secretary of War Stanton launched a funerary train—basically a railway-facilitated parade of the president's casket—across the country on April 21. The train stopped in many major cities en route to Springfield, Illinois, where President Lincoln would ultimately be buried in May.

Booth's surviving conspirators were quickly jailed in Washington, D.C., where they went on trial one by one throughout May and June at the Old Arsenal Penitentiary. Each sat before a nine-person military commission, which acted as a jury and only needed to turn in a majority decision to achieve a guilty verdict. And if six guilty votes were cast by the tribunal, the death penalty could be issued for the defendant.

Even at the time, use of a military trial was controversial and seen as eliciting a less fair result than one achieved with a civilian jury. But the powers that be got away with the decision, mostly because Confederate troops were still hanging around the capital at the time of the assassination. This meant Washington, D.C., was under martial law back in April, allowing the assassination to be categorized—and litigated—as an act of war.

A whopping 366 witnesses were called to the stand during the conspirators' trials, and the eight defendants were not permitted to *defend* themselves. Their alleged contributions to Booth's plan varied, suggesting different levels of involvement and severity. For instance, Mary Surratt was the owner of a boardinghouse used by Booth and his coconspirators as a meeting place, and she also delivered Booth's field glasses and supplies to her Maryland tavern in advance of the assassination.

Then there was David Herold, who visited Secretary of State Seward's home the night of April 14 with the intention of killing him before chickening out last minute. Even so, Herold helped Booth survive and hide out following his escape from Washington, D.C. Lewis Powell got closer to finishing Herold's murderous assignment at the secretary of state's home, since Powell posed as a prescription delivery man and stabbed Seward in the face and neck. At the time, Seward was wearing a brace because of a recent carriage accident, and this medical device probably saved his life.

George Atzerodt was the conspirator tasked with assassinating Vice President Andrew Johnson at the Kirkwood House hotel, but the man got too drunk to follow through. Dr. Samuel Mudd was initially tried as a conspirator for his role in treating Booth's leg, and he later admitted to knowing Booth prior to the assassination. A lesser-known name, Edman "Ned" Spangler, was in trouble for watching Booth's horse outside Ford's Theatre during the assassination, though it was later agreed that he probably didn't have anything to do with the plot.

The familiar foes Michael O'Laughlen and Samuel Arnold also ended up on trial; recall that both men were initially part of Booth's kidnapping plot, but neither was involved in the assassination. In fact, at the time of the incident, O'Laughlen and Arnold were verifiably nowhere near the theater.

Ultimately, Arnold, O'Laughlen, and Mudd received sentences of life in prison owing to the revelation of their involvement in the kidnapping scheme. Spangler received the lightest punishment—six years of hard labor while imprisoned—for his part in inadvertently helping Booth escape the theater on the night in question. John Surratt, a final alleged conspirator and Confederate spy who spent much time overseas, would later be extradited to the United States, where his case ended in a hung jury and was never relitigated.

Four of Booth's coconspirators would be issued the death penalty after being found guilty of "conspiracy to assassinate." Atzerodt, Herold, Powell, and Mary Surratt were executed by hanging on July 7, 1865. As a result, Mary Surratt became the first woman in history to be put to death by the US government. Today, it is agreed that Atzerodt, Herold, and Powell definitely knew about Booth's plan and intention to assassinate the president. Mary Surratt's knowledge of the full plot remains up for debate.

LISTEN TO RILEY

Since John Wilkes Booth died before he could be thoroughly interrogated, historians have needed to look elsewhere to infer his true motivations for becoming one of the most notorious criminals in American history. As a result, much attention has been paid to his small, red appointment book, which was among the items found on his person after he died. This collection of objects included five women's photos (four of actresses and one of his rumored fiancée), the dagger with which he slashed Major Rathbone, a compass, keys, a switchblade knife, and a pistol.

Over time, the appointment book has become better known as the Booth diary, since he used it as a makeshift journal during his time on the run. In it, Booth made numerous entries contradicting the media's accusations of his cowardice, simultaneously recording thoughts that embellished his own actions. From an outsider's perspective, the Booth diary is filled with self-pity, self-aggrandizing, and a perceived need to justify the writer's actions to the world.

While the first entry in the diary is dated April 14, the day of the assassination, it's likely that Booth wrote his complete series of reflections between April 17 and 22. Highlights of his writings include Booth's adamant belief that he "struck boldly and not as the [news]papers say," subsequently sharing all the reasons why he believed onlookers should laud him (not the least of which were his broken leg and all the other challenges he purportedly had to overcome to accomplish his dark deed). He shared his "despair…For doing what Brutus was honored for" and for being "looked upon as a common, cutthroat." Theatrical even in death, Booth assured readers that he assassinated President Lincoln on behalf of his country.

You might believe any controversy associated with the Booth diary would revolve around the assassin's bold—even egregious—statements of self-importance. Yet the real reason the diary has been a source of intrigue is because, at some point, a set of its pages went missing. As if simply to make things *more* interesting, no one seems to know where they went or what was written on them.

This sounds impossible. Clearly one of the most important pieces of tangible evidence in a notorious crime wouldn't have ever been misplaced or mishandled . . . especially since it would need to be presented at any trials related to said crime. Right? Nope.

Not only was the diary *not* presented as evidence during the coconspirators' trials in 1865, but Secretary of War Stanton was put in charge of the diary and soon lost it amongst the files of the War Department. Fortunately (or suspiciously, depending on your take), it turned back up in 1867 right before the delayed trial of John Surratt, at which point someone realized a number of pages had been excised with a knife.

At the time, Stanton and others vehemently agreed these pages had been missing back when the diary was first located two years earlier. However, there remains some disagreement about whether the same number of pages was missing before and after the diary's mysterious disappearing act. And whenever such a controversy exists surrounding an important document, conspiracies are sure to follow. Some people believe additional pages were removed because they contained information that would have vindicated, or at least reduced the perceived guilt of, coconspirators like the Surratts.

In 1977, more than a century later, the Federal Bureau of Investigation (FBI) conducted a thorough forensic analysis of the Booth diary in an attempt to quell a growing conspiracy theory that its pages contained secret, hidden writing. The agency's examination included ultraviolet, fluorescence, infrared, and X-ray spectroscopies, techniques that were used to examine a Booth diary page in *National Treasure: Book of Secrets* but, in real life, turned up no such writing. However, the FBI also used this opportunity to verify Booth's handwriting in the book and confirm that twenty-seven sheets of paper were missing from the binding.

Digging even deeper, the FBI report indicates that at some point the diary had been unbound and rebound, with pages missing from the middle section where Booth issued his confession-type statements. This assessment was supported by closely tracking the natural indentations created on consecutive pages by pressing down when writing. To this day, conspiracy theorists believe the removal of pages from the center of Booth's sequence is evidence that the diary was forged or altered by the US government.

Adding fuel to the fire is the fact that somehow, even after the FBI's analysis, there is little consensus regarding the exact number of sheets missing from the diary; the numbers eighteen, twenty-seven, and forty-three have all been suggested. Naturally, people throughout history have come forward at different times to claim they have found missing pages; equally naturally, none of these claims have been verified, and the pages remain officially lost. In fact, the assertion that eighteen pages are missing seems to stem from a claim that eighteen pages were later found in the home of Stanton's descendant, which conspiracy theorists took to mean the secretary of war had actually been the ringleader of the assassination.

Perhaps surprisingly, it is not a small, fringe group of people who maintain that Booth wasn't solely responsible for the assassination plot. Many history enthusiasts share this belief even today, though their alternative explanations vary substantially. A popular assertion is that the assassination was an elaborate plan of the Confederate government, with some theorists trying to make connections between Booth and Jefferson Davis or Judah Benjamin, the Confederate president and secretary of state, respectively.

These and other Booth conspiracy theories ramped up in frequency and intensity following the publication of the book *Why Was Lincoln Murdered?* by chemist, oil executive, and author Otto Eisenschiml in 1937. In his book, Eisenschiml purported that Stanton led the assassination conspiracy with the aim of taking control of the country.

In support of his claim, Eisenschiml asserted that Stanton was the reason Union General Ulysses S. Grant didn't attend the theater with President Lincoln on the night of the assassination (which was originally intended), as well as the reason why a notoriously tough bodyguard failed to tag along with the Lincolns. Plus, Eisenschiml said, one couldn't ignore the fact that Stanton was the man in control of the Booth diary before the public discovery of its missing pages.

But as Ben Gates accurately points out in *Book of Secrets*, Eisenschiml's theories have been widely refuted by historians since their initial publication. One of the most discredited points in his book is the supposition that Stanton had ordered all bridges out of Washington, D.C., to be closed on the night of the assassination with the exception of Navy Yard Bridge—the one Booth used to escape. Despite the thorough rebuttal of his points, the creativity that Eisenschiml's text inspired in its readers was beyond suppression: conspiracies regarding the origin of the assassination plot were—and continue to be—pervasive.

But that isn't even the extent of the *scope* of conspiracy theories related to the assassination. Take, for example, the fact that a nonzero number of people strongly believe Booth never died on the Garrett family's property on April 26. These people maintain that Booth had already left the barn by the time the Union troops arrived in pursuit, and that Corbett's gunfire actually struck and killed someone else who was posing as the assassin. The root of this theory is the fact that Booth was not captured alive, which many found—and still find—suspicious. Indeed, following his death, reports of Booth being spotted alive and well poured in from across the country and around the world.

This theory was given enough credence that in 1866 during a debate on the Senate floor, Kentucky Senator Garrett Davis asserted Booth might still be at large. Moreover, modern-day descendants of Booth confirm that a story passed down through their family for generations suggests their infamous ancestor did escape.

> **Riley's Next Hunt:** A new treasure hunt would necessarily bring unexpected characters out of the woodwork. Perhaps a Booth descendant—one who could "prove" his ancestor *did* escape the barn ambush—could hold a critical clue that doubles as a *Book of Secrets* callback!

Perhaps one of the oddest coincidences related to the Booth survival theory is related to a man named James William Boyd. A captured Confederate soldier, Boyd was released by Stanton on February 14, 1865, after promising he would head straight home to care for his children following his wife's passing. But shortly after his release, Boyd disappeared without a trace. Interestingly, Boyd was said to exhibit an uncanny resemblance to John Wilkes Booth, even sporting a tattoo similar to one Booth had that was used to identify his body after he was killed. While the details differ from theory to theory, their premise remains the same: some believe the body examined and determined to be Booth's was actually Boyd's, while Booth either escaped to rural America or fled the country.

Somehow, that theory isn't even the most intriguing. In the early 1900s, a Texan known as John St. Helen feared he was on his deathbed and used the opportunity to confide in his friend and lawyer, Finis L. Bates, that his real name was John Wilkes Booth. St. Helen issued a full confession related to the assassination, including details that only Booth would seemingly know. Unexpectedly, however, St. Helen recovered from his illness and surreptitiously skipped town. When a supposedly different man, David E. George, died by suicide in Enid, Oklahoma, in 1903, his body was (for some reason) embalmed and put on display at a mortuary, leading many to determine he looked suspiciously like Booth. When lawyer Finis L. Bates happened to visit Enid, he was taken aback to find that the window-displayed body of David E. George was actually that of his friend, John St. Helen.

As if that wasn't strange enough, George-slash-St. Helen's preserved remains would end up being paraded around state fairs and related social gatherings, only to eventually go missing. At some point, Bates published the details that St. Helen shared with him regarding his past life as John Wilkes Booth, and some of those details were found not to accord with federal records associated with the Lincoln assassination. Yet when the embalmed body of George-slash-St. Helen reappeared in the 1930s, doctors who examined it found striking similarities between it and what would be the expected condition of Booth's body, including evidence of a broken leg, broken thumb, and a scar on his neck. However, the wrong leg was broken. (And if all that isn't enough coincidence for you, I'll leave you to chew on this: Thomas "Boston" Corbett, the Union soldier who supposedly killed John Wilkes Booth, is himself buried in Enid, Oklahoma. Mind. Blown.)

With time comes advancements in technology, and in 2020, facial recognition software developed at Virginia Tech was used to compare known photographs of Booth's face with those of not only John St. Helen, but also James William Boyd. According to the test results, neither face was a match to Booth's. Regardless, for decades, the FBI has received innumerable letters from people around the United States sharing details about Booth's supposed life postassassination. The letter writers would often purport that their neighbor (or a similar contact within a few degrees of separation) was Booth himself, or that said person had been in contact with Booth throughout the early 1900s.

But what cannot be argued is this: Booth's body was identified by family members, as well as colleagues from Ford's Theatre and a doctor who had previously performed surgery on him. While he was initially buried in the basement of the Old Penitentiary (the government sought to prevent desecration by both critics and admirers alike), his body was exhumed in 1869 and reburied in an unmarked grave within his family's plot at Green Mount Cemetery, located in Baltimore.

In the 1990s, a contingent of Booth's descendants called for the body to be exhumed yet again so that genetic testing could be performed. However, various logistical issues created barriers to this course of action, not the least of which was the fact that no one knows exactly where in the plot Booth's unmarked grave is situated. Plus, it was assumed that other family members had been buried atop older graves in more recent years, making it impossible to remove the body without disturbing others even if its location could be pinpointed.

Naysayers also note that in order to be effective, DNA testing would require comparison to known dental records or the genetic information of Booth's matrilineal descendants. The body of Edwin Booth could be exhumed for this purpose, and these results could be compared to DNA gleaned from the vertebrae removed from John Wilkes Booth's body during his autopsy. However, the family that now owns the land where Edwin was buried refuses to consent to digging requests, and the US Army Medical Command, which is currently in possession of John Wilkes's vertebrae, has denied requests to test the samples on numerous occasions.

Perhaps some mysteries are meant to remain unsolved, even if the broader historical community has already arrived at its own conclusion.

And then again, maybe there is some value in keeping mysteries alive. After all, it's those pesky mysteries from long ago that are mostly likely to succeed in drawing in even the most disinterested observers of the past.

Chapter 12

Seward's Folly

We're all human. We all make mistakes. But the most painful mistakes are the ones that onlookers—our families, friends, the Internal Revenue Service (in Riley's case)—never let us forget. As if detrimental impacts to our health, financial situations, or the trust of the people around us aren't enough punishment, the constant reminder of our follies is what haunts us in the wee hours of the morning as we lie awake at night. Just me? Frankly, I'm not sorry if you can't relate.

If we're deemed important enough to be remembered in textbooks and taught in schools for generations after we've passed on, our mistakes can truly take on a life of their own. For someone like Riley, who presumably aspires to achieve some degree of notoriety in a world characterized by social media and "DIY fame," it's the possibility of history remembering their failures with greater gusto than their successes that occasionally provokes heartburn. And if you think such a possibility is far-fetched, allow me to reintroduce you to US Secretary of State William H. Seward, who is probably most remembered for an event colloquially known as "Seward's folly."

This man was a secretary of state—one of the most powerful positions within one of the most powerful governments in the world. And yet more than a century after serving, his most famous contribution to his country is something dubbed a folly. I'm no English major, but I'm pretty sure "folly" is synonymous with something that is stupid, foolish, or reckless. Pay no attention to the fact that the moment in history assigned this moniker inspired a popular dessert (baked Alaska), or that the historical event is still feted in the state of its origin. Because once a catchy slogan or cutesy tagline is embedded into the brains of Americans, it's hard to get it out. (Ask me about particularly memorable car insurance or canine medication commercials from my youth.)

I take it back. Riley's biggest fear in becoming famous is probably not that his mistakes will be remembered for all of eternity, but rather that one of his *good* deeds will be misremembered as a bad deed for all of eternity.

I like to think that in his distaste for the blander bits of American history, Riley was never acquainted with Secretary Seward's plight. If he was, he'd be terrified by the cautionary tale of Seward's most famous act having such a negative connotation in circles of nonhistorical experts. This reality is exclusively due to the perception we have of how the event was viewed at the time of its occurrence. And yet somehow that perception is wildly incorrect; the story most of us think we know is a total lie. It turns out the real circumstances surrounding Seward's folly—the purchase of Alaska by the United States—were hardly illogical at all.

> **Why Riley Would Care:** Riley—who probably dreams of going viral on social media—should learn about Seward's folly as a cautionary tale of what *not* to do if you'd like to be remembered fondly by future generations.

HUNT DOWN THAT HISTORY

For millennia, prior to the colonization of the New World and the establishment of the United States, the northwestern corner of North America—present-day Alaska—was home to the Inuit and many other Indigenous tribes. In fact, Alaska was the first location in the Americas to have been populated when early humans crossed into the region from Asia about 15,000 years ago.

Fast forward several thousand years. In the 1500s, Russia had been toying with the idea of expanding its territory into North America, and the country's geographic location offered an ideal home base from which to enact such a plan. Once the Russians crept into Siberia, they literally followed their primary source of income—pelted animals—into new locations to expand their fur trade, spread the Russian Orthodox sect of Christianity, and gain access to new, fruitful resources.

One of the most well-known early explorers of Alaska on behalf of

Russia was Vitus Jonassen Bering, a Danish adventurer and cartographer. By the time Bering died in 1741, succumbing to a case of scurvy during his final expedition, his documentation of Alaska was state-of-the-art and had made the region, its populations, and its natural resources known to the world. Unsurprisingly, his discoveries piqued the interest of some of the era's other formidable powers, including Great Britain, France, and Spain. As the late 1700s approached, these countries, as well as the freshly minted United States of America, began their own explorations of the land.

But these countries were at a disadvantage; they couldn't change the fact that Russia had gotten there first. In 1799, Russia's Tsar Paul I granted the new Russian-American Company control over the territory's economic operations. In practice, this meant the company was responsible for standing up a trade monopoly while establishing settlements for their traders.

Alaska was, of course, already home to around one hundred thousand Indigenous people from numerous tribes, but their numbers would quickly begin to decline. With Russian permanent settlement came subjugation of the native communities, aided by the Russians' firearms and other weaponry that allowed for ease of overpowering. The Russian settlers killed or enslaved many of the Indigenous people they encountered, while others succumbed to unfamiliar diseases.

By the mid-1800s, Russia discovered it had committed a folly of its own. Despite the deceptive appearances of maps, the Russian homeland was actually rather far from its new territory, a reality that perpetually threw wrenches into Russia's plans to maintain its newest chunk of permafrost. From both cost and logistical perspectives, Russia couldn't effectively communicate with or provide much-needed supplies to its own countrymen occupying the region. It quickly became economically untenable to maintain the large parcel of land, for a laundry list of reasons.

For starters, Russia was already in significant debt from the Crimean War, which had lasted from 1853 to 1856 and left the nation with very little financial flexibility to do things like take care of what was practically a whole separate country hundreds of miles away. For example, while it might have been helpful for Russia to establish a protective military installation on the Pacific Coast of North America, this simply was not economically possible. Plus, once the Russians had obliterated Alaska's local sea otter population in the name of the fur trade, they could literally no longer justify being in the territory with no more fur profits to be had.

But the problems didn't stop there. Russian settlers increasingly encountered conflicts with the Tlingit tribe of skilled warriors. And since the Russians relied on various native communities to provide them with much-needed supplies, a souring relationship with nearby groups only made their lives more difficult. I may be biased by the contents of my own book, but the situation feels somewhat akin to "Roanoke 2.0."

Russia ultimately ceased sending settlers to live and work in Alaska; there were never more than several hundred, and they primarily lived on the Aleutian Islands, Kenai Peninsula, Kodiak, and Sitka. The land wasn't exactly amenable to agriculture, so it was challenging to ensure those living in the area had adequate food to survive. This harsh reality had initially prompted the Russian-American Company to establish Fort Ross as a trade and agriculture outpost on the California coast earlier in 1812. The goings-on at and around the fort would be used to feed and provide other necessities to Alaska's settlers when it became clear that those supplies wouldn't reliably arrive from the Russian mainland.

After decades of struggle, the Russian-American Company was in severe need of monetary support from home, and Russia simply couldn't afford to subsidize its Alaskan operations any longer. While the country was still interested in expanding its land holdings, it had grown to view advancing across the *Asian* continent as more logistically appealing. Russia had once boasted North American assets as far south as San Francisco Bay, but when the country eventually offloaded the Alaskan territory from its holdings, this event formally marked the end of Russia's attempts at trade proliferation and settlement along the Pacific Coast. But alas, we're getting ahead of ourselves, as the story of said offloading is what we're really here to explore.

In December 1866, a year after the American Civil War's conclusion, Russian envoy to the United States Baron Eduard de Stoeckl received permission from Tsar Alexander II to begin discussions about the theoretical sale of Alaska. As de Stoeckl pursued his negotiations, he was instructed not to accept an offer valued at less than $5 million.

But why was Russia so keen to sell Alaska to the *United States* specifically? Surely the would-be sellers could have shopped around for the best offer, agreeing to terms with the highest bidder. While that may have been true, Russia saw the United States's eventual acquisition of the land as a foregone conclusion, likening the situation to the takeover of Texas a few decades earlier. Plus, of all the countries that could potentially control Alaska, the United States was seen as a best-case scenario from Russia's perspective. After all, Great Britain, which owned nearby Canada, had just defeated Russia in the Crimean War, and perhaps selling to the United States could even invoke a truce between US and Russian traders operating on the Pacific Coast.

Armed with his negotiating authority, de Stoeckl chose to contact William H. Seward, who served as the US secretary of state during the administrations of Presidents Abraham Lincoln and Andrew Johnson. Seward's political career began as a New York state senator; he later became New York governor and eventually US senator. During the 1860 presidential election, he was a candidate for the Republican nomination. After landing the secretary of state role, Seward often butted heads with President Lincoln at the onset of the Civil War, but over time the two grew to work well together, and Seward was allegedly responsible for ensuring Great Britain's Civil War neutrality. He would become the only secretary of state to survive an assassination attempt; as a reminder, this took place on the night of Lincoln's assassination.

Seward had long been a vocal advocate not only of westward expansion, but specifically of the United States subsuming Alaska. At one point, Seward was publicly quoted as saying that Alaskan settlements would "yet become the outposts of my own country." President Johnson gave Seward written permission to meet with de Stoeckl and begin negotiating the acquisition, a process that began on March 11, 1867. In a matter of weeks (shockingly fast, I know), a treaty that would give the northwestern land to the United States had been fully drafted.

Said treaty outlined the boundaries of the intended land transfer, as well as a specific set of guidelines to govern what would happen to Russians who were currently living in the Alaska territory. These settlers had options: either return to Russia within three years' time or stay and become citizens of the United States. The futures of Indigenous tribes living in Alaska were also outlined (without their input); the treaty stipulated that while native people could not earn US citizenship, they still had to abide by US laws. And since textbooks often forget the nitty-gritty administrative details, it's worth noting here that in accordance with the treaty, the written records of the Russian-American Company would be transferred to the United States in the deal.

This so-called Treaty of Cession, which would see the United States paying Russia $7.2 million for a total land area of 586,412 square miles (a rate of approximately $0.02 per acre), was approved by Seward on March 30, 1867. For comparison's sake, this vast expanse of land was about 20 percent of the size of the rest of the United States at the time, or about twice the size of Texas. Needless to say, the transfer would expand the total land area of the country significantly. Adjusted for inflation, the cost for Alaska would have been more than $120 million today.

The next step for the treaty was its presentation to the US Senate for approval; ratification would require a two-thirds affirmative vote. During the Senate's deliberations, one of the treaty's strongest and most vocal advocates was Senator Charles Sumner of Massachusetts, who served as the chair of the Senate Foreign Relations Committee. Interestingly, Senator Sumner's support for the Alaska purchase wasn't always so staunch.

In fact, Sumner allegedly *opposed* the acquisition when it was first presented to him as a possibility. Like many of his contemporaries, he didn't understand why the land would be of value to the United States and, worse, he worried that taking over Alaska would set a dangerous precedent for annexing new lands that came at a high financial cost. But instead of doubling down on his concerns, Sumner opted to dive headfirst into researching the territory when the treaty came to the Senate Foreign Relations Committee for consideration.

His deep dive focused on the findings of the Smithsonian Institution, which had surveyed the land in 1859 and 1865 and published detailed records of Alaska's vast natural resources. The Smithsonian's research was powerful enough that it completely changed Sumner's perception of the proposal. When he finally addressed the committee, Sumner waxed philosophical for three hours about all he had read: details regarding the region's climate, mineral deposits, fish stocks, and Indigenous communities. He also advocated that the land be named for the cultures of its native inhabitants, and it was during this speech that the name Alaska (derived from the Aleut word *Alyeska*, or "great land") was first used to describe the territory.

The US Senate ultimately approved the Alaska purchase on April 9 by an overwhelming majority, and President Johnson signed the Treaty of Cession on May 28. Later that year, on October 18, the United States formally took possession of Alaska during a flag-changing ceremony at Sitka, which was attended by contingents of both American and Russian troops, as well as a handful of local Indigenous leaders. An amusing fact (though probably not amusing for residents at the time) is that Alaskans lost eleven days of their calendar on October 18, since they would be required to transition from the Julian calendar (which Russia observed) to the Gregorian calendar (which was customary in the United States). (Once again, this may be the result of my own bias, but the situation has serious Mecklenburg Declaration vibes.)

As is so often the case, politics swiftly got in the way of making the transition of Alaska from Russia to America as smooth as it could have been. President Johnson's public approval rating wasn't high at the time, so some members of the US House of Representatives tried preventing the appropriations necessary for the "purchase" part of the Alaska purchase from going through. These congresspeople largely viewed the acquisition as a gross overreach of the Johnson Administration, going so far as to question whether it was even legal for Seward and the Senate to have agreed to the treaty without first consulting the purse strings-holding House. The House voted on the impeachment of President Johnson in February 1868, but the measure didn't pass.

Even so, the House of Representatives succeeded in delaying appropriations for the Alaska purchase for more than a year. But everything worked out in the end because, allegedly, de Stoeckl engaged in a vast campaign of bribes targeting congressmen, lobbyists, and journalists; this might (again, allegedly) have happened under Seward's watch. Later, de Stoeckl himself apparently admitted to paying a total of $200,000 to various parties, but investigations into these payments failed to conclusively determine who received the money, how much each person received, who was aware of the payments, and other key details. Wherever the truth lay, the House of Representatives finally agreed to appropriate the necessary funds in July 1868.

In retrospect, it appears that once the United States took control of the Alaska territory, it faced some growing pains (like those felt by Russia) as it determined how to actually manage the distant land. Numerous US government entities took turns administering the territory's oversight. It remained under the purview of the US Army until June 1877, at which point it was turned over to the Department of the Treasury and then other US military branches.

Under the auspices of the Treaty of Cession, most of Alaska's Russian citizens opted to leave and return to their homeland. But when Seward first visited Alaska after his retirement in 1869, he took note of the territory's melting pot aesthetic, with inhabitants donning the garb of Russia, local native tribes, the US military, and traders from San Francisco. In May 1884, the territory's first government was appointed, and on January 3, 1959, Alaska became the forty-ninth US state under the purview of President Dwight D. Eisenhower.

Significantly, when President Eisenhower signed the Alaska Statehood Act, he approved a landmark clause that forbade the state's citizens from claiming the lands of Alaska Natives. This language is what led President Richard Nixon to give forty-four million acres of federal land, as well as $1 billion, to Indigenous populations in Alaska in 1971.

And while the preceding paragraphs describe the real story of the Alaska purchase and its aftereffects, history books tend to remember the landmark event quite differently. Just as a few "loud" accounts on social media can chart the course for a given narrative in the present day, a few "loud" news outlets lambasted the Alaska purchase when it took place. These news outlets mostly criticized the large sum of money spent on the land and used various derogatory monikers to describe the acquisition, such as Seward's icebox, Walrussia, and President Johnson's polar bear garden. Contrary to popular belief, "Seward's folly" wasn't popularized in the immediate aftermath of the deal; it didn't appear in the vernacular until 1877, a decade later.

In any case, the leader of the pack of loud news outlets was the editor of the *New York Tribune*, Horace Greeley, who made headlines when he claimed Alaska was a "burden . . . not worth taking as a gift." He and his supporters believed Alaska was just a mass of snow, ice, and glaciers that had no economic or settlement value. But the newspaper contingent wasn't the only group skeptical of the acquisition. Maine Senator William Pitt Fessenden famously joked that for him to vote in favor of the Treaty of Cession, it would need to include a clause mandating that Secretary Seward live in Alaska. Other detractors had somewhat reasonable hesitancies, like the concern that any natural resources worth pursuing would have already been depleted by the Russians (just as they had done to the otters).

Critics also pointed out that the treaty with Russia was negotiated under a shroud of secrecy, something that didn't jive with a spirit of government transparency. However, this concern mostly disappeared once the Senate was briefed on the territory's value. Today, it isn't totally clear why Seward committed the bureaucratic faux pas of pursuing the acquisition so clandestinely, though concern that government and public skepticism might have prevented its success *could* have been a logical reason. Purportedly, de Stoeckl had offered to socialize the idea of the sale with his friends in Congress before negotiations advanced too far, but Seward asked him to remain mum until he could ensure the presidential cabinet was on board with the acquisition.

> **Riley's Favorite Fact (Probably):** Alaska purchase skeptic Senator William Pitt Fessenden sarcastically scoffed that Secretary Seward should have to live in Alaska—something Fessenden perceived as wholly unpleasant—if the sale went through.

While the critiques of the Alaska purchase were varied, it bears repeating that detractors represented the minority of onlookers. In other words, the belief that all of America agreed Seward's efforts constituted a "folly" is completely erroneous. In fact, a review of forty-eight major news outlets that covered the purchase in 1867 and 1868 found that only three (the *New York Tribune*, the *Sun*, and the *Independent*) wrote in opposition. At the time, most everyday Americans did not feel strongly one way or the other about the purchase of Alaska, while those who believed the United States should expand northward (potentially even taking control of Canada one day) actively supported the acquisition as a step in the right direction—literally and figuratively.

Seward collected quite a bit of memorabilia from the Alaska purchase era, and amongst his personal effects were many newspaper articles that could only be described as glowing reviews. Some of these articles highlighted how the treaty exemplified good relations between the United States and Russia, a bilateral relationship that had been strengthened years earlier when the United States supported Russia during the Crimean War, and when Russia followed suit by siding with the Union during the Civil War. As the secretary of state in charge of US diplomatic relations, this was potentially a point of pride for Seward.

It was therefore unsurprising that most other world powers at the time of the Alaska purchase reacted with a fair amount of alarm.

Many European countries expressed concern that the Treaty of Cession represented a big step toward strengthened bonds between the United States and Russia. European newspapers went on to share unsubstantiated claims that the treaty included an agreement that the United States would support Russia in its quest to expand throughout Europe and Asia. Onlookers from other countries also saw the acquisition as proof that the United States was recovering—both economically and politically—from its recent Civil War without issue.

LISTEN TO RILEY

Perhaps it would be useful to set the record straight once and for all, especially since the majority of the minority thought the Alaska purchase couldn't possibly benefit the United States. Plus, after the transfer of land became official, the plot's proud new owners largely ignored Alaska for about thirty years. So why did the United States want to acquire Alaska? Why did Seward aim to annex the territory since early in his political tenure?

It turns out the Alaska purchase was not only *not* a folly, but the reason for wanting the territory to begin with wasn't very mysterious. First and foremost, by the 1840s, the United States was deep in the throes of expansion, having recently acquired Oregon, Texas, and California. The country's westward creep was outwardly justified by the government's use of the term "manifest destiny," a belief popularized in the nineteenth century and claiming that the United States had a right to expand from the Atlantic Coast to the Pacific Coast. Not only was the expansion of the young yet powerful country justified, but it was inevitable (according to purveyors of the manifest destiny mantra).

In fact, the country's interest in taking control of Alaska predated Seward's time as secretary of state, tracing back to the presidency of James Buchanan. So real was this early interest that an offer of $5 million for the land had been tossed around at the highest levels of government. At the time, however, one of the acquisition's most vocal advocates, Senator William Gwin of California, cautioned against making the move during President Buchanan's term. After all, Buchanan wasn't exactly a fan-favorite president, and the politics of his unpopularity might have made the Alaska proposition dead on arrival with Congress. Surely, according to Senator Gwin, the United States shouldn't pull the trigger until a new president was elected.

Russia's hopes of offloading Alaska to the United States were therefore delayed, though Russia eventually reinitiated talks in 1859. But once the Civil War got underway, the proposed purchase was obviously the last thing on the Union's mind, and negotiations once again stalled until the war concluded. Enter Secretary of State Seward, who (as previously discussed) had already made his intentions for Alaska abundantly clear.

Seward was interested in Alaska not only because of its abundant natural resources, but also because the land's geographic location made it a perfect outpost for trade with China and Japan. Like Russia, Seward favored the idea of the land *not* falling into the hands of the British, since he didn't want Great Britain to be able to capitalize on these perceived economic benefits.

While most of the country either didn't really care about or actively supported the Alaska purchase at the time of its occurrence, for the sake of the doubters, Seward was vindicated by the late 1800s when large deposits of gold began popping up in and near Alaska. In 1880, gold found at the Silver Bowl Basin led to the establishment of the Juneau-Douglas mines and, later, the entire city of Juneau. Within ten years, Juneau would boast a population of more than twelve hundred residents who were serviced by a full suite of infrastructure and community services, including schools, stores, hospitals, and bars.

But the discoveries didn't stop there. In 1896, another site rife with gold was identified nearby in Canada's Yukon territory, launching what would become known as the Klondike Gold Rush. Swarms of people migrated into the region, establishing new urban centers such as Dawson City. Soon after, in 1902, yet *another* gold deposit in Alaska's Tanana Valley led to the development of Fairbanks. These discoveries of gold, taken on their own, would have been enough to make the Alaska purchase seem like a good investment on the part of the United States, but this precious metal wasn't the only valuable resource literally hiding beneath the surface. By the 1900s, Alaska and its surrounding area became synonymous with lucrative oil reserves.

Seward's vision of Alaska as a strategic location also came to fruition, but not always for the reasons he predicted. For example, during World War II, the distance between Alaska and Japan seemed shorter than ever. Japan would end up bombing and invading the Aleutian Islands in 1942; events like these during wartime led the United States to invest more heavily in Alaska's infrastructure. Soon, the government developed the state's Alcan Highway and established additional military installations on-site.

> **Riley's Next Hunt:** What if natural resources weren't the only lucrative reason Seward sought to purchase Alaska? Riley and team could uncover a more literal treasure—one that might even explain why the acquisition was pursued with such secrecy.

All in all, the US government's ownership of Alaska would ultimately help the country establish itself as a significant economic and military player within the Asia-Pacific region. Even today, Alaska's status as a US state will play a role in ensuring that the United States has access to any new Arctic sea-lanes that may open as glaciers melt, a strategic outcome from both commercial and security perspectives.

While history has largely maligned Seward for his Alaska purchase, this *is* the event for which the former secretary of state is most remembered. The state of Alaska seems to think fondly of Seward, as one each of Alaska's cities, highways, and peninsulas bears the secretary's name. Two state holidays relating to the Alaska purchase are still observed; this includes Seward's Day (the last Monday in March), which commemorates the initial signing of the Treaty of Cession.

By all accounts, Alaska was a beneficial addition to the United States. The northernmost state in the union boasts about 220 million acres of federal parks and wildlife refuges. A great example is Tongass National Forest, which—since its dedication by President Theodore Roosevelt in 1907—holds the distinction of being the country's largest federally protected woods. About 25 percent of America's oil and more than 50 percent of America's seafood can be traced back to Alaska today. The state's rich natural resources extend beyond gold, petroleum, timber, and fish to include fur, copper, platinum, zinc, and lead, and they help to make Alaska one of the wealthiest US states.

In total, Alaska's natural resources have amounted to hundreds of billions of dollars in value. Compared to the $7.2 million spent on the state's acquisition in 1867, or even the $120 million equivalent in today's economy, it's safe to say the United States got more than its money's worth when it purchased Alaska from Russia. It's truly a shame that such a beneficial outcome still retains the derogatory moniker "Seward's folly" in the minds of much of the US population, especially when the term Seward's *bargain* would be much more appropriate.

And all of this leads me back to our conversation that helped us set the stage for this chapter. If one of the best financial decisions with the most lucrative return-on-investment in recorded history can be remembered so unfairly, what hope do the rest of us have?

Chapter 13

The President's Secret Book

Sometimes I wonder whether Riley would secretly like to serve as president of the United States, especially since the role promises fame and dangles the possibility of glory. But at the same time, could you *imagine* sidekick-energy Riley Poole making decisions that would mean the difference between war and peace? It's a sacrifice he might just be willing to make in exchange for the opportunity to function as a human repository for all our nation's secrets.

Disclaimer: I don't believe for a second that Riley would want to bear a country's deepest secrets to use them in some nefarious way. (He is, after all, a loyal teammate to one of the most noble characters in action-adventure cinema history.) As a matter of fact, he'd probably rather exude cognitive dissonance than acknowledge how real-world villains might threaten him to obtain the secretive information that intrigues him so.

That said, we know without a shadow of a doubt that Riley thinks conspiracy theories are pretty darn cool. There's even a part of him, tucked behind the logical left hemisphere of his brain, that believes some conspiracy theories are true. Maybe he just *wants* them to be true, because that would make life so much more interesting.

If anyone knows whether the biggest mysteries on Earth are true, I've got to believe that person is the president of the United States. If only there was some way for the president to record all this knowledge for posterity—only to be revealed if and when doing so wouldn't threaten national security. You could bet Riley would be first in line to buy such a book, and that's why he practically wills it into existence in his own text, *Templar Treasure.*

In true *National Treasure* fashion, I'd be lying if I said Riley Poole was the first person—fictional or otherwise—to suggest that an "unofficially official" presidential record of events must exist. Like Riley, millions of people are intrigued by conspiracy theories, and millions of people think the rich and powerful know more about these theories than they're letting on. The result of this collective belief is itself a conspiracy theory: the existence of a president's book of secrets. It's a legend that has captured the public's imagination so effectively that President Barack Obama once joked about it during an interview with a radio talk show. In other words, it's a theory with staying power.

> **Why Riley Would Care:** As the subject of one of the only known chapters of *Templar Treasure*, the urban-legend President's secret book—and the alleged government cover-ups contained within—is Riley's not-so-secret passion.

HUNT DOWN THAT HISTORY

The legend that the president of the United States gains access to a mythical book of national secrets calls into question the broader history of secrecy within the US government. By all accounts, secrecy has played a role in governance since the beginning of time—and certainly since the beginning of the United States, given that the Constitutional Convention was a closed-door convening. It was public knowledge that the Constitutional Convention had been called to order with a goal of adjusting the Articles of Confederation, but behind those closed doors, the Founding Fathers ended up drafting an entirely new system of government. Today, historians generally agree that if the Constitutional Convention had been open to onlookers, it would have been far more difficult—and perhaps impossible—to reach consensus on a governing document.

From that point forward, secrecy has had its role to play, for better or worse, within the governments of the United States and basically all other countries. To some extent, this secrecy was formalized in the American context when President Harry S. Truman rounded up a handful of government employees to establish the Central Intelligence Group, which later became the Central Intelligence Agency (CIA), an organization tasked with gathering intelligence. "Intelligence" is governance speak for "secrets."

For these reasons, it's probably not surprising that a salient urban legend has perpetually existed in the ether of Washington, D.C. Namely, the conspiratorially minded would swear that the nation's greatest secrets, and the true answers to the country's prevailing conspiracy theories, are stashed in a single book that is passed from one president to the next. Those who believe in the book's existence even have ideas about where it is hidden, ranging from the stacks at the Library of Congress to inside a bust of President Abraham Lincoln at the White House.

But where did the legend of this president's secret book originate? Like so many mysteries, the beginnings of this conspiracy theory are themselves contested. Some believe its origins date back to 1778 with the establishment of the Culper Spy Ring, an intelligence unit formed by George Washington in his capacity as commander of the Continental Army. The spy organization was based in New York City and, for five years, collected information about British movements, defenses, and unit strength during the American Revolution. Under the auspices of Major Benjamin Tallmadge, Washington's appointee as director of military intelligence, the Culper Spy Ring infiltrated British headquarters and relayed learnings to Washington via a sophisticated courier system.

One of the unit's most notorious successes came in 1781 when it acquired a copy of Great Britain's naval codes, an event that helped the French score a decisive sea victory that led to Washington's triumph at Yorktown to end the war. Just as you'd expect based on any good thriller, the Culper Spy Ring's members used code names, wrote ciphers with invisible ink, and were unknown even to Washington himself. Not a single member was revealed during their service, and the public didn't become aware of the unit's activities until more than a century later, in 1929.

Riley's Favorite Fact (Probably): George Washington's Culper Spy Ring was instrumental in collecting British military secrets that would ultimately propel the Continental Army to a Revolutionary War victory. It also helped inspire an undying legend related to presidents' best-kept secrets.

Surely any information gleaned by the Culper Spy Ring would warrant inclusion in a president's secret book if such a book existed. But some theorists point to more recent presidential actions as a potential starting point for the urban legend in question. An example is the tradition of outgoing presidents leaving incoming presidents notes in the Oval Office. Typically, these presidential messages are handwritten words of encouragement deposited at the Resolute desk, and they have historically served as a symbol of unity and hope, especially when a transition of power from one political party to another is at hand.

But words of encouragement are hardly secrets, and many of these presidential messages have been shared with the public postinauguration. Perhaps this is why another modern origin for the president's book legend has been suggested: the President's Daily Brief, affectionately dubbed "the book" by those within the intelligence community.

According to public knowledge, the President's Daily Brief began in 1961 during the administration of President John F. Kennedy. The CIA is responsible for coordinating this daily collection of the most pressing issues and context the president needs to know, though other agencies that make up the intelligence community have contributed over the years. In brief (pun most definitely intended), we're talking about highly classified information, including threats to US national security, but contents are also tailored to the policy priorities of the president. Other common inclusions are more mundane but still pressing matters, such as upcoming decisions, meetings, or travel.

The President's Daily Brief has taken various physical forms over the years based on each president's reading preferences. For instance, President Kennedy chose to receive his "book" as notecards that could be stowed in his pocket and consulted throughout the day. President Jimmy Carter, on the other hand, requested large margins on the full-size pages of his brief so he could jot down notes. A digital version was provided to President Obama, leading to the implementation of a secure iPad and allowing for the incorporation of graphics and other multimedia alongside the requisite text.

Different presidents have been known to spend more or less time reviewing their brief. President Richard Nixon simply glanced over the material, while President George W. Bush tended to spend a great deal of time with it. The sitting president also determines who else might read the compiled content. While President Bush invited just six readers to partake (particularly before the events of September 11, 2001), Presidents Bill Clinton and Barack Obama had twenty-four and thirty people on their reading lists, respectively. President Carter's rationale for keeping his own list limited was a fear that the best intelligence was not included when many readers were involved.

If intelligence a president deems important is *not* included in "the book," they can request additional material. Examples of highly classified information a president may wish to access include details about suspected terrorists and their activities, entities the government is paying in exchange for information or surveillance, the status of the country's nuclear arsenal, and news about classified aircraft.

Given the vast number of secrets a president—or others within the government—may keep or utilize in the conduct of official policy, the Freedom of Information Act (FOIA) was passed in 1966 to ensure the concept of secrecy isn't abused within the government system. Under FOIA, journalists and members of the public can request access to government documents whose exposure wouldn't cause harm to the country. As a result, FOIA serves as somewhat of a checks-and-balances system so that those who are not in positions of power can confirm that processes taking place within government are aboveboard.

LISTEN TO RILEY

If you're wondering whether the president's secret book exists, I have some bad news for you: it does not. But it's still quite fun to use real stories from history to justify the public's persistent belief. Take, for instance, the events surrounding the British setting Washington, D.C., ablaze during the War of 1812. The day was August 24, 1814, and the White House was one of the capital's critical structures threatened by the flames. Before evacuating, First Lady Dolley Madison famously ensured the White House's Gilbert Stuart-crafted painting of George Washington, known as the Lansdowne portrait, was saved, alongside official papers of the presidential cabinet, a copy of the Declaration of Independence, and her silver.

The recovery of the portrait, in particular, is most remembered by history, perhaps because of the importance of this piece of art; when it was painted in 1797, it was the first effort to depict Washington as a president as opposed to a military figure. Since the portrait was securely mounted to the wall, the First Lady asked the White House staff and enslaved people to break the canvas out of its frame if necessary. In her mind, the thought (and symbolism) of the British getting their hands on or burning the Lansdowne portrait was an absolute nonstarter.

Dolley Madison and White House workers weren't the only ones to prioritize saving government materials. Clerks at the Department of State acted quickly to rescue as many records from the citywide fire as they could. What they managed to smuggle out included official department papers, unpublished congressional journals, George Washington's letters, the Articles of Confederation, and other documents dating back as far as 1789. Congress also saved as many of its own files as possible. As evidenced by the fact that the original Declaration of Independence, Constitution, and Bill of Rights can be viewed at the National Archives today, protecting these documents from the fire was obviously another top priority.

But how do the events of the fire relate to the legend of the president's secret book? The answer is simple but takes a creative mind to identify. If First Lady Dolley Madison was adamant about removing a painting and other materials from the burning White House, what else might she have smuggled out of the building? What unknown records did the State Department and Congress save? Could the president's secret book have been among them?

And although all signs point to the answer being a resounding no, Riley spends the thirteenth chapter of *Templar Treasure* hypothesizing what information would be contained in the pages of a secret book if it *did* exist. It is quite the thought experiment to predict what truths would be so secretive and so classified that only a sitting president could know about them. In other words, what information could be so protected that it wouldn't be governed by legal classification and archiving rules? Wracking my brain (and the transcript of Riley's own words) yielded a few possibilities.

Riley's Next Hunt: *National Treasure* fans would riot if Riley's next adventure failed to reveal what's on page forty-seven of the president's secret book as popularized by the franchise—even if the book's real-life existence is a myth born out of facts.

One moment in time that could reasonably be preserved in a president's secret book is the infamous Roswell incident. In the summer of 1947, at the onset of the Cold War, the US military published a press release claiming that a flying saucer had been recovered at a ranch in Roswell, New Mexico. The remnants of the supposed craft, which consisted of tinfoil, rubber, and sticks, had been found by W. W. "Mac" Brazel on his property, and he immediately notified authorities due to recent reports of flying saucers in the region.

But just as quickly as the military declared the acquisition of its supposed saucer, it made a second announcement stating the wreckage was actually that of a weather balloon. This sudden backtracking led many Americans to believe something fishy was afoot. In the years that followed, numerous hoaxes surrounding this "Roswell incident" cropped up, including a widely circulated video that claimed to portray an alien autopsy.

The public wouldn't get their answers about Roswell until the 1990s. First, in 1994, the US Air Force published a report conceding that the debris collected in New Mexico was not that of a weather balloon, but was instead a collection of high-altitude balloons the US government had been using to spy on Soviet Russia under a top-secret mission called Project MOGUL. A 1997 publication put to bed conspiracy theorists' claims that alien bodies had been removed from the Roswell site: the bodies people *thought* they saw were test dummies manning the high-altitude balloons.

Still, some observers have remained dissatisfied with the conclusion of the Roswell case. These skeptics don't understand why the US government publicly recognized the crash site, let alone drew public attention to it with a flying saucer-centric press release, given all the secret military installations in Roswell's vicinity. In other words, the initial report must have been real for such drastic action to have been taken when the incident first occurred. Other theorists have claimed the crash was the work of the Soviet Union's Joseph Stalin intending to induce mass panic in America.

If Roswell is in contention for inclusion in a hypothetical president's secret book, then Area 51 would definitely warrant a chapter. Area 51 is well-known as a US Air Force base at Groom Lake, Nevada, purportedly used as an aircraft flight-test facility. Over time, the public has concluded that the site is also used (or *actually* used) for research on alien life, owing to the fact that an unusually high number of unidentified aerial phenomena (UAP) have been reported in the base's neighborhood.

Suspicion came to a head in the late 1980s when an alleged former employee of the base publicly proclaimed the government was using the site to investigate alien aircraft.

To this day, many UAP sightings around Area 51 have been chalked up to the secret testing of U-2 spy planes in 1955 and, later, other technologically advanced military aircraft such as the A-12 reconnaissance plane and F-117 stealth fighter Nighthawk. U-2 planes could fly much higher than the common aircraft of the time, so it would make sense for uninformed citizens viewing the high-flying vessels to suspect something at least odd, if not sinister. It wasn't until 2013, thanks to a FOIA request about the military's U-2 plane program, that the US government formally acknowledged the existence of Area 51.

But not all conspiracy theories worthy of a president's book entry are related to aliens. In fact, fans and followers of pop culture might hope for a chapter dedicated to the odd circumstances surrounding the autopsy report of Hollywood star Marilyn Monroe. The famous actress's body was discovered unclothed on her bed at home in Brentwood, California, on August 4, 1962. Next to the body sat an empty bottle of sleeping medicine.

An autopsy revealed a cause of death consistent with what the scene suggested: an overdose of Nembutal, a barbiturate prescribed for insomniacs and taken by mouth. The official determination, supported by a postmortem psychiatric evaluation, was that Monroe had died, perhaps accidentally, by suicide.

It didn't take long for onlookers to raise concerns about this official cause of death, particularly because the autopsy failed to detect drugs in the stomach or small intestine of the deceased. In fact, Monroe's stomach contents and other organ samples mysteriously vanished while the investigation into her death remained active. For this reason, naysayers believe the actress was murdered by lethal injection (disclaimer: no injection marks were found on her body) or by enema, since a toxicological study found barbiturates in her blood and liver.

Why would someone have wanted Marilyn Monroe dead? The hypothesized answer traces back to the actress's "red diary," a journal that has been missing since Monroe's body was found. Conspiracy theorists believe Monroe recorded incriminating information about powerful people in her red diary, including details about her long-suspected affairs with President Kennedy and his brother, Senator Robert Kennedy. Also allegedly contained in the diary was information about the CIA's plans to assassinate Fidel Castro of Cuba, as well as mafia members in San Diego.

From here, it's quite easy to predict where conspiracy theorists are headed with their version of events. In short, they believe Monroe was murdered to conceal the swaths of damaging information she had collected and recorded over the years. They have even speculated about Monroe's possible intention to go public with the Kennedy affairs. In this iteration of the story, the identity of the murderer (as well as who planned the murder) remains up for debate, though various names and organizations have been floated.

Perhaps most interestingly, the homicide investigator from the Los Angeles Police Department who was first on the scene of Monroe's death expressed his belief postretirement that the actress was murdered. He went as far as to say the murder was purposefully covered up, a claim supported by the deputy coroner who admitted to having signed the death certificate "under duress." Monroe's ex-husband Joe DiMaggio reported that Monroe had shared with him her suspicions of being targeted for murder. DiMaggio admitted freely his supposition that his ex-wife had been deliberately killed.

But the reliability of the LAPD retirees has been called into question, especially since one of them was accused of having fabricated his newer testimony to profit off the story. In 1982, a reexamination of the available evidence in the case came to the same conclusion as the original, 1962 investigation: death by suicide.

Even if Monroe wasn't murdered, a second question lingers: could she truly have known as much damning information and as many national secrets as conspiracy theorists suggest? Potentially lending validity to this question is the fact that the Federal Bureau of Investigation (FBI) maintained a robust file on the actress.

In the 1980s, a FOIA request prompted the FBI to publish the file, but the paperwork within was heavily redacted. When, in the early 2010s, journalists issued a second FOIA request to secure versions with fewer redactions, the original documents temporarily went missing. The FBI claimed the files had been sent to the National Archives and Records Administration, while the National Archives and Records Administration claimed to have never received them.

Fortunately (and oddly), the files were only "missing" for a short period of time, and they were subsequently published. They reveal that the FBI began monitoring Monroe in 1955 because of her association with several individuals linked to the Communist Party. The agency's surveillance involved tracking the actress's movements, which is why the FBI knew she was among a group of entertainment industry professionals seeking visas to visit Russia. The FOIA request also exposed that the FBI had been tracking conspiracy theories regarding Monroe's murder, though the agency never opened its own investigation into her death.

While Monroe's death was *suspected* by many to be a murder, a *definite* murder has been the subject of innumerable conspiracies and would therefore have a logical home in a president's book of secrets. I am referring, of course, to the assassination of President John F. Kennedy on November 22, 1963. It's a tale as old as time, but for those who are less familiar, President Kennedy and his wife were riding in a convertible through the streets of Dallas, Texas, as part as an official visit. Lee Harvey Oswald, stationed on the sixth floor of the nearby Texas School Book Depository, fired the shot that killed the thirty-fifth president of the United States.

Frustratingly, no one knows Oswald's motivation, as he was himself murdered just two days later by local nightclub owner Jack Ruby. But the Warren Commission, established by executive order to investigate the assassination, confirmed in 1964 that Oswald had acted alone; he was not part of any larger plot of domestic terrorism, nor was he commissioned by a foreign adversary.

The incident was shocking enough that the public began suggesting its own theories to explain Oswald's actions, such as asserting that President Kennedy's successor to the Oval Office, Lyndon B. Johnson, was the mastermind behind the attack. Another popular theory was that the Cuban government had schemed up the assassination; this supposition gained traction once it was revealed that President Kennedy's administration had considered or attempted attacks on Fidel Castro. From the opposite perspective, some conspiracy theorists believe Oswald's action reflected a belief that President Kennedy wasn't doing *enough* to subvert threats by Cuba.

Naturally, many conspiracies that have captured widespread attention in the intervening decades are those that insist Oswald was not a lone actor. Footage of the assassination focusing on the movement of President Kennedy's head upon bullet impact suggest the gunshot originated in front of the president, not behind him, where Oswald was located. Supporting this theory are at least a few eyewitness accounts from observers seated in a park in front of the car who claimed to have heard and smelled gunshots.

Another piece of evidence suggesting more than one shooter had been active was the presence of numerous bullet entry and exit wounds. Oswald would not have been able to fire off multiple shots in such quick succession, implying that he was not the only one shooting a weapon. These multiple puzzle pieces that just don't seem to fit together have influenced the perspectives of some individuals close to the investigation. Over time, three of the seven members of the Warren Commission *plus* President Johnson came to reject the investigation's conclusion.

In fact, when a reinvestigation into the assassination was completed in 1979, the House Select Committee on Assassinations agreed President Kennedy "was probably assassinated as a result of a conspiracy." Part of this determination was attributed to the revelation that both the FBI and CIA had not revealed critical information—including details about the United States's plots against Fidel Castro—to the Warren Commission during the initial investigation. This has led to one of the most popular conspiracy theories of all, in which the CIA was at worst responsible for, or at best tangentially involved in, the assassination.

Even decades after the official reinvestigation, rumors surrounding President Kennedy's tragic fate live on. Interest in official documents related to the event was reignited in 2017, when all the files were set to be declassified—but weren't. In 2025, President Donald Trump released a swath of case files that at the time of this writing were still being scrutinized to determine whether they contain information that is new to the public. At the very least, files that have been available for some time indicate that the CIA was monitoring Oswald for a substantial period prior to the assassination, and the agency knew of the man's associations with both pro- and anti-Castro organizations.

Yet another modern mystery that could feasibly find its way into a president's secret book is the truth behind the 18.5 missing minutes of the Watergate tapes, something that has indefinitely intrigued onlookers of American history. The story goes something like this: Five people broke into the Watergate headquarters of the Democratic National Committee on June 17, 1972, just five months before a presidential election. The perpetrators, including one person involved in President

Richard Nixon's reelection campaign, were arrested trying to place recording devices in the office.

In the days following the break-in, the White House's recording system logged discussions between President Nixon and his chief of staff, H. R. "Bob" Haldeman. This is where President Nixon's peculiarities may have led to his own demise, as he insisted that every conversation at the White House be recorded—a practice that was quite unconventional. While the president intended for his recording system to remain a secret (he wanted to use the audio files to correct official records, when needed), the tapes were ultimately subpoenaed as part of the investigation into the Watergate break-in.

President Nixon was reluctant to turn over the recordings, so an agreement was reached in which the president's secretary, Rose Mary Woods, would transcribe the audio. But partway through a recording dated June 20, 1972, a span of 18.5 minutes mysteriously disappeared, treating listeners to only buzzing and clicking sounds. This, of course, raised eyebrows, and when pressed, Woods claimed that she accidentally erased part of the recording while completing her transcription. Investigators became increasingly skeptical when they asked the secretary to recreate the accidental erasure event, which involved her reaching for a phone placed at a distance, and they witnessed her almost comical struggle to do so.

Naturally, the Watergate investigation turned much of its attention to the missing 18.5 minutes of tape. Expert testimony suggested the complete erasure consisted of at least five consecutive segments of audio. Some suspect President Nixon of erasing the recordings himself, either intentionally or accidentally.

Much time and effort has been spent attempting to predict what information the missing minutes contained. Nixon Administration officials have conjectured that the lost recordings included one or a few comments connecting President Nixon to the Watergate event. But other, not-erased tapes also prove this connection, such as a recording dated June 23 that reveals the president and his chief of staff devised a plan to convince the FBI to end its investigation. As a result, the lost minutes aren't thought to be particularly important, especially since President Nixon resigned on August 8, 1974, for fear of impeachment.

Today, it's largely believed that President Nixon had no advance knowledge about the events of Watergate, but that he was involved in covering up the incident as soon as it happened. His personal view was that if someone could be held accountable for the incident, his actions could not be considered a cover-up. Regardless, the missing 18.5 minutes of tape that brought down a sitting president remain a tantalizing mystery. In 2009, new technology was deployed to try recovering the missing recordings, but the effort was unsuccessful. We may never know what was erased and why.

A final, lesser-known conspiracy theory that could belong in a president's secret book is one surrounding the oft-theorized, never realized water-powered automobile. In 1975, inventor Stanley Meyer patented the concept for a fuel cell that uses an electrical current to hydrolyze, or split, water into hydrogen and oxygen gases. Meyer claimed he could use the fuel cell to generate hydrogen for powering a car's engine. He also insisted the fuel cell could reverse the reaction, combining hydrogen and oxygen back into water to perpetually run the car (which is completely impossible because of conservation of mass: he'd need to burn off the hydrogen for the car to operate).

The inventor swore his water-powered prototype car, a glorified dune buggy, could travel forty-five kilometers per liter of water. He embarked on a tour across the United States with the prototype in tow to galvanize interest and attract investment, but he was quickly met with controversy when he couldn't prove the car actually functioned. For as much public attention as he sought to draw, there were no videos or other evidence of the car running. Adding to the controversy were scientists who suggested Meyer was invoking electrolysis technology that already existed, and that more energy would be needed to split the water than the energy generated to power the car.

The situation came to a head when a scientist asked Meyer to perform a verification test to show that his technology was operational. Cognizant of the inventor's concerns about his advancement being stolen, the scientist agreed that Meyer didn't have to open the secret box containing the hydrolysis components as long as he could produce a running vehicle. Meyer patently refused to perform the test. As a result, in 1996, Meyer was sued for fraud and instructed to refund all his investors.

On the surface, there's nothing terribly mysterious about a con man masquerading as an inventor to gain a buck. But Meyer died under mysterious circumstances on March 21, 1998, during a business meeting in Ohio with potential investors. In the moments leading up to his death, Meyer began vomiting uncontrollably and claimed, with his dying words, that he had been poisoned. The official autopsy report contradicts his suspicion by stating the cause of death was a cerebral aneurysm.

In the preceding years, Meyer allegedly received several death threats and bribery attempts, the latter of which asked him to destroy his work, and he pointed to oil companies as the guilty parties. After all, oil companies' earning potential would have been threatened by a water-powered vehicle. Conspiracy theorists and Meyer supporters alike speculate that he was indeed murdered to prevent his technology from harming the automobile industry if it had ever seen the light of day.

Following Meyer's death, his prototype dune buggy was locked in a room away from the prying eyes of a curious public. Somehow, a Canadian family took possession of the vehicle in 2014, and this is where the story ends . . . for now. In any case, Meyer's patents have since reached the public domain, and no scientist or engineer has yet been able to replicate his work.

Conspiracy theorists and history enthusiasts have jointly clamored for the answers to the preceding mysteries for decades, but that's only because the mysteries made national or even international headlines at some point in time. Other secrets that could be found in a president's secret book might be considered "unknown unknowns." After all, there exists at least one robust portfolio of secrets the public knows little or nothing about: presidents' *personal* secrets.

Consider, for instance, the fact that President Kennedy was known to escape his security detail in disguise, disappearing for hours on end. It's largely agreed that his excursions facilitated extramarital affairs, but the Secret Service feared that one or more of the women could eventually blackmail or murder him. Similarly, President Clinton was said to have been carrying on affairs when he claimed to be going to the gym. Such secrets might not be important enough to national security to warrant inclusion in a president's secret book, but they do offer a serious reminder that presidents are people too—people whose mundane actions can have far more serious consequences than the same actions taken by ordinary folks.

Another category of personal presidential secrets is related to health. President Franklin Delano Roosevelt was suffering from heart failure during his time in office, though the official diagnosis shared with the public was "a touch of bronchitis." He died a year later. President Woodrow Wilson experienced a serious stroke, which was said to have impacted his rationality in decision-making, yet the health event was kept secret. Some people believe President Ronald Reagan developed Alzheimer's disease during his tenure, while President Kennedy was taking strong medications for Addison's disease with serious mental and physical side effects. Given that to some extent the health of a president is the health of a nation, many have called for increased transparency regarding presidential medical diagnoses, especially since several recent presidents have assumed office at an advanced age.

Ultimately, the fact that a president's secret book doesn't exist means speculating about what could be included in it is a fool's errand. But mainstream interest in this longstanding conspiracy theory can be taken as evidence that the public seeks transparency in governance—both in the United States and around the world. And because there exists no shortage of topics that could be explored in such a book, curious members of the public will continue sleuthing for decades to come.

Chapter 14

The Mary Celeste

Have you ever stopped to consider just how many mysterious incidents in history are tied in some way to ships? Even *National Treasure*'s fictional storyline is based on a nonfictional ship, the *Charlotte*. Not only did one of the most infamous real-life tragedies take place on a boat (I'm talking about the *Titanic*, of course), but innumerable smaller mysteries that haven't had the luxury of being commemorated by Hollywood have *also* centered on seafaring vessels. These stories tend to follow either the "ship lost at sea" or the "abandoned ship" motif, and even though such stories feature little to no plot diversity, each is somehow just as enthralling as the last.

In retrospect, it's not terribly surprising that ships provide the exposition for so many legends that have burrowed their way into the mainstream. After all, ships spend long stretches of time sailing across vast oceans, and before modern communication technologies were available, these ships—and the people who piloted them—were truly on their own before reaching their destinations. Who's to say what mysterious occurrences took place aboard these ships that were beyond communication range for weeks or months at a time?

Sickness—of the "sea" variety or otherwise—could make long voyages even more dramatic, imperiling entire crews or causing individuals to hallucinate fanciful things that have been memorialized in journals and captains' logs. Severe storms over the ocean, which can be truly perilous, only added to the drama, turning a simple excursion into an arduous fight for survival. Between the seemingly contradictory danger and monotony of a life at sea, it's no wonder that sailors have reported spotting all sorts of mythical creatures, ranging from mermaids to megalodons. And when no one else is present to validate a purported sighting, it becomes the eyewitness's word against the word of science. In other words, it's the birth of a pop culture legend.

You may disagree with me here, but I'd suggest that mysterious sea creatures and other perils of the high seas are not what would interest Riley most about this genre. I suspect his fascination would be piqued by an entirely different ocean-based mystery—the discovery of "ghost ships." For those who are new to the lore, a ghost ship is a vessel found abandoned at sea, devoid of crew for no apparent or logical reason. The Riley-based appeal stems from the absolute reality yet inexplicability of ghost ships, as instances have occurred in maritime history more often than you might imagine. And there's no better way to orient an audience to ghost ships than with the tale of the most intriguing one of all: the *Mary Celeste*.

You see, the *Mary Celeste* is your classic ghost ship mystery that has puzzled historians and enthusiasts for decades. To add to the intrigue, the chance to truly and irrefutably solve the mystery has passed . . . It quite literally can no longer be solved with any degree of provable certainty. For some, this is a shame, but for others, it's cause for salivation. This was a ship whose occupants literally disappeared without a trace. It's the maritime version of the lost colony of Roanoke—without the luxury of "CRO" carved into the timbers. And we will never really know what happened to its crew.

> **Why Riley Would Care:** Hypotheses about the fate of the *Mary Celeste*'s crew can no longer be proven, but Riley could certainly apply his favorite science and tech tools to inch closer to a satisfying solution.

HUNT DOWN THAT HISTORY

In the mid-1800s, Nova Scotia was a world leader in ship construction, so it makes sense that our story about a famous—or perhaps infamous—ship begins on Nova Scotia's own Spencer's Island. In 1861, the *Mary Celeste* was crafted as a 282-ton, double-masted brigantine measuring just over one hundred feet long and twenty-five feet wide. The ship's original name was *Amazon*, but it would be renamed after changing hands in 1868 following what can only be described as a series of unfortunate events.

In retrospect, those who believed the *Mary Celeste* was cursed—and plenty of people did—were pretty justified in their Riley-approved superstition. For starters, the ship's initial captain, Robert McLellan of Nova Scotia, fell suddenly ill as cargo was being loaded onto the vessel for its first commercial voyage. Said voyage, intended to transport timber from the United States to London, truly wasn't meant to be, as Captain McLellan soon succumbed to his illness.

A new captain, John Nutting Parker, eventually succeeded at piloting the craft to the United Kingdom, but the trip was not without its share of drama. Upon departing its home port, the ship sailed into just enough fishing gear floating off the coast of Maine to create some unnecessary navigational challenges. Then, after unloading its cargo in London and beginning its return voyage across the Atlantic Ocean, the ship was involved in a collision in the English Channel.

Despite Parker's eventful early reign as captain, his remaining time with the soon-to-be-named *Mary Celeste* was filled with far fewer hysterics. After several years of facilitating cargo shipping in the West Indies, Parker concluded his tenure and made way for a new captain, William Thompson, who promptly ran the ship aground in Cow Bay of Cape Breton Island during a storm in October 1867. Thompson abandoned ship.

In the months that followed, the grounded vessel changed hands numerous times, first coming into the possession of Alexander McBean of Nova Scotia, and then becoming the property of an American businessman named Richard W. Haines. When Haines managed to transport his ship to New York in 1868, the condition was so poor that it was deemed wrecked (or as Riley, a car connoisseur, would probably think of it, *totaled*). But Haines refused to admit defeat, taking on the costly repairs and upgrades (which, from a car connoisseur's perspective, would seem like a wild choice). It was at this point, under the ownership of Haines, that the ship became formally known as the *Mary Celeste*.

> **Riley's Favorite Fact (Probably):** The disappearance of the *Mary Celeste*'s crew wasn't the only strange occurrence to befall the ship. Before its fated journey, the vessel was plagued by mysterious crew deaths and a series of unlucky collisions.

At long last, on October 20, 1872, the *Mary Celeste*'s repairs were not only complete, but she was ready to begin taking on cargo for the first journey of her new era. On November 3, the ship's latest captain, Benjamin Spooner Briggs, penned a letter to his Massachusetts-based mother commenting on the beautiful quality of the renovated vessel and sharing his hopes and expectations for a safe intercontinental voyage. If you've ever sought evidence in support of the concept of jinxing things, Captain Briggs might just be your guy.

The captain and his ship departed New York Harbor on November 7, 1872, carrying just over seventeen hundred barrels of alcohol—the kind used in fuel and for other industrial purposes—destined for the port of Genoa, Italy. Captain Briggs was joined on board by his wife, Sarah, their two-year-old daughter, Sophia, and a handful of crewmen. In total, ten souls sailed aboard the fated ship. Not accompanying the family was the Briggs' seven-year-old son, who was left behind in America to continue his schooling. Descendants of this son would later become the sought-after subjects of interviews attempting to unravel the voyage's mysterious outcome.

If anything could have saved the *Mary Celeste* from future infamy, it would have been her new captain. Born in 1835 in Massachusetts, Benjamin Spooner Briggs was the son of a seafaring family but not always destined for a life on the ocean. In fact, he had considered going into business with his brother Oliver—they intended to open a hardware store—until pivoting to invest his life savings in two-fifths ownership of the *Mary Celeste*. Soon after taking partial ownership, Captain Briggs signed up to pilot the voyage from New York to Genoa. I'm no expert, but a trip from a bustling early American metropolis to a beautiful Italian destination sounds like a lovely way to break in your new ship.

But even from the start of the voyage, this peaceful vision was certainly not reality. The *Mary Celeste* battled severe weather for the duration of its known journey. Because maritime life is lonely and, during the era in question, was largely devoid of communication with ports, the next moment of clarity in the ship's story is when it was found abandoned at sea on December 5. The perplexing discovery was made by the crew of the *Dei Gratia*, a British brigantine of Canadian origin captained by David Morehouse.

If we were to anthropomorphize the ships in our story, it would be fair to say that the *Dei Gratia* was plenty familiar with the *Mary*

Celeste. After all, when the *Mary Celeste* left New York Harbor, the *Dei Gratia* was docked at a nearby port, where workers loaded her bowels with petroleum cargo. Both ships shared Genoa as their final intended destination, though their departures from New York were staggered by a few days (the *Dei Gratia* departed later, on November 14). As such, the *Dei Gratia* was just a few days behind the *Mary Celeste*, so the crew of the former ship expected to see that of the latter only after both had finally docked in Italy.

You might therefore imagine the surprise of the *Dei Gratia* captain and crew when they spotted the *Mary Celeste* drifting a few hundred nautical miles east of the Azores, a Portuguese archipelago in the Atlantic Ocean. Adding to the perceived strangeness was the appearance of the ship bobbing around uncontrollably on the water, not to mention the fact that it was scheduled to have arrived in Genoa days earlier.

A seasoned captain, Morehouse knew something was off even from a distance. He suspected the crew of the *Mary Celeste* needed assistance, so he sent a boarding party onto the ship to investigate. What awaited the sailors was truly shocking—but in an eerie sense, not a gruesome one. Not a single passenger—dead or alive—was found aboard the *Mary Celeste*.

The ship's bowels were filled with approximately three feet of seawater, yet rations of food and drinking water—enough to last six months—were found intact. The cargo of industrial alcohol remained in place. The possessions of the Briggs family and the ship's crew, including poor-weather outdoor gear, were still sitting in the individuals' respective rooms. The ship and everything it housed, ranging from a sewing machine to a small organ, were simply abandoned. Left. Ditched.

Externally, the ship wasn't in terribly bad shape. Sure, its rigging and sails were somewhat damaged, and a few were even missing, but what else would you expect from a ship being tossed around in the middle of the ocean for some indeterminate amount of time? This is also the explanation assigned to the galley being somewhat messy, with utensils and other objects dislodged and damp. A makeshift tool to measure the amount of water in the ship's hull was found lying outside on the deck. Aside from a single dismantled pump, the ship didn't appear damaged to the naked eye.

All that was missing from the *Mary Celeste* was a set of captain's tools—a sextant, chronometer, and navigation book—as well as the ship's register and a lifeboat. Oh, and her passengers.

Upon making their curious discovery and recording their observations of the ship's abandoned state, the *Dei Gratia*'s crew sailed their prize eight hundred miles to the port of Gibraltar, arriving on December 12. The fact that the *Mary Celeste* could make such a journey further proved it was in fine shape, which was probably the first reason authorities regarded the ship's discovery with suspicion. A formal three-month investigation was launched by the British vice admiralty court on December 17 to determine whether the crew of the *Dei Gratia* should receive the insurance payment associated with the *Mary Celeste*'s recovery.

Authorities—and the insurance company—were not about to unquestioningly reward the *Dei Gratia* team under such baffling circumstances. For all they knew, Captain Briggs and Captain Morehouse could have conspired together to commit insurance fraud and split the resulting profits. This supposition was quickly abandoned (pun intended), as investigators realized Briggs would have needed to do away with his wife, daughter, and crew to make such a scheme work.

The investigation uncovered some visible anomalies on the ship that a cursory inspection had failed to identify. For instance, a captain's sword was found on board, and for a short time a stain on its blade was thought to be blood (chemical testing eventually proved otherwise). Similarly, robust gashes in the ship's railing were purported to be from an axe until investigators determined the markings not only predated the journey in question, but they weren't even manmade. Ultimately, authorities were forced to accept an unsatisfying conclusion: no foul play was involved in whatever happened to the ship's passengers.

When the investigation concluded in early 1873, the *Dei Gratia* crew was awarded a partial payment for the *Mary Celeste*; the amount received was just one-sixth of the $46,000 for which the ship and its contents had been insured. After all the drama, each sailor pocketed only a few hundred dollars. This outcome, which was obscure for the time, suggested the court wasn't fully convinced that the *Dei Gratia* team held no responsibility for whatever happened. In the eyes of the court, something fishy (pun intended again) was going on between the two ships.

LISTEN TO RILEY

The nature of the mystery surrounding the *Mary Celeste* is quite simple, really. What happened to her passengers and crew? To attempt an answer, we must examine the material objects left aboard the vessel to construct a timeline of events. But to be a detective in this case, you'll need to be comfortable with more than a few holes in your story.

To begin, let's consider the notes found within the ship's log, whose final entry was dated the morning of November 25 and claimed that the crew had just spotted the coast of Santa Maria, the easternmost island of the Azores. This land spotting had followed yet another night of awful storms, complete with wind gusts that clocked in at more than thirty-five knots. According to the logbook entry, the last known location of the *Mary Celeste* with her crew still onboard was between four hundred and five hundred miles away from where the abandoned ship would eventually be recovered just over a week later.

These details give us a hazy picture—but a picture nonetheless—of the ship's final occupied moments, though it is worth questioning why a crew departing its ship under no duress wouldn't pause to jot down one final note sharing what in God's name happened to them. Due to this oversight by the crew, we're left wondering why Captain Briggs, his family, and his crew abandoned the intact, well-stocked vessel.

On first glance, the missing navigational equipment suggests Captain Briggs had enough time to collect his tools before departing, making a hasty departure unlikely. Plus, testimony shared by the *Mary Celeste*'s majority owner, James H. Winchester, during the admiralty court investigation indicated that Briggs "would not desert his ship to save his life." Winchester also vowed that Briggs's deputy, Albert Richardson, was skilled enough in navigation that he could have captained the ship on his own if needed.

With so little evidence, the mystery of the *Mary Celeste* can be broached only with theories, plenty of which have been floated over the years. Some have accused natural phenomena such as waterspouts and underwater earthquakes of having something to do with the crew's disappearance, while supernatural explanations range from an attack by a sea creature (most commonly cited as a giant squid) to encounters with another ghost ship to abduction by extraterrestrials. But the theories that have gained the most traction—or have seemed most feasible—are those with a social angle.

For instance, the prevailing belief during the admiralty court's investigation was that the passengers of the *Mary Celeste* were the victims of an attack by the *Dei Gratia*'s crew. Numerous pieces of hearsay evidence were presented to refute this theory, with the strongest being the fact that Captains Briggs and Morehouse were known friends. In fact, the two men had shared a meal together in the days preceding Briggs's departure for Genoa. Plus, no tangible proof of violence could be identified onboard the ship (especially once the supposed axe markings were debunked).

Another social explanation that has gained some traction is mutiny, whereby one or more members of the crew attempted a hostile takeover of the *Mary Celeste*. Those who believe this explanation point to the alcohol in the ship's cargo hold as having emboldened crew members—who could have been under the influence—to perform their alleged drastic action. At one point during the admiralty court process, the lead investigator suggested the *Mary Celeste*'s crew took things one step further by drunkenly *murdering* the entire Briggs family, then intentionally damaging parts of the ship and sails to thwart suspicion. According to this theory, the crew tossed their victims' bodies overboard before departing the ship on the small lifeboat.

With little evidence to tangibly *disprove* this theory, interviews were conducted with descendants of the *Mary Celeste*'s crew members to determine whether such an event would accord with the general psychology of any of the men. The results of these conversations indicated that mutiny was unlikely. It was also unlikely that Captain Briggs would have hired untrustworthy crewmen—or even crewmen who were unknown to him previously—particularly because his wife and daughter were accompanying him on his journey. Then there's the fact that if the crew *had* mutinied, it wouldn't have made sense for them to subsequently abandon the ship they had just acquired. And, once again, no evidence of violence or even a skirmish was discovered during the investigation.

Despite these irregularities, some investigators and observers grew suspicious of two crewmen in particular, German brothers Volkert and Boye Lorenzen. This skepticism stemmed from the men being the only two passengers whose belongings were not found aboard the ship. However, their names were cleared later by a descendant who revealed the brothers had previously lost most of their possessions in a shipwreck; in other words, their possessions were not found onboard because they simply didn't have any.

What if someone other than the ship's own crew was responsible for its demise? This is the premise underlying the theory that *pirates* encountered the *Mary Celeste* and murdered or captured every living soul on board. But this explanation is even more spotty than the mutiny one, since pirates *certainly* would have taken the ship itself as a prize—or at least its barrels of cargo and any personal possessions that may have had value. These inconsistencies did not prevent the *Boston Post* from publishing the pirate hypothesis in February 1873; the article's main piece of evidence was that pirates were active in the region of the ship's abandonment.

Other attempts at explaining the *Mary Celeste*'s mysterious fate are less social and more scientific in nature. One technical explanation points an accusatory finger at the ship's cargo, suggesting the hot climate of the Azores did not mix well with the seventeen hundred barrels of volatile alcohol below deck. This explanation purports that vapor from the alcohol expanded in volume, increasing the pressure in the cargo hold and creating enough force to blow open the main hatch. Such an event could have been seen as an explosion, or it could have caused the passengers to fear an explosion, leading them to evacuate. Those who favor this theory note that nine of the below-deck alcohol barrels were empty, and these nine barrels were made from red oak instead of white, the former of which is known to leak.

But this explanation certainly hasn't been considered completely satisfying, especially because the *Dei Gratia* crew did not report smelling fumes when they boarded the vessel. Plus, at least two hatches were found unlatched on the ship, but the latch securing the cargo hold was not one of them. All in all, the alcohol explosion theory has been largely dismissed, especially because the *Mary Celeste* showed no indication of having experienced even a small explosion or fire.

However, the explosion hypothesis has led some to question whether, even if an explosion did not happen aboard the *Mary Celeste*, the family and crew might have feared an explosion was imminent. Perhaps they had begun smelling alcohol fumes and suspected the worst was yet to come. But investigators are quick to point out that if this was the case, Captain Briggs likely would have ordered a *temporary* evacuation of the ship, sending all passengers into the lifeboat until the fumes dissipated. The line connecting the lifeboat to the main ship would have had to break or become detached for the theory to hold water (more puns). By this explanation, the lifeboat and her passengers would have floated away at sea, but like most theories, no actual evidence exists to support this version of events.

For over a century, maritime enthusiasts and conspiracy theorists have dedicated an enormous amount of time to devising a satisfactory solution, but it wasn't until the early 2000s that what is now considered the most likely story was elucidated. Documentarian Anne MacGregor spearheaded research that now suggests the final position recorded in the log of the *Mary Celeste* may have been completely wrong. In fact, MacGregor believes the *Mary Celeste* and her crew were actually 120 miles west of where they *thought* they were at the time of the logbook entry's writing.

MacGregor came to this significant conclusion by plotting the ship's changing position against the associated dates and times in its complete log and then comparing these points with environmental conditions at the time of the voyage. According to this analysis, the *Mary Celeste* should have been in a different position on the morning of November 25 (compared with where the book says it was). MacGregor chalks up the crew's navigational inaccuracy to a broken chronometer, a device used to measure a ship's location.

But even more details can be added to this account and, taken altogether, paint a picture of an increasingly dire situation onboard the seemingly serene, but perhaps secretly cursed, *Mary Celeste*. Once upon a time, the ship had transported a cargo of coal; in fact, the ship's massive repairs occurred not long after this particular haul. Dust remnants from the coal, combined with sawdust from the renovations, may have clogged the ship's pumps, which would help explain why one such pump was found dismantled. If the pumps were clogged, Captain Briggs would have been unable to determine how much water filled the ship's hull (remember that makeshift water-measuring device found on the deck?), potentially leading him to erroneously believe the ship was taking on water in dangerous quantities.

A deeper look at the ship's log, combined with the notes of the admiralty court investigators, also reveals that Captain Briggs steered the *Mary Celeste* off course—due north toward the island of Santa Maria in the Azores—the day before the ship was presumably abandoned. This has led some to believe the ship's crew was seeking respite from the latest in a constant barrage of storms at sea.

With all these recently unveiled clues taken together, a slightly less foggy view of the crew's final day comes into focus. With his ship potentially at risk of sinking in the middle of the ocean and finally catching sight of a coastline as many as three days after he was expecting to, Captain Briggs may have opted for a drastic solution. He might have ordered his family and crew to abandon ship out of an abundance of caution, opting to row the lifeboat to the shores of Santa Maria.

The fact that new theories regarding the fate of the *Mary Celeste* are still being formulated in the twenty-first century is proof positive that this mystery is one for the ages. Even some famous historical figures found themselves mystified by the seemingly inexplicable occurrence, further embedding the *Mary Celeste* in pop culture. I am referring to legendary author Sir Arthur Conan Doyle. While most readers know him for imagining the character of Sherlock Holmes, his literary beginnings were much humbler. Before Doyle gained worldwide recognition, his first piece to be published in a major publication, *Cornhill Magazine*, was a short story called "J. Habakuk Jephson's Statement" (1884).

"J. Habakuk Jephson's Statement" was, at its core, a fictionalized retelling of the case of the *Mary Celeste*. In it, a formerly enslaved man from New Orleans was among the ship's passengers, and he murdered the captain and crew in an act of revenge. The character subsequently sailed the empty vessel to West Africa.

At the time of the story's writing, Doyle was a twenty-five-year-old surgeon working aboard a ship, and his work of fiction was so well-received that it functionally launched Doyle's career as an author by inspiring him to quit his medical profession. Doyle's first Sherlock Holmes novel, *A Study in Scarlet*, would be published merely three years later.

What was so special about Doyle's version of the *Mary Celeste* story? First of all, he did his best to emphasize that the tale was sensationalized compared with its historical reference point, even going so far as to change the name of the ship from *Mary Celeste* to *Marie Celeste*. Plus, anyone who had closely studied the original case would know that the story's format—a dramatic retelling by a survivor of the ordeal— did not accord with history, since no survivors were ever found. The problem was, not every reader was well studied in *Mary Celeste* lore, and fiction authors of the era enjoyed widespread readership from general audiences. As a result, readers were enamored by Doyle's tale, and they found the story so convincing that the governments of Great Britain and the United States were forced to issue statements assuring the public it wasn't true.

Yet in 1935, Doyle's story had retained enough popularity that it became the source material for a movie called *The Mystery of the Mary Celeste* (in Great Britain) or *Phantom Ship* (in the United States). In the film, actor Bela Lugosi portrayed the murderous sailor who ultimately killed the ship's crew. Some people believe Doyle's story—and therefore its later adaptations or retellings—may have been loosely inspired by the suspicions that once surrounded the German brothers who were members of the crew.

Despite the ongoing debate surrounding the fate of everyone on board—and the mystery's permanent remembrance in pop culture—the details of the *Mary Celeste*'s final years are comparatively clear. After Captain Morehouse and his team recovered the ship and received their measly partial insurance payment, the *Mary Celeste* returned to cargo service in 1873. The ship would be used continually for twelve more years under a variety of owners.

Now, I'm no expert, but twelve years doesn't seem like a long enough time to warrant numerous ownership changes under ordinary circumstances, and this is where the supposed curse of the *Mary Celeste* returns to rear its ugly head. It has been said that each of the ship's subsequent owners suffered encounters with misfortune. For example, Captain George Blatchford, who piloted the craft as it shuttled cargo between Indian Ocean ports throughout 1874, was ultimately met with financial failure and sold the ship in 1879. With each additional mishap, it became increasingly difficult for the *Mary Celeste*'s new owners to secure shipping contracts and attract crewmen who were willing to staff its journeys. Clearly, the maritime community had bought into the idea that the *Mary Celeste* was doomed.

By the time the ship's final captain, an American by the name of Gilman C. Parker, realized the dire impact of the ship's reputation on business (in other words, he couldn't sign a shipping contract to save his life), he became a tad desperate. Seeing little other recourse, Captain Parker intentionally grounded the *Mary Celeste* on the Rochelais Reef off the coast of Haiti sometime between late 1884 and early 1885. Ironically, he sought to do exactly what the British admiralty court had initially suspected of Captains Briggs and Morehouse years earlier: Parker was attempting to commit insurance fraud.

Parker undoubtedly believed he had concocted an effective plan. He loaded up worthless cargo and insured the ship and its contents for far more than the collective lot was worth. But he failed to account for one important factor: the coral reef prevented the ship from sinking in a timely fashion, giving insurance investigators plenty of opportunity to appraise the wreck and realize the cargo's true value. Parker's attempt was entirely unsuccessful, and he and several Bostonian coconspirators were arrested and put on trial. All parties were eventually acquitted for lack of evidence, but Parker's name was already mud. The story of his attempted insurance fraud stuck in the court of public opinion, and he suffered financially and socially for the rest of his life.

> **Riley's Next Hunt:** Under the tutelage of trained salvage diver Ben, Riley could play a role in discovering the long-lost wreck of the *Mary Celeste*, finding evidence that the ship's pumps had been clogged by past cargo, renovation debris, or—in true *National Treasure* fashion—something intentionally hidden.

While it is known that the *Mary Celeste* met a wrecked end, and while the general location of the wreckage event was also well-documented, somehow the remnants of the craft still haven't been recovered (as of the time of this writing). An ocean explorer thought he had identified the ship's deteriorated structure on Rochelais Reef as recently as 2001 because the wreck's dimensions and the composition of its fastenings were found to match those of the *Mary Celeste*. Additional analysis even found that the submerged vessel's remaining bits of timber seemed to match the type of wood used for shipbuilding in New York at the time the *Mary Celeste* underwent major repairs.

However, excitement over the discovery was short-lived, as modern scientific tools were deployed to analyze the findings. Dendrochronological analysis, or the study of tree rings, applied to the wreck's wooden components offered the final nail in the coffin and proved that the ship, while old, was certainly not the *Mary Celeste*.

The timber used to construct the found vessel originated in a forest of longleaf pines—trees that were not native to Nova Scotia or New York—and the trees in question were still alive and well a full decade after the *Mary Celeste* sank in the Caribbean.

And with that, the mystery of the *Mary Celeste* lives on. We will never know for certain what happened to her missing crew, and we might never learn the location of the ship's watery grave. Even if the wreck was eventually discovered, every additional day underwater between now and then adds to its disintegration. But it's not as if finding the ship, which had operated continually for years postmystery, would offer any insight into what happened on that fateful, incomplete journey from New York to Genoa. Alas, the theorizing shall continue!

Chapter 15

Winchester Mystery House

We know it; we love it—and we return to it for the second time in this book. It's the classic Hollywood trope of the dark, mysterious house down the street! It's probably inhabited by a reclusive widow (a woman, because such tales are both sexist and predictable) whose very existence is shrouded in rumors perpetuated by the local townspeople. Maybe the house is boarded up. Maybe it's haunted. But every fictional town has one, and it's our favorite place to set a mystery, a murder, and the macabre.

Surely these foreboding facades that live in the recesses of our minds are entirely attributable to pop culture classics. Whether you're drawn to Boo Radley's home in *To Kill a Mockingbird* or the quintessential mansion in any given episode of *Scooby-Doo!*, it's somewhat more difficult to imagine a real-life version of the dark, mysterious house down the street. I'd even argue the ones that do exist aren't *physically* dark and mysterious, but rather that they have played host to various dark and mysterious events over time.

But every rule has an exception. Enter the Winchester Mystery House, an architectural enigma whose existence sits somewhere on the spectrum between "mysterious home straight out of a Hollywood blockbuster" and "real-world amusement park funhouse." In fact, it's the rare anomaly that bears more similarities to the film and television trope than to the very real houses around the world that are "dark" because of activities they've witnessed.

Everything about the Winchester Mystery House is exactly that: a mystery. From its curious interior to its imposing size to the reclusive woman who both inhabited the home and was responsible for its construction, you'd be hard-pressed to ask a question about the house that has a clear or easy answer.

Yet if you ask what I think is the most interesting part of the house's story, I'd point out that when you get to know the Winchester Mystery House, you'll find that its mystery is fueled by legends that are themselves born out of social stigmas. I can't help but notice how, more often than not, by the end of the movie, the dark, mysterious house down the street is revealed to have been not so scary after all. The house—and its inhabitants—may have simply been misunderstood. That just might be the reality of the Winchester Mystery House as well.

> **Why Riley Would Care:** The Winchester Mystery House story features the unexpected intersection of history, psychology, and public relations. There's no shortage of legends for Riley to investigate in this objectively strange structure.

HUNT DOWN THAT HISTORY

Situated in a busy, bustling corridor of San Jose, California, the Winchester Mystery House is surrounded by the Interstate-280, a mobile home park, and a former movie theater. Its urban location is truly unexpected, especially given the large plot of land on which it sits. But a plot of land—ripe for construction—is exactly what Sarah Winchester sought when she acquired the property and began renovations on what would eventually become her personal abode.

Sarah Lockwood Pardee was born in 1839 in New Haven, Connecticut. As a child, Sarah received a good education, eventually learning to speak four languages and play three instruments. She was just two years younger than Baltimore-born William Wirt Winchester, whom she married on September 30, 1862.

Her nuptials made Sarah a wealthy young woman because William was the heir to the Winchester Repeating Arms Company, one of the most profitable weapons manufacturers of the nineteenth century. Oliver Winchester, William's father, had been co-owner of a successful shirt-making company and then turned his attention to a young repeating arms company, of which he became majority shareholder.

The Volcanic Repeating Arms Company, as it was initially known, would eventually be reorganized as the New Haven Arms Company, and this version of the business quickly made a name for itself. The Henry rifle of 1860, one of the company's most widely used models, was the weapon of choice for Union soldiers during the Civil War. At the war's conclusion, Oliver Winchester renamed the business once more, and Winchester Repeating Arms would quickly become famous as the manufacturer of the repeating rifle.

The concept of a repeating rifle was game-changing, as it allowed the operator to fire, reload, and fire again at a pace previously unknown to everyday riflemen. Winchester Repeating Arms would ultimately sell more than eight million repeating rifles, with its most famous variant, the Model 1873, remaining in production until 1923. The Model 1873 was marketed as "the gun that won the West," and for good reason: the repeating rifle was responsible for a slew of casualties—blowing the death tolls of alternative weapons out of the water—because of the speed with which ammunition could be fired.

By the time Sarah and William Winchester married and settled in New Haven, their fortune was already secure due to Oliver's business ventures. The young Winchester couple made their home on Prospect Hill at a site that is now part of Yale Divinity School. In July 1866, they welcomed a daughter, Annie Pardee Winchester, who passed away less than six weeks after birth due to marasmus, an illness characterized by severe malnutrition. But this wasn't the last sad fate to afflict Sarah Winchester, as her father and mother subsequently died in 1869 and 1880, respectively.

Everything changed for Sarah just one year later, in 1881, when, at the age of forty-three, her husband succumbed to tuberculosis, and one of her sisters met an untimely end shortly after. Following this string of unforeseen family deaths, Sarah went into mourning and, for lack of better terms, simply never reemerged. She channeled her energy into a new hobby, architecture, which was facilitated by her newfound wealth.

Not only had William Winchester passed away, but so had his father, which left the entire fortune of the Winchester Repeating Arms Company to Sarah. In the 1880s, the value of this inheritance was said to be $20 million plus approximately 50 percent ownership of the still-thriving weapons company. The value of her business ownership alone was believed to have afforded Sarah an income of about $1,000 per day (or $26,000 per day adjusted to inflation in the year 2019).

Her foray into architectural experimentalism began in 1885, when Sarah put some of her monetary holdings toward relocating to California. The following year, she purchased and immediately began renovating an eight-room San Jose farmhouse, a modest piece of a vast forty-five-acre property. Her machinations transformed the farmhouse into a Victorian mansion that she would dub Llanada Villa in honor of the site's Spanish lineage and her passion for the country's Basque community.

It is at this point in the story that I should be overviewing what the mansion looked like once it was complete, but that would be quite an impossible task. You see, Sarah's renovations were never actually finished, both literally and figuratively. Construction began in 1886 and lasted for the duration of Sarah's life, but activities at the site were most intense for the ten-year period spanning from 1890 to 1900.

Early in the renovation process, Sarah met with numerous architects but failed to hire a single one of them, instead opting to design each expansion and alteration on her own. She lacked formal training in design or architecture, but she was not a woman willing to sacrifice her vision for the benefit of a more experienced hand. As a result, she built and rebuilt elements of the home, especially when new additions failed to fulfill her artistic vision. After all, money was no object, so she could afford to make multiple attempts if her desired outcome wasn't achieved on the first try.

Despite local lore attesting to the contrary, construction at Sarah's estate paused at various intervals. For instance, in a letter to her family, Sarah shared that she once suspended construction because she recognized it was too hot for the builders to safely operate. She seemed to be a fair employer, having her workers cycle out in sixteen-person shifts given the generally ongoing nature of the renovations.

In 1906, Northern California was struck by an infamous earthquake, wreaking havoc across urban centers. Sarah's mansion was affected like any other building; the structure experienced such damage that an imposing tower attached to the home needed to be demolished, and the entire mansion was reduced in height from seven stories to four. For the most part, Sarah ceased work on the front-facing portion of the house following the earthquake, but interior and exterior efforts around the rest of the property continued.

A few years passed, and by 1910, Sarah was only a part-time resident of her beloved Llanada Villa, choosing to occupy most days with her sister and niece in Atherton. In truth, Sarah's money was well spent on several properties throughout the Bay Area. Even so, Sarah slept peacefully at her continuously under-construction mansion when she passed away, likely due to heart failure, on September 5, 1922. It was only after her death that renovations finally ceased.

While the house should still technically be considered incomplete, the final and present-day version of Llanada Villa comprises twenty-four thousand square feet, but the impact of the monstrosity is truly in the details. The home is made up of ten thousand windows, two thousand doors, 160 rooms, forty-seven stairways and fireplaces, thirteen bathrooms, six kitchens, and two basements. In 1923, the total value of the renovations was estimated to be $5 million, the equivalent of more than $70 million today.

Embedded throughout the house are traditional elements of Victorian architecture, such as gold-plated fixtures and stained-glass windows set in silver. The interior was crafted from redwood trees, but Sarah specified that visible timber should be stained a different hue. In some ways, Sarah was ahead of her time as a novice designer, incorporating infrastructural elements that were uncommon in buildings of the era, such as indoor plumbing, hot running water, and button-operated gas lighting. Heating and remote communication systems were designed to reach all corners of the house, while three elevators had been installed for ease of passage.

Llanada Villa's foundation also exhibited strange characteristics that aged well from an architectural perspective. One of the reasons the building remains structurally sound today—despite withstanding a second significant earthquake in 1989—is likely due to its implementation of a floating foundation. A house with a floating foundation isn't permanently affixed to its base, leaving an appropriate amount of wiggle room to endure movements like those introduced by tremors and quakes.

You're probably wondering why an entire chapter of this text has been dedicated to a massive California mansion. Sure, it's weird that the construction was never formally complete, and it's also cool that an ambitious woman chose to spend her money on experimenting with new techniques in architecture and design. But these realities don't themselves constitute a legend or mystery. To discover the true curiosity of Llanada Villa, one must attempt a walk through its innumerable halls.

If you do, you'll likely find yourself unsettled at best—and uncomfortable at worst. Llanada Villa has taken on the popular name of the "Winchester Mystery House" largely because its interior was crafted—intentionally or unintentionally—in the style of a perpetual labyrinth, and its list of design-related peculiarities is equally endless.

Within the confines of the Winchester Mystery House, you'll discover that some doors and cabinets open onto blank walls. If you peer out certain windows or step out onto certain balconies, you'll find yourself overlooking other rooms in the mansion. At least one staircase, should you happen upon it, leads straight into a ceiling. (Watch your head.)

Walking through doors at the house is an equally tedious, even dangerous, affair; after all, one door opens to nothingness, creating a steep drop to the floor of a room below. Another room has neither a floor nor a ceiling—a clear remnant of a room that existed in an earlier version of the structure. When following passageways, visitors might round a corner only to find a dead end, or they might ascend multiple flights before a staircase simply stops.

Some larger rooms are home to smaller rooms nestled within. Some chimneys don't make their way up to the roof. Some floors are interrupted by skylights. Some doors open in only one direction.

Adjacent doorways are markedly different sizes. Adjacent linen closets and cabinets differ dramatically in depth. Nothing seems to make sense; trying to determine the rhyme or reason for any one design element is an exercise in futility.

The result of what seems to be a combination of incompatible architectural elements is an aura of confusion affecting those passing through the structure. Adding to this sense of uncertainty is the way light interacts with the windows in the different rooms. In some spaces, light shining through a window lends the optical illusion that the floorboards are alternating in color. Some oddly shaped windows, including those fashioned like bull's-eyes, create an upside-down perspective for those peering through.

As Dr. Pamela Haag so aptly described in *Smithsonian Magazine*, "I came to think that if a mind were a house, it would probably look like this," owing to the fact that Sarah's creation represented an amalgamation of fleeting ideas. Her house was a puzzle to be assembled, but some of the puzzle pieces connected in multiple ways, while others didn't fit together at all.

To best understand the complexities of the Winchester Mystery House, it is worth exploring a few of its most famous—and, by many accounts, most bewildering—rooms. One such compartment is the grand ballroom, whose construction cost $9,000 in the late-nineteenth or early-twentieth century. After Walt Disney paid a visit to the mansion, he took inspiration from this room when designing the ballroom portion of Magic Kingdom's famous *Haunted Mansion* attraction.

> **Riley's Favorite Fact (Probably):** The Winchester Mystery House's grand ballroom—one of the home's many architecturally unconventional chambers—was the inspiration for parts of the *Haunted Mansion* ride at Magic Kingdom.

The number thirteen appears repeatedly within Sarah's grand ballroom, just as it appears throughout the house. For example, thirteen hooks are found in some closets, thirteen ceiling panels hover above the entrance hall, thirteen panes comprise most windows, thirteen palm trees line the driveway, thirteen lights sit in a chandelier, and thirteen steps make up the staircases. Taylor Swift would probably feel at home.

The séance room is also notable, as it was thought to be off-limits to anyone but Sarah during her time living at the mansion. Legend has it she would frequently ring the bell in the tower adjacent to the séance room when trying to summon and then release spirits following communication sessions. However, historians who have studied Sarah and the Winchester family disagree with this mystical theory, instead suggesting that the room served as private quarters for a gardener. These historians also argue that spiritualism was a communal practice, and Sarah was notoriously reclusive, making it unlikely that she practiced séances.

Regardless of the room's functionality, its real oddity lies in the fact that it has one entrance and three exits, though one of the exits would require the user to take their life into their own hands. Allow me to explain. The first exit, of course, is through the entrance. The second is a one-way door leading to a secret passageway. And the third is an eight-foot jump into a kitchen situated one floor below.

The strangeness of the Winchester Mystery House could have easily made the structure obsolete after Sarah's passing. Since the property was not explicitly mentioned in her will, it was eventually sold at auction. Despite its vast size and advanced innovations, the house was valued unfathomably low because of its many peculiarities, and the person who won the auction ended up paying less than the value of the land on which the home sat. Its next inhabitants, who took over in April 1923, were lessees and eventual owners John and Mayme Brown.

The Browns had big plans for the Winchester Mystery House once they became its full-fledged owners. They sought to create an amusement park on its grounds, believing the site to be the perfect home for a Backety-Back Railway, an early wooden roller coaster that John Brown had designed. However, the Browns' plans were foiled by a combination of local regulations and swelling public interest in the mansion. They soon shifted their focus to finding a way to welcome tourists onto their strange new property.

That's why, in June 1923, the Winchester Mystery House first opened its doors to the public, while its grounds and gardens accepted picnickers. Mayme Brown served as a tour guide ushering visitors through the winding interior passageways, a role she developed by creating entirely baseless stories to explain away the house's features. She not only started rumors that the home was haunted, but she was also likely the source of many urban legends about Sarah Winchester that persist to this day.

Visitors to the Winchester Mystery House are treated to interior furnishings that match the time period of the home's construction era, though the rooms' adornments are not Sarah's originals. (Any of Sarah's possessions not kept by her niece were sold at auction.) Plus, because few people were granted access to the home during Sarah's lifetime, little photographic evidence exists to confirm what Sarah's furnishings looked like; it would therefore be impossible to replicate her chosen layouts. But such minor complications haven't deterred tourists from stopping by. To date, Winchester Mystery House has welcomed more than twelve million visitors from around the world.

LISTEN TO RILEY

It's almost comical to begin our discussion of Winchester Mystery House *intrigue* at this point in the story. To be honest, where to begin said conversation is somewhat of an arbitrary decision given all the unexplained elements found within the house's walls. But I'll defend my decision to begin our exploration of curiosities at this very point, because in my opinion, the real mystery of the site is the strange collection of circumstances that ultimately produced years of bizarre renovations.

After all, at no point did a master plan or blueprint exist to guide builders toward a final, intended outcome. No one—perhaps not even Sarah Winchester herself—had a clue what the completed structure was supposed to resemble. To this day, we don't know when Sarah would have stopped adding rooms, staircases, and other repetitive elements to the home. Maybe she hoped the construction would continue forever.

One of the reasons we know so little about her intentions is because after moving to California and commencing the renovation process, Sarah Winchester became withdrawn. It's almost too predictable, is it not? The widow locked up in the big, strange house—the concept straight out of one of those movies or television shows with which we started this chapter. But despite having all the money in the world, which could have easily qualified her as a socialite, Sarah simply didn't care to engage with society.

As a result, society viewed her from a distance as eccentric. Since Sarah refused to speak with the press, which became increasingly curious as new wings and towers popped up on the house seemingly overnight, the press concocted its own stories about her. Readers of myriad articles absorbed those stories and drew their own conclusions.

One prime example of this dynamic dates back to 1895, when articles in the *San Francisco Chronicle* and the *San Jose Daily News* claimed the reason Llanada Villa's construction seemed perpetual was because its owner believed she would die if the renovations stopped. The public took this story and ran with it, some morphing the tale into a quest for immortality. Even today many people locally and around the world believe some version of this urban legend—itself born out of shoddy reporting.

In the case of the Winchester Mystery House, the public salivated when answers to their unyielding questions seemed within reach, and the more bizarre the answers, the more traction those answers seemed to achieve. Colin Dickey, author of *Ghostland: An American History in Haunted Places* (2016), suggests this mainstream reaction may have been a manifestation of the country's economic woes of the 1890s. According to Dickey, Sarah Winchester provided the perfect mold out of which to craft a villain: she was a widow who kept to herself and seemed infinitely wealthy. At a time when many in the middle class were struggling, Sarah was a natural recipient of ire; a 1909 *San Francisco Chronicle* piece lambasted her construction as wasteful.

Dickey wonders whether societal gender norms could be partially to blame for not only the public's curiosity, but also their anger. He notes that during her lifetime, Sarah was the stereotype of a social outcast: a single woman living alone. One could argue that a woman in Sarah's position would still be regarded questioningly by some onlookers even today. And when the public deems something unnatural or odd— whether in the 1800s or 2000s—lashing out is unfortunately a common response.

If curious Californians chalked up Sarah's actions to psychological explanations during her lifetime, their assessments pivoted to the supernatural after her death. One rumor purported that Sarah built the immense home per the instructions of a spiritualist or psychic whom Sarah had visited while grieving. According to this version of events, the psychic informed Sarah that the reason her family members died in rapid succession was because of the ghosts of those who had been killed by the Winchester repeating rifle. Put bluntly, the ghosts sought revenge. The psychic supposedly went on to say these angry spirits would continue to haunt Sarah until her death. To appease the spirits, she was to build a home that could contain them all.

But is there any truth to the tale? Word of this supposed meeting with a psychic first appeared in 1967 when author Susy Smith published a book titled, *Prominent American Ghosts*. Yet no one has been able to prove that the meeting ever occurred, and Sarah's employees and friends claimed this version of events was patently untrue. At the very least, there is no record of Sarah Winchester having participated in local spiritualist gatherings in California, and we do not know whether she believed in spiritualism (though this practice was definitely popular with wealthy Americans in the decades following the Civil War).

A different supernatural theory underpinning Sarah's construction is also popular, and it too invokes the ghosts of the Winchester repeating rifle's victims. Some believe Sarah's mansion incorporated an endless labyrinth of doors, windows, staircases, and rooms in an effort to confuse these spirits, so they'd have trouble finding her. Rumors circulated that

Sarah used secret passageways to navigate the house, alternating which room she slept in at night to keep the spirits on their transparent toes.

Still other reports claim Sarah engaged with psychics during the ongoing construction in order to learn new ways to appease the spirits surrounding her. But since she invited so few visitors into her mansion, this seems unlikely. That's probably why a different version of this supposition suggests Sarah held personal séances in the middle of the night, during which time she collected the spirits' instructions regarding what her next home addition should be. This theory stemmed from the fact that whenever she had new plans to share with her builders, they always seemed to crop up overnight.

All in all, it's my personal belief that theories associating Sarah's actions with fear of or remorse for the repeating rifle's victims would be more plausible if she *hadn't* chosen to remain an active board member of the Winchester Repeating Arms Company after her husband's passing. Plus, in the late-nineteenth and early-twentieth centuries, Americans didn't tend to feel a great deal of guilt over guns, which were viewed as necessary utilities. It's quite likely that when we reflect on Sarah Winchester's story today—in the twenty-first century—we project our modern, conflicting feelings about guns onto the mystery. As a result, we create an interpretation that makes quite a bit of sense to us but likely would have made very little sense to Sarah herself.

If our interpretations and assumptions are erroneous, that hasn't stopped Hollywood from adapting the Winchester story to make a buck. In 2018, actress Helen Mirren (also known as Dr. Emily Appleton in the *National Treasure* universe) starred as Sarah Winchester in the eponymous horror film *Winchester*, which is inspired by an amalgamation of the previous supernatural theories.

In the end, the truth of Sarah Winchester's story may be far more benign (dare I say boring?). Sarah's father was a Victorian-era carpenter, and Sarah had a longstanding passion for building design, even subscribing to numerous architecture magazines. At one point, she had devised a plan to build a medieval-style castle—complete with a moat and drawbridge—in San Mateo County, California, though this desire never came to fruition.

So we know that Sarah was interested in building, but she had no formal experience with it. That doesn't really matter when you have endless funding and can effectively implement large-scale trial and error as you experiment with your new craft. In sum, it's highly likely the eccentricities found within the mansion today are simply mistakes—evidence of her architectural novice. In a letter written to her sister-in-law in 1898, Sarah lamented that "my upper hall which leads to the sleeping apartment was rendered so unexpectedly dark by a little addition that . . . a number of people had missed their footing on the stairs." Whoops.

> **Riley's Next Hunt:** What if Sarah Winchester's obscure construction choices weren't mistakes after all? Riley would be all too eager to discover a treasure hunt clue hidden in her home, perhaps tied to an "innocent" optical illusion or "accidental" stairway to nowhere.

Additionally, recall that the 1906 earthquake resulted in the shortening of the mansion's height by three whole floors. At least some of the house's odd features may therefore have been caused by this reduction; stairs that lead to nowhere may have once led to somewhere. And then there's the question of practicality. Narrow staircases and other smaller-than-usual dimensions may have been chosen strategically because Sarah was only four-foot-ten and suffered from arthritis that could hinder basic mobility.

When there is very little record of an individual's life from their own perspective, the best thing to do is collect testimony from whomever knew that individual on a personal level. Sarah Winchester's friends, family, and construction workers unanimously agreed she was a fiercely independent, grieving widow, while her lawyer was vocally impressed with her business aptitude. As for why she was reclusive, insiders point to her ailing health combined with the fact that she was a bit more on the reserved side. In today's terms, Sarah was simply an introvert.

But why did Sarah choose to move out west in the first place? She relocated not because a psychic told her to, but rather because that's where the remaining members of her family lived. Since Sarah had recently lost so many loved ones in rapid succession, it's no surprise that she wanted to be around family. Her doctor may have even encouraged her to move westward, believing that a warmer climate would be an effective antidote to both grief and health challenges.

Accordingly, many people believe Sarah Winchester purchased a farmhouse sitting on lots of land to facilitate the construction of a larger home that could house not just her, but also her sisters and their families. Some historians even suspect the reason she kept the construction going was, in part, to keep her builders employed in an economically tumultuous time. It's said that she paid her carpenters handsomely and treated them like family, and as a result her staff exhibited extreme loyalty to their employer. That's why these employees never shared a peep about the home's interior with the press, even after Sarah passed.

Records that do exist seem to support the conclusion that Sarah Winchester was a pretty darn good person. A philanthropist in life, she donated to numerous causes anonymously, and her will provisioned $1 million for a hospital located in her hometown back east, alongside other charitable contributions. In retrospect, it's astonishingly unfair that Sarah Winchester is remembered for the rumors and legends that ceaselessly swirled about her when in reality she might have been just a woman ahead of her time.

Today, the Winchester Mystery House is a popular destination for paranormal investigators, as the structure has never been able to shake the speculation that it's haunted. The first person to explore this theory was none other than Harry Houdini, who visited during his 1924 tour attempting to negate the concept of spiritualism. The Winchester Mystery House was his destination on Halloween night, and he was supposedly the person who assigned it the "mystery house" moniker. By the 1930s, the nickname had stuck.

Employees and visitors alike claim to have experienced encounters with spirits. One oft-referenced figure is Clyde, who has been spotted pushing a wheelbarrow in the basement or fixing a fireplace in the ballroom. Some tour guides and guests have reported seeing a woman in period-specific black garments amongst their tour groups; this is presumed to be the ghost of Sarah Winchester herself.

In 1974, the Winchester Mystery House was designated as a state historic landmark and made its way onto the National Register of Historic Places. In 1996, it was declared a landmark of the city of San Jose. Over the last century, the house and grounds have undergone numerous renovations—but not renovations like Sarah's. These modern repairs have primarily focused on restoring the site. For example, in 2016 and 2017, Sarah's personal wallpaper stockpiles—which were 130 years old in the 2000s—were used to freshly line the walls of the parlor hallway and south twin dining room.

Curiously, discoveries are *still* being made within the walls of the Winchester Mystery House. A room that many believe Sarah forgot about and built over was rediscovered in 1975, revealing two chairs and a phonograph speaker. The door to the room had been locked from the inside. In 2016, a previously unknown attic was found to contain a pump organ, couch, dress form, sewing machine, and paintings. Even more recently—in 2019—renovators discovered a century-old envelope from the Pacific American Decorative Company stashed in a wall. This find confirmed what historians had previously only been able to speculate: the house's stained-glass windows were made by well-known crafter John Mallon.

Who's to say what discoveries are next to befall the Winchester Mystery House? When a setting is mired in so many unanswered questions, the information provided by even the smallest, seemingly insignificant find can mean the difference between an incomplete understanding and a crystal-clear picture. But even if we could answer every lingering question about Sarah Winchester and her mysterious home, would the public ever relinquish its grasp on the supernatural, reclusive version of Sarah that resembles pop culture stereotypes? That might be the most puzzling question of all.

Chapter 16

Jack
the
Ripper

As previously discussed, since the dawn of podcasting, society has developed a morbid fascination with serial killers. Perhaps that fascination has constantly existed—hiding deep within the recesses of the human mind. After all, horror movies have always been popular, but they've never been slapped with a social stigma because they're typically labeled as "fiction." Real-life horror stories—murders committed individually or en masse—seemed taboo for years, probably because of society's unspoken agreement that interest in something so horrific was unsavory.

But all that changed with the rise of podcasts and, specifically, the "true crime" genre. Suddenly, our deepest, animalistic desires to understand the psychologies of serial killers had permission to leave the depths of our brains. It became acceptable, even trendy, to discuss long-forgotten cold cases, while the most dedicated listeners took it upon themselves to launch their own investigations. Before long, general knowledge of just about every serial killer in history seemed greater than ever before.

Given such a modern interest—and the sheer number of serial killer mysteries that persist in the zeitgeist—this text would seem quite incomplete without examining at least one historical, murderous foe. And since we're prioritizing the examination of people, places, and things that fail to yield clear answers, it's only fair that we consider arguably the most infamous anonymous murderer known to man: Jack the Ripper.

Now, I must confess something: my education related to Jack the Ripper's story began far before the advent of podcasts—and therefore far before it was considered socially acceptable to study such a story. But the reason for my research was purely academic (okay, fine, it was middle school) when my class was learning about the legal system by acting out the mock trial of a famous figure. Our "client" was Jack the Ripper, and I—always the overachiever—was tasked with serving as his defense attorney.

I learned later (many years after getting a fictional version of Jack off the hook in my classroom court) that this particular killer had captured the attention of more than just my former teacher. As an adult, I came to realize that the way history has remembered this faceless criminal has resulted in not only his immortalization, but his glorification. Society's morbid fascination has turned Jack the Ripper into a popular Halloween costume while his victims—those who should probably be centered in the story—have been largely forgotten by comparison.

> **Why Riley Would Care:** While I don't envision Riley as a true crime junkie, I do believe he'd be motivated to solve the most famous whodunit in history. By unmasking Jack the Ripper, Riley would be celebrated as this century's Hercule Poirot.

HUNT DOWN THAT HISTORY

In the year 1888, London grappled with citywide fear and uncertainty. This so-called Autumn of Terror was characterized by the dastardly actions of an unknown figure who murdered at least five women between late August and early November. Some believe the true number of victims rises to double digits, likely because a single police file contains these and other murder mysteries dated from April 1888 to February 1891.

Jack the Ripper, as the culprit came to be known, committed his five definite crimes within a mile of one another near the East End's Whitechapel district. In the period under discussion, Whitechapel was rife with violence and illicit activities, while its residents suffered high rates of alcoholism, diphtheria, tuberculosis, and other diseases. The impoverished community—consisting of many skilled workers who settled there after immigrating—lived in overcrowded quarters with poor access to clean water and adequate sanitation.

At the time, the social and economic conditions of the East End were a far cry from the situation in the West End, which was filled with shops and theaters that hosted London's wealthy elite. The Royal Navy's impressive ships docked at the piers, while countless merchant ships navigated their way into and out of the ports. The late 1800s were characterized by a tale of two Londons, and the East End had gotten the short end of the stick.

In these poverty-stricken neighborhoods, individuals accepted whatever jobs they could find as a matter of survival. Women predominantly earned low wages as domestic help and sweatshop employees, while those desperate for income commonly turned to sex work. Sadly, violence toward sex workers was extremely common, but it was rarely discussed in public due to the stigma surrounding the practice as a whole.

Ironically, Jack the Ripper had a hand in bringing that very conversation to the forefront, as all his known victims were women sex workers. Jack's cases gained national—and even international— attention because they were quite different from other murders of the era. Jack's crimes featured such extreme brutality and gruesomeness that there was no question about whether they were committed by the same deranged person. Allow us to review the evidence.

Jack the Ripper's first victim, Mary Ann "Polly" Nichols, was found dead—her throat slashed and abdomen cut open—on a street corner at 3:40 a.m. on August 31, 1888. As investigators interviewed local sex workers hoping to identify a perpetrator, they learned that a man, dubbed Leather Apron because of his consistent apparel, had been extorting the women. Specifically, Leather Apron threatened to cut them open if they didn't meet his demands, which included monetary payment.

A literal leather apron would eventually turn up near the deceased body of Jack's second victim, Annie Chapman, who was murdered on September 8. But the apron belonged to the owner of the house alongside which Chapman's body was found; in other words, it wasn't evidence at all. Investigators' pursuit of the "real" Leather Apron led them to arrest a man named John Pizer, whose answers during interrogation revealed ironclad alibis for the nights in question. Pizer was formally cleared of suspicion during the inquest for Chapman's murder.

Nichols and Chapman, in addition to Elisabeth Stride, Catherine Eddowes, and Mary Jane Kelly, make up the "canonical five" victims of Jack the Ripper; the association of their murders with Jack is uncontested. Stride and Eddowes were slain within an hour of one another on September 30, while Kelly's murder occurred more than a month later on November 9. It is worth noting that some in-depth studies of the killer suggest his first victim was actually Martha Tabram, who had been found fatally stabbed in the throat and abdomen in early August 1888.

Jack the Ripper's victims shared numerous traits. Not only were they all women—and specifically current or former sex workers—but all were also associated with at least one additional social stigma of the time. They were alcoholics, had failed marriages, were of low socioeconomic status, or exhibited other stereotyped characteristics. Plus, they all lived a quarter of a mile from one another.

If true crime podcasts have taught us anything, the details of a murder—and especially a set of connected murders—must not be ignored. Jack's killings were collectively perpetrated after traditional pub closing hours and on weekends. Their locations were confined to secluded inlets of comparatively more crowded spaces, making it easy for someone to lie in wait or escape unnoticed by blending in amongst the throngs. Despite the hustle and bustle, no one nearby ever reported hearing screams or calls for help.

> **Riley's Favorite Fact (Probably):** Jack the Ripper's unfortunate victims all lived within the same quarter-mile radius and exhibited numerous sociodemographic similarities.

While the victims' deaths were officially attributed to hemorrhage, it has long been believed they were first strangled. And when the bodies were examined postmortem, no evidence was found to suggest the women had tried to defend themselves from their attacker.

It is at this point that we must address the elephant in the room. If there's one thing that even uninterested members of the public tend to know about Jack the Ripper, it's that he had a distinct calling card—the type of calling card that makes his cases prime real estate for podcasters. Jack's modus operandi involved mutilating the bodies of his victims (all but one), but this heinous act was not conducted haphazardly. In fact, the mutilations were carried out with great precision, leading investigators to believe early on that their killer was studied in human anatomy.

I must now offer a trigger warning to readers before discussing the details of the killer's characteristic—and now infamous—mutilations.

Jack the Ripper routinely removed entire organs from his victims' bodies, and these organs were typically missing from the scene of the crime. In many cases, the women's intestines were carefully cut away and placed over their shoulders, which is how their bodies were found. Two distinct exceptions to this rule were the cases of Nichols and Stride. When investigating Stride's murder, in particular, authorities suspected the killer had been interrupted—nearly caught in the act—by the carriage of the man who would end up discovering the victim's body. This interruption occurred before any organs could be excised.

Some cases exhibited additional, unique defacements. Chapman's body was devoid of a uterus, while Kelly's face was disfigured, and her heart was missing from the scene. In fact, Kelly's murder was the most gruesome, perhaps because she was the lone victim murdered indoors, giving the killer more time to operate without risk of being spotted. Much of her body had been skinned, and additional interior and exterior body parts were cut away. Sadly, it's said that her partner could identify her body based only on the unmarred appearance of her eyes and ears.

Given that the victims' bodies were found shortly after the nighttime killings, Jack the Ripper was clearly able to remove organs quickly and precisely without the luxury of lighting. Consider, for example, the case of Catherine Eddowes. Just fourteen minutes elapsed between the moment one police officer passed the scene (before the crime had been committed) and another walked by during his own patrol (ultimately discovering the body). In this short window, Jack murdered Eddowes, cut her throat, produced a large incision from her groin to her chest, removed her kidney and uterus, and added additional, smaller cuts to her face.

As the gruesome nature of the murders and their aftermath spread throughout the city, rumors began circulating that Jack the Ripper was a doctor by trade. Onlookers agreed that the nature of the mutilations indicated a pure, unyielding hatred for at least sex workers, if not women as a whole. Jack's penchant for mutilations earned him an early nickname of the Whitechapel Butcher, which predated his more famous moniker.

One of the lesser-known interesting facts about the case is that police were aided in their investigation by a local committee formed in September 1888. The group of concerned citizens served as somewhat of a neighborhood watch and fundraised so that authorities could offer a monetary reward for information leading to the murderer's identity and capture. Unemployed men were hired to monitor the streets at night. This "Mile End Vigilance Committee" was run by local builder George Lusk, who quickly became a small-town celebrity.

Soon, Jack the Ripper began taunting both the committee and the police . . . or so we think. Scotland Yard was suddenly on the receiving end of numerous letters allegedly authored by the vicious murderer, with the letters' contents foreshadowing future attacks. In retrospect, it's unclear how many of these letters, if any, were actually penned by Jack.

The letter that appeared to be most legitimate arrived alongside a specimen: a piece of human kidney preserved in ethanol. A hospital examiner determined it had been removed from a woman, around forty-five years of age, sometime within the preceding three weeks. This assessment accorded with the age (forty-six) and death date of Catherine Eddowes.

In the accompanying letter, the author claimed to have consumed the other half of the kidney and was considering sending a bloody knife to the police. This letter, addressed to Lusk and purporting to be sent "From Hell," contained many curious misspellings, including the word "kidney," which seemed to be an unlikely mistake for a medical professional or student—the killer's presumed profession. Still, police and medical practitioners believed the letter and kidney were sent as part of a sick prank conducted by a medical student living nearby.

Despite questions surrounding their legitimacy, the letters proved influential to the case, even giving the Whitechapel Butcher his better-known pseudonym. The "Dear Boss" letter, sent to a local news outlet, was written in red ink and boasted about all the murders committed up until that point. The letter was signed "Jack the Ripper," and the police opted to share the letter's contents with the public. The moniker stuck.

But that wasn't the only effect of the letter's publication. By revealing the correspondence to the masses, the police jeopardized their ability to advance the investigation. That's because seeing the letter inspired a whole host of bored or troublemaking citizens to author their own fake letters and send them to authorities, making it next to impossible to identify which were real and which were counterfeit. To make matters worse, the Dear Boss letter was soon thought to be a hoax itself, penned by a journalist seeking attention.

Despite the frenzy surrounding them, Jack's murders ceased just as abruptly as they had begun, and while no one knows why, many theories have been suggested. These include suppositions that the murderer died either by suicide or by some other means, that he was imprisoned or institutionalized for a reason *other* than being Jack the Ripper, or that he fled the city—perhaps even the country.

Nonetheless, the investigation continued—and found very little success. It suffered from scarce quantity and quality of evidence, rampant misinformation, and unreliable witness testimony. Another confounding factor was that crime scene investigation wasn't much of a thing in the late-nineteenth century, so catching a killer largely relied on being able to identify personal effects left at the scene (assuming an eyewitness didn't literally *observe* the murderer committing the crime).

It's worth noting that while fingerprinting was a known technique at the time of Jack the Ripper's murders, it wasn't until 1905 that the first-ever criminal conviction was made using fingerprint evidence. Plus, genetic analysis of blood samples found at a crime scene was not yet possible, meaning blood evidence was largely useless. Another obstacle was the inexplicable fact that many people apparently enjoyed falsely admitting to Jack's crimes.

As London's Autumn of Terror progressed, each subsequent murder's inquest became the talk of the town, with coverage appearing in local newspapers ranging from the *Daily Telegraph* to *The Times*. London's most popular outlet, the *Star*, was selling up to three hundred thousand copies every day at the height of the Jack panic. Perhaps by necessity, each paper tended to take a slightly different angle when covering the crimes. For example, the *Daily Chronicle* and *The Times* explored the outcast nature of the victims, while the *East London Observer* took a more sympathetic tone, particularly after sending a reporter to witness the condition of Polly Nichols's body.

Even so, nearly all the newspapers made a final assessment that was aligned with popular discourse at the time—one that would attract vehement disagreement today. The journalists concluded that as sex workers, the victims put themselves in a position to be violently murdered and (to use a phrase that's rightfully lambasted in the modern era) were effectively "asking for it." In covering the stories, the newspapers were sure to add details regarding whether the women were thought to be alcoholics or otherwise seen as "lesser than" members of society.

The press coverage spread far and wide across the city, creating a story onto which rampant fears and prejudices of the time could be easily projected. For example, antisemitism and xenophobia loomed large, and many accused perpetrators would end up being Jewish or immigrants. Unfortunately, these sentiments were not new, having risen substantially after journalist Henry Mayhew's 1840 publication of *London Labour and the London Poor*, which generalized the inhabitants of the Whitechapel community as "a strange amalgamation of Jews, French, Germans, and other antagonistic elements" and deemed them "suspicious."

Among the many horrible impacts of Jack's crimes, one positive outcome rises to the fore. (After all, if anything even remotely beneficial can come of such a terrible series of events, it's certainly worth taking a moment to consider.) In this case, the situation in Whitechapel forced London's elite to finally pay attention to the impoverished East End. A nation celebrating its economic heyday under Queen Victoria was plagued by a bona fide serial killer, and there was seemingly nothing anyone could do about it. It was a forceful shove back to reality, and it led to a contingent of community members beginning to seek social reform for Londoners facing poverty.

But that's officially where the good news begins *and* ends. Reports of Jack the Ripper quickly spilled beyond British borders and inspired copycat killings. By December 1888, a month after the murders ceased in London, hysteria—and possibly Jack himself—had crossed the Atlantic Ocean. A murderer in Philadelphia, Pennsylvania, reportedly replicated or even expanded upon Jack's practices, dismembering victims and separating the body parts into distinct packages. Back in Europe, numerous public figures received letters claiming that Jack would soon strike in Belgium. As late as April 1891—several years after the killer's last known attack—New York police reportedly believed he or his copycat were to blame for a local murder spree.

LISTEN TO RILEY

The story of Jack the Ripper is a classic case of whodunit, though it's perhaps grislier than your typical mystery. To this day, the identity and motive of Jack have never been definitively clarified, yet more than one hundred people have been either suspected or accused since 1888. Unfortunately, all leads quickly fizzled out shortly after the killings ceased, and efforts to explain the cases seemed unsatisfactory in one way or another. Maybe this is why Jack the Ripper remains one of the most notorious unidentified serial killers in history, with the cases surrounding his murders being officially closed in 1892.

Naturally, this hasn't stopped the public from speculating, and some speculations have been more grounded in the initial investigation than others. For example, the Macnaghten Memoranda, an official document sent to Scotland Yard by Chief Constable Sir Melville Leslie Macnaghten, pointed to three prime suspects, all of whom were accused because of prejudices running rampant within society.

The first suspect identified in the Macnaghten Memoranda was Montague John Druitt, a barrister and assistant schoolmaster. Fingers pointed at Druitt because he was suspected of homosexuality (many people believe this is why he was dismissed from the school where he worked), and in late-1800s London, gay men were considered mentally unsound. In addition to the social stigma surrounding Druitt, he also disappeared shortly after the last Jack the Ripper murder occurred and was later found drowned.

Michael Ostrog, a Russian doctor, convicted thief, and patient at a mental hospital, was the second suspect noted in the memoranda.

Aaron Kosminski was identified as the third and final suspect. At twenty-three years of age, Kosminski was a Jewish, Polish immigrant who worked as a barber. He spent much of his life in and out of mental institutions and was widely believed to hate women—and particularly sex workers.

Interestingly, recent DNA analysis of blood recovered from a shawl purportedly found next to Catherine Eddowes's body added fuel to Kosminski's accusation. As the story goes, the shawl disappeared for years because it had been stashed away by the wife of a Scotland Yard sergeant and remained untouched for years. Apparently, the sergeant had gifted the shawl to his wife after soliciting permission from the relevant authorities, and it was subsequently passed down in the family for generations. It wasn't until 2007 that the shawl reappeared to the public at auction.

In 2014, the person who won the auctioned scarf revealed they had conducted DNA testing on blood samples that still tainted the article after all these years. They printed the test results in a book, stating that the mitochondrial DNA, examined by credentialed researchers, was a positive match to descendants of both Eddowes and Kosminski. The book also suggested the researchers found evidence of organ damage "consistent with kidney removal." It wasn't until 2019 that the results were further published in a scientific journal.

The implication that the data prove Kosminski's guilt has been widely contested. The methodology of the study has been called into question, since mitochondrial DNA should theoretically only exonerate suspects, not prove a match. Furthermore, given that the scarf had disappeared for more than a century and had presumably not been preserved in any way, the samples had probably been contaminated, not to mention no one could actually confirm the scarf was at the scene of Eddowes's murder.

Many have doubted that Eddowes would have owned such a scarf to begin with, since it was of high quality and she was poor. To further examine this wrinkle, the fibers of the scarf were studied and found to be consistent with fabrics manufactured near St. Petersburg, Russia; Kosminski's Polish homeland was a region under Russian control. Needless to say, the jury is still proverbially out regarding whether Kosminski committed the murders, and the twenty-first century analysis of this mysterious scarf begs the question as to whether additional pieces of dubious evidence may reveal themselves in the future.

For better or worse, suspects were not confined to those identified in the Macnaghten Memoranda. Another name that floated in the ether was Francis Spurzheim Craig, the estranged husband of Jack the Ripper's fifth victim, Mary Jane Kelly. Craig worked as a courtroom reporter during the inquest for one of the earlier murders, and some have suspected he conducted the first four killings to throw suspicion away from himself as he pursued his one true target: Kelly. Craig would eventually die by suicide, slashing his own throat in a manner that was strikingly similar to how Jack's victims were found.

Another variation of this theory suggests the murderer was Joseph Barnett, the man who lived with Kelly at the time of her death. Barnett butchered fish for a living and supposedly matched the physical and psychological profiles associated with the killer. Whether Barnett or Craig was the guilty party—and indeed whether the string of killings revolved in some way around Kelly—remains uncertain. Like most of the accused in this case, only speculation links either of the men to the crimes.

Circumstantial evidence was and still is the name of the game when attempting to link historical figures with Jack the Ripper's modus operandi. For instance, barber George Chapman was a known murderer, having been convicted of poisoning three of his common-law wives, and his schedule was said to have accorded with Jack's. He worked during the day, and he had some amount of physician training. George Chapman even departed for America around the time the murders stopped. But these facts are all circumstantial—perhaps just coincidental—and naysayers have pointed out that his killing method of choice, poisoning, was vastly different than Jack's.

Some theories ventured into the outlandish but, because of the scandal they implied, were heavily favored by the press. One such accusation landed on Prince Albert Victor, Duke of Clarence and grandson of Queen Victoria. According to the local rumor mill, Prince Albert Victor had an illegitimate child in Whitechapel, so the royal family sought to do away with the child and anyone who knew of its existence. A different version of this story was that the prince suffered from syphilis, which affected his mental capacities and incited him to commit the murders. While no tangible evidence supported these tales, newspapers (and later a graphic novel by Alan Moore) enjoyed sharing them.

At least some people believe Jack the Ripper was actually Jill. The "Jill the Ripper" theory—which states that the murderer, or at least his scribe, was a woman—is supported by modern DNA analysis of the case's famous letters (at least some of which may have been real). However, most experts agree that a woman would have been physically incapable of committing the murders, since the killer would have needed extreme strength to overpower the victims so swiftly.

A theory that has emerged in more recent years suggests that H. H. Holmes, America's first known serial killer, was behind the Jack the Ripper murders. No one knows exactly how many people Holmes killed in the United States in the late 1800s, but the true number could be upward of two hundred. Holmes had fashioned a "murder castle" during the Chicago World's Fair in 1893, and it housed innumerable torture devices, implements with which to conduct mutilations, and tools needed to destroy criminal evidence.

The first person to publicly suspect that Holmes and Jack the Ripper could be one and the same was Holmes's own descendant. A great-great-grandson pointed out that not only had Holmes received medical training at the University of Michigan, but analysis of the "Dear Boss" letter revealed an exact match to Holmes's handwriting. The descendant also suggested that diary entries by Holmes may connect him to the Whitechapel murders.

> **Riley's Next Hunt:** Jack the Ripper's letters contain clues to his identity and exhibit numerous peculiarities, but maybe those oddities weren't accidental. Could Riley find a different kind of clue—a cipher, perhaps—concealed within Jack's notes?

It would be impossible to efficiently analyze every accusation that has ever been made in the Jack the Ripper file, especially since those accusations span more than a century of time. But to demonstrate the sheer breadth of people tied—erroneously or not—to the case, consider this brief sampling. Walter Sickert, an English artist of the Victorian era, was allegedly connected to Jack's letters via DNA evidence and, even more shockingly, based on the subject matter of his paintings. Then there was Robert Mann, the Whitechapel mortician whose only known connection to the cases was the fact that he examined the bodies of the victims. On the more famous side, Charles Dodgson, better known by pseudonym Lewis Carroll of *Alice's Adventures in Wonderland* (1865) fame, was suspected of having integrated anagrams related to Jack's murders in his books.

Fascination with the case, alongside an overall sense of dissatisfaction with its outcomes, led the US Federal Bureau of Investigation (FBI) to develop a psychological profile of the killer in 1986. It was hoped that a profile crafted using modern techniques would allow for a more effective comparison to records of known individuals at the time of the murders. The profiling process included considerations like geography, motive, requisite knowledge, and emotional factors.

Based on this process, the FBI predicted Jack was a single white man between the ages of twenty-eight and thirty-six. He was never married and had no remarkable features, lending him an ability to blend in with a crowd. From a personality perspective, he was likely withdrawn and antisocial. He was probably poor and *definitely* hated women. It has also been suggested that Jack was employed in a daily job, given that his murders never occurred during standard working hours. Potentially complicating matters, the profile indicated Jack would not be one to challenge authority figures, which means he never would have taunted them via letters.

After the profile was developed, the FBI conducted comparisons with the many suspects who lived in the late 1880s. They noted strong similarities to a suspect of American origin, Francis Tumblety, who traveled to England just two months prior to Jack the Ripper's first crime and returned to the United States shortly after the final murder. Since he was staying in Whitechapel while in London, Tumblety would have had the necessary spatial awareness to commit the crimes, and he was believed to have left his wife after finding out she was a sex worker. Plus, his job as a medical assistant meant he could perform surgical dissections with precision, and he was known to carry surgical knives in his trunk.

But over time, Jack the Ripper's medical prowess has increasingly been called into question. Recent analysis of a mortuary sketch of Catherine Eddowes points to Jack being not a doctor, but rather a butcher or someone who worked at a slaughterhouse. For one thing, the incision to Eddowes's abdomen was made in the opposite direction of one made by a medical professional, alongside other inconsistencies with common surgical practices. And while hasty removal of organs required some degree of anatomical knowledge, a butcher or slaughterer would have been familiar with the subject.

It turns out that several slaughterhouses were operational around Whitechapel, and Jack's first victim's body was found not far from one. Many slaughterhouse employees worked at night and may have known local sex workers due to their mutual odd hours, potentially making the victims less likely to suspect danger. Plus, a man working at a slaughterhouse would have certainly possessed the physical strength necessary to overpower the women in question.

Some have taken additional steps to determine at which slaughterhouse the killer could have worked. Citing the specific type of neck incisions Jack made on his victims, it has been suggested that the murderer was a shohet, someone trained in kosher animal slaughter practices. Shohets are also responsible for examining an animal's organs to ensure no abnormalities are present, meaning they're skilled at locating said organs within the body. Could Jack the Ripper have been a slaughterman—and more specifically, a shohet—or are all these factors simply coincidental?

The unyielding mystery has resulted in the development of an untold number of movies, television series, and books keeping Jack's story alive. And since the popularity of true crime podcasts and related forms of media has grown, there's no chance of Jack the Ripper disappearing from our collective imagination anytime soon. Now all that's left is for an armchair expert to crack the case once and for all.

Chapter 17

Bermuda Triangle

As a "tech guy," **Riley** must have a healthy respect for science. For centuries, the scientific method—meticulous investigations guided by careful hypotheses and culminating in evidence-based conclusions—has helped humanity understand the way the world works. To be fair, gravity (for example) would exist whether or not we knew what it was, but there's still something comforting and empowering about *knowing* why our feet are figuratively glued to the surface of the earth.

Science has given us the lay of the land for such a long time that we've become completely reliant on it to explain everything with which we interact. See, hear, or smell something? Science has had a role in helping you pinpoint the cause. The opposite is also true: if science hasn't explained something, that something is presumed by many people, at least publicly, not to exist.

The two greatest examples of this are the paranormal and the extraterrestrial. If you assert to friends, family members, or coworkers that you have seen either a ghost or a UAP, they'll probably discount your claim at best—or ridicule you mercilessly at worst. I've got to believe Riley knows this from experience.

But as a scientific individual who also dabbles in superstition, Riley would probably also feel the need to defend witnesses of the unexplained: just because science hasn't successfully unraveled certain phenomena, does that really mean they don't exist? What if the way we currently conduct scientific research isn't conducive to laying bare explanations for these strange happenings? If we maintain such a narrow-minded view of what is and what is not, our collective worldview will be shockingly limited.

Until science finds ways to poke, prod, and prove the existence (or nonexistence) of that which we do not understand, those who experience the incomprehensible are left to cope with a new reality. And one of the ways they do that is by sharing their story with believers and skeptics alike—an errand that often leads to some of the juiciest, longest-lasting legends that perpetually occupy our Internet search histories.

One of the most notorious examples of the unexplained is the Bermuda Triangle. In it we find a case that science has failed to satisfyingly close, and individuals, keen to explain away the situation for their own comfort, have responded by crafting their own solution. That solution is a place you'll never see demarcated on a map, but you'll know its name—and location—all the same.

> **Why Riley Would Care:** The Bermuda Triangle combines maritime isolation, mysterious disappearances, paranormal hypotheses, and just about every other ingredient required to cook up a long-lasting legend. From Riley's perspective, what's not to love?

HUNT DOWN THAT HISTORY

The "Bermuda Triangle," a tenuously outlined section of the North Atlantic Ocean, has been known by several turns of phrase. These aliases have ranged from the Devil's Triangle to the Hoodoo Sea to Limbo of the Lost, but its most famous name was adopted in 1964 thanks to an article by Victor Gaddis in science fiction magazine *Argosy*. The boundaries of the five hundred thousand square mile expanse of ocean remain somewhat contested, but the corners of the so-called triangle are generally accepted as eastern Florida (approximately Miami), the Greater Antilles (approximately San Juan, Puerto Rico), and, of course, Bermuda.

Poetically, the Bermuda Triangle first made a name for itself in western records during the voyage that accidentally discovered the New World. Christopher Columbus's expedition traveled along the present-day East Coast of the United States, eventually reaching the Caribbean Sea. The expedition's journals reveal that the crew observed a "great flame of fire," widely believed to be a meteor, falling into the ocean in the vicinity of the Bermuda Triangle. Columbus and his team also recorded inconsistent readings on their compasses while in this region. Since science likes repeatability, we cannot ignore that these magnetic oddities were witnessed as far back as the late fifteenth century (and they'll reemerge in much more recent times, but hold that thought for now).

By 1610, famous playwright and poet William Shakespeare penned *The Tempest*, a play that would first be performed in November of the following year. Many historians and scholars suggest the tale was inspired by a real-life shipwreck occurring off the Bermuda coast. Ships and planes of all shapes and sizes have disappeared within the Bermuda Triangle under mysterious circumstances, with a commonality being the inability of search parties to recover their wreckage. While exact numbers are hard to pinpoint, more than fifty ships and twenty planes have likely met this fate in the region since the mid-1800s.

Riley's Favorite Fact (Probably): Christopher Columbus was the first maritime navigator to report mysterious incidents—including a falling comet and magnetic anomalies—in the Bermuda Triangle region.

An early example of one of these mysterious incidents occurred in 1881 when a ship named *Ellen Austin* was sailing from Liverpool to New York and happened upon a ghost ship fully stocked and floating in the Sargasso Sea. With no obvious reason for the ship to have been abandoned, the *Ellen Austin* crew climbed aboard their find in the hopes of sailing it back to New York for salvage. But according to legend, a storm separated the *Ellen Austin* and the trailing ship, and the next time they met, the mysterious vessel was once again crewless yet chock-full of supplies.

Another Bermuda Triangle story dates back to 1895, when a man named Joshua Slocum found himself lost at sea. What sounds like a simple case of an inexperienced or unprepared sailor meeting an unfortunate end is quickly complicated by the fact that Slocum couldn't possibly be considered inexperienced or unprepared. Slocum was the first person to complete a solo sailing trip around the world, so he really had no business getting lost on a simple journey from Martha's Vineyard to South America. The Bermuda Triangle had struck again, but the public wouldn't really begin latching on to the site's mysteries until the 1900s.

The eye-catching moment that would first grab the public's attention occurred in March 1918. The ship in question was not only a military vessel, the *USS Cyclops*, but it was also—and I cannot emphasize this enough—*massive*. A cargo ship of the US Navy, the *Cyclops* reached over 540 feet in length, housed three hundred crewmen, and carried ten thousand tons of cargo. And at some point on its route between the Chesapeake Bay and Barbados, it sank.

An unfortunate incident to be sure, the capsizing was shrouded in mystery. For starters, the *Cyclops* was a reliable vessel with a robust history. Having been in operation for eight years, the ship had successfully navigated routes between the Baltic Sea, Caribbean Sea, and Mexico on cargo transport and refugee assistance duties. During World War I, it provided troop and coal transit services. When it sank, the *Cyclops* had been completing a routine route from Brazil to Baltimore, toting manganese ore destined for steel manufacture.

Those who are invested in the *Cyclops*'s story are quick to point out that the final signal received from the ship was an unassuming (and yet ominous, given the vessel's fate), "Weather Fair, All Well." The crew never issued a distress signal, and despite exhaustive search, rescue, and eventual recovery efforts, the wreckage was never found. To this day, the sinking of the *USS Cyclops* remains the largest mass-mortality event in the history of the US Navy outside of active combat scenarios.

At the time of the *Cyclops*'s demise, popular opinion contended that a German submarine took out the vessel as part of a World War I attack. But after the war concluded, Germany publicly refuted that claim, stating that none of their submarines or mines were in the vicinity at the time of the ship's disappearance. Others believed whatever happened to the *Cyclops* was the fault of its captain, whose name was mud after being accused of alcoholism and experiencing a mutiny at one point in his career.

What became of the *Cyclops* remains a mystery, but researchers have not failed to suggest answers. One such researcher, a descendant of one of the ship's crewmen, believes a combination of onboard mechanical failures, new cargo (which the crew wasn't familiar with handling), and a large wave tipped over the ship. According to this descendant, if this series of unfortunate events had occurred over the Puerto Rico Trench, whose depths reach 27,500 feet below sea level, the wreckage of the vessel would surely be lost forever. A simpler version of this story is that the ship succumbed to a wicked storm at sea, though if this was the case, it's hard to comprehend why the crew never issued a distress signal.

The case of the *USS Cyclops* is both tragic and intriguing, yet it could easily be chalked up to a freak accident—*if* it was a one-off mystery. But a little over twenty years after the *Cyclops* vanished, two similar vessels disappeared under comparable circumstances while traveling a nearly identical route. The first was the *USS Proteus*, which carried fifty-eight people and cargo of ore on a journey from St. Thomas to the East Coast of the United States in 1941. Then, just a month later, the *USS Nereus* and its sixty-one crew members vanished.

But the tales of the Bermuda Triangle extend beyond the maritime. In late 1945, several military planes disappeared in the region. A set of five TBM Avengers—navy torpedo bombers collectively known as "Flight 19"—departed from Fort Lauderdale, Florida, on a training mission that was set to last three hours. During their flight, they planned to drop fake bombs in a preconfigured formation.

There was nothing unusual about the planes' flight path, which was itself triangular and involved navigating east from Fort Lauderdale, releasing the bomb stand-ins at Hens and Chickens Shoals, turning north over the Bahamas, and finally returning to the origin point. Flight 19's crew, all members of the US Navy and Marines, were experienced navigators. This included the training mission's leader, Lieutenant Charles C. Taylor, who had gained repute while serving in World War II.

The beginning of the mission went off without a hitch. The practice bombs were dropped, and the planes turned north according to plan. But before long, the cohort became inexplicably yet hopelessly lost, prompted by strange readings on Lieutenant Taylor's compass and the onset of a sudden storm. Despite explicit instructions to do so from their ground-based team, those aboard the planes failed to turn on their ZBX receivers, which would have collected stable signals from terrestrial US Navy radio towers and helped them navigate back to home base.

In the moments that followed, Lieutenant Taylor made some questionable leadership decisions, including refusing to abide by standard protocols for lost planes over the Atlantic Ocean (i.e., using the sun as a guide to fly west, which would help the planes reach land). It is widely believed Taylor thought he was flying over the Gulf of Mexico, which was his rationale for turning *east* instead. But Taylor was terribly wrong, and the planes headed out over the open ocean (as evidenced by the crew's radio signal becoming increasingly faint).

As the planes flew farther and farther out of range, their last communications trickled into the receivers of the Fort Lauderdale team. The final transmissions paint a grim, eerie picture in which Lieutenant Taylor instructed all five planes to crash into the Atlantic Ocean as soon as one plane's fuel reserves dipped below ten gallons. The next transmission consisted of only static.

Two rescue planes were immediately deployed, but one of them was just as doomed (superstitious folks might say "cursed") as Flight 19 itself. This rescue plane, a PBM Mariner, as well as its thirteen onboard crewmen, immediately vanished without a trace. A closer examination suggests that shortly after takeoff, the PBM Mariner exploded in midair; it turns out this type of seaplane was known to catch fire. A nearby ship later claimed to have witnessed a "fireball" in the sky, and when the ship passed the fireball's location, the crew noticed an oil slick on the water—taken as evidence of the PBM Mariner's fate.

But this unlucky instance didn't prevent the rescue mission from continuing. More than three hundred boats and aircraft were deployed to search for survivors, victims, and wreckage of both Flight 19 and the PBM Mariner. The convoy scoured three hundred thousand square miles yet failed to locate any evidence of the planes or their crews. In a frustrating final report on the incident, the US Navy seemed baffled, asserting that it was "as if [the planes] had flown to Mars." Adding to the incredulity was the fact that Navy investigators could never pinpoint an exact reason why Lieutenant Taylor became irrevocably disoriented during the training mission.

Between the time of Flight 19's disappearance and the establishment of the Bermuda Triangle moniker in 1964, plenty more mysterious incidents occurred in this portion of ocean. The list includes the crashes of three passenger planes (all of which transmitted no issues during their radio communications) in 1948 and 1949. And in February 1963, the *SS Marine Sulphur Queen*, a tanker hauling molten sulfur, sank off the coast of Key West, Florida, while traveling from Texas to Virginia. You guessed it: no distress signal was sent, its wreckage and crewmen's bodies were never found, and a cause was never identified.

For completeness, it's worth noting that the case of the *SS Marine*

Sulphur Queen exhibits some distinctions from the rest. For instance, a few of its life preservers were found bobbing in the ocean (so there's at least one tiny piece of evidence that the ship didn't disappear into thin air), and the area in which it sank is rife with sharks and barracuda (potentially explaining the lack of recovered bodies). Some are also quick to point to the ship's cargo as the reason for its demise, postulating that sulfur gas leaked from the tanks onboard, poisoning the crew and rendering them unable to issue a distress signal before the ship exploded. This theory is supported by the observations of a nearby Honduran boat crew, who reported an "acrid" scent characteristic of a sulfur explosion on the day of the *SS Marine Sulphur Queen*'s disappearance.

Collectively, these stories represent just a sampling of the purported power of the Bermuda Triangle. Some believers even assert that the triangle can influence people in addition to vessels. For example, in August 1969, the only two inhabitants of Great Isaac Rock in the Bahamas seemed to disappear. These individuals were the keepers of the island's lighthouse, and after several calls to the lighthouse were left unanswered, a boat was sent to check on the duo. But no one was home, the residence exhibited no damage, and no evidence of foul play was detected. While the superstitious chalk up this disappearance to the Bermuda Triangle, others believe the lighthouse keepers perished in a storm (to which the superstitious reply, *why wasn't their house damaged?*).

Officially, according to the US National Oceanic and Atmospheric Administration, the swath of ocean comprising the Bermuda Triangle does not exhibit unusual occurrences—including lost ships or planes—at rates that exceed other highly traversed open waters. Additionally, Lloyd's of London, a global leader in the issuance of maritime insurance, does not implement high-hazard rates for ships passing through the region. In other words, if money talks, it doesn't have much to say about the perceived dangers of the Bermuda Triangle.

Believe it or not, these governmental and economic assertions are borne out by evidence. A World Wildlife Fund study conducted in 2013 concluded that the Bermuda Triangle doesn't even make the top ten list of most dangerous water bodies in the maritime shipping industry. Indeed, plenty of brave souls pass through the region daily without encountering a single challenge, and that's a distinctly good thing since the Bermuda Triangle is part of a popular route for ships traveling between the US East Coast and the Gulf of Mexico. So inconsequential is the Bermuda Triangle to navigators that the region isn't even recognized on any official maps.

LISTEN TO RILEY

Despite these official rulings, to most onlookers, the Bermuda Triangle represents a case of concentric mysteries. At the forefront is understanding what happened to the many vessels that vanished without a trace in or over its waters. But having already discussed the leading theories (or lack thereof) for each of the triangle's most famous disappearances, we must now turn our attention to a broader question. Even if these strange occurrences are not happening more frequently in the Bermuda Triangle than in other locations, why are they happening at all?

In pop culture, supernatural explanations have long taken center stage. Extraterrestrials are the most commonly invoked paranormal culprits, as believers suggest the Bermuda Triangle is a portal used by aliens to reach Earth. Once arrived, these theories contend, the aliens kidnap people and ships, taking them back to their home planets for study or observation. Another supernatural conspiracy theory suggests the lost city of Atlantis sits in the ocean depths beneath the Bermuda Triangle and sucks ships and planes toward it. Other variants include sea creatures snatching vessels from the ocean's surface, wormholes transporting them to other dimensions, or reverse gravity sending them hurtling into space.

Supernatural assertions like these accompany just about any half decent legend or conspiracy theory. When considering the Bermuda Triangle, they seem particularly popular because the vessels in question didn't just vanish—they vanished *without a trace*. Most shipwrecks or downed planes result in the discovery of at least some small debris, but that hasn't typically been the case for vessels that have been victimized by the Bermuda Triangle.

Of course, scientists have also tried their hands at devising a satisfactory, nonsupernatural explanation for the mysterious incidents surrounding this swath of sea. And while many agree that geophysical and environmental explanations likely offer the truth, so many of them exist that it's next to impossible to know which account is correct (or, at minimum, which is the least wrong).

One of the most common geophysical explanations is that

aberrations in the earth's magnetic field are commonplace in this region, detrimentally affecting navigators' instruments. (Remember what we learned from Christopher Columbus's expedition journals?) Yet the US Navy's "Project Magnet," which has surveyed magnetic fields at different latitudes and longitudes for decades, insists it has never recorded strange magnetic readings in the Bermuda Triangle despite having recorded data in the area on hundreds of occasions.

An alternative magnetism-related rationale invokes the eightieth meridian, also known as the agonic line. Along this longitudinal line, which passes near or through the Bermuda Triangle, magnetic north and true north are fully aligned. What does this mean in practice? If the ships' captains and planes' pilots had accidentally ignored this reality—failing to consider impacts on their compasses—they may have strayed significantly off course and eventually capsized.

In support of this theory, odd events have been reported at the only other location on Earth affected by the agonic line. Visualize the line extending north from the Bermuda Triangle, passing through the North Pole, and then extending south into the Eastern Hemisphere. Here, a part of the Pacific Ocean slightly east of Japan just so happens to be the location of "Devil Sea," nicknamed as such by Japanese and Filipino ship captains based on the host of strange happenings that have been recorded there.

Magnetism isn't the only possible natural antagonist in this story. One environmental explanation includes methane emissions spewing out of the seafloor. When a pocket of methane shakes loose from the bottom of the ocean, methane bubbles rise to the surface and can reduce the density of the surrounding surface water, causing boats (or other objects) floating nearby to sink. Furthermore, if a plane encountered a methane mass midair, it could explode. Even so, these methane eruptions are incredibly rare, and we have no real reason to believe they would happen with greater frequency in the Bermuda Triangle region. Indeed, the last known methane release from this area occurred fifteen thousand years ago.

While magnetism and methane provide attractive solutions, the most popular theories to explain away the Bermuda Triangle's unyielding mysteries involve extreme weather events. For starters, most tropical storms and hurricanes originating in the Atlantic Ocean pass straight through the region in question. Back in the day, before weather forecasting was as good as it is now (which is saying something, since it's still pretty bad), unexpected storms capsized ships with ease.

Even today, while large, well-tracked storms can be documented, forecast, and ultimately planned around (if you're the seafaring type), smaller but equally intense incidents called meso-meteorological storms can crop up at a moment's notice. Meso-meteorological storms can span several miles at sea, and they're known to disappear just as quickly as they begin—leaving very little evidence of having ever occurred in the first place. Making the case even more compelling is the fact that these storms are exceedingly common over the Gulf Stream, a powerful ocean current that passes through the Bermuda Triangle.

> **Riley's Next Hunt:** In its adamance to distance itself from the supernatural, *National Treasure* could shed light on the Bermuda Triangle's environmental phenomena by having Riley and team contend with magnetic anomalies or severe storms during their next treasure hunt.

Another very real danger of the region is the rogue wave. Reaching up to one hundred feet in height in the middle of the ocean, rogue waves are most likely to form in locations where storms converge from multiple directions. And yes, this absolutely describes the Bermuda Triangle, where storms arrive from Mexico in the west, the equator down south, and the open Atlantic Ocean in the east.

If a rogue wave encounters an unfortunate ship or even a low-flying plane, it could not only bring the vessel crashing into the ocean, but it could also swallow up any evidence of the vessel having been there at all. Advocates of the rogue wave theory point out that large tankers and cargo ships have also disappeared off the coast of South Africa, another destination where rogue waves are common due to the convergence of the Atlantic, Indian, and Antarctic Oceans.

But storms and rogue waves are matched by a third natural danger in the Bermuda Triangle: waterspouts. Waterspouts are basically tornadoes that suck water out of the ocean to generate a cyclone in midair—potentially thousands of feet above the surface. Taken together, these extreme weather events made the Bermuda Triangle a terribly difficult place to navigate before the modern era. To make matters worse, the region is filled with islands of all sizes, meaning the local ocean depth shifts from extremely deep to extremely shallow over small distances.

Navigational obstacles abound.

There remains, however, the question of where the ships' and planes' wrecks may have ended up if they were never found (assuming that rogue waves weren't responsible for swallowing them all whole). Like the descendant of the *USS Cyclops* crewman, many researchers have pointed to the Puerto Rico Trench as the debris' final resting place, while others have suggested the Gulf Stream quickly carried any floating materials away. All in all, it's safe to say that a fatal combination of environmental conditions and human error could easily have caused most—if not all—of the infamous disappearances attributed to the Bermuda Triangle.

If we've all but solved *that* mystery, how about we consider a smaller but equally curious one? Of all the water bodies in the world, why has the Bermuda Triangle gained so much misplaced attention as a hotspot for ship disappearances? Perhaps this has something to do with the tourist-heavy nature of the region in question, which would inherently result in more attention to what is going on—or what has gone on—nearby. Plus, as previously discussed, the Bermuda Triangle is heavily traversed by ships and planes. Based on probability alone, the more ships and planes navigate a given area, the more emergency events happen there (even if the percentage of emergencies isn't significantly greater than in other locations).

Then there's the psychology of the situation, which we used to launch this very chapter. Very little concrete scientific research has been done to understand the Bermuda Triangle's historical anomalies. As a result, curiosity and imagination have been left to fill in the blanks, and those blanks seem to get bigger with confirmation bias. In other words, once we become familiar with or notice something (for instance, ships sinking in the Bermuda Triangle), we witness more and more instances of that thing in our daily lives. The result is an illusion that the event in question is incredibly common, when in reality we've just subconsciously trained ourselves to notice it. This is known as the Baader-Meinhof effect.

To prove my point, consider this: unless you live in the Last Frontier, I bet you've never heard of the *Alaska Triangle*. It has received far less publicity over the years (probably because it's located in such a remote place), and as a result we aren't trained to identify its incidents.

The Alaska Triangle is a vast wooded region roughly bordered by Anchorage, Utqiagvik, and Juneau. Upward of twenty thousand locals and tourists alike have mysteriously disappeared here since the 1970s, while many planes have vanished in its airspace. The wrecks of these planes and the bodies of the victims tend not to be located—a situation that is reminiscent of the Bermuda Triangle.

Case in point was the plane crash of US Representative Hale Boggs in October 1972. Expansive search and rescue efforts were immediately deployed to the Alaska Triangle in search of the wreck, and when they came up empty, conspiracy theories emerged to explain away the conundrum. One such theory suggested Boggs was murdered because he publicly disagreed with the Warren Commission's verdict on the assassination of President John F. Kennedy. We can always count on conspiracy theories to fill voids left by our understanding of reality.

Like the Bermuda Triangle, the Alaska Triangle has been the site of numerous military aircraft disappearances. Unlike the Bermuda Triangle, the Alaska Triangle actually offers a fraction of evidence in support of extraterrestrial explanations. A Japan Airlines flight passing over the area once purported to witness three UAP, whose existence in the nearby airspace was later confirmed by civilian and military radar. Beyond the supernatural, it's also intriguing to note that magnetic variations and compass errors have been recorded in the Alaska Triangle for years, and locals and tourists have reported feeling disoriented (a common reaction to electromagnetic anomalies).

In the end, however, just as the Bermuda Triangle is home to seemingly every type of open-water weather oddity, the Alaska Triangle has its own perilous nature to contend with: open wilderness. The parallels continue, because the Bermuda Triangle's ability to hide its wreckage in deep ocean waters is matched by the Alaska Triangle stashing its own collections in hidden caves and crevasses. These terrestrial chambers could easily swallow up entire planes and certainly the bodies of unfortunate passers-by, who probably wouldn't be located by search parties before succumbing to injuries, hunger, or the elements.

While it may be tempting to do so, it would be quite unwise to assume the many mysterious occurrences of the Bermuda Triangle (and even its Alaskan counterpart) can be chalked up to a single explanation. After all, each of these incidents was probably nothing more than an accident, and we don't traditionally assume *other* accidents that happen in one place—like a city or country—have the same underlying cause. The next time a ship disappears in the Bermuda Triangle, we'd all do well to remember that correlation does not necessarily equal causation.

Chapter 18

Camp David

As evidenced by some of our previous discussions, history's most compelling mysteries are often shrouded in seclusion and privacy. In situations where even a few concrete details are available, well, that's when fascination blends into *speculation*. I still remember growing up near neighborhoods inhabited by professional athletes, and rolling past their properties was a rite of passage when you were issued your first driver's license. Part of it was the novelty of driving the car, for sure, but wondering what went on beyond the gates was equally compelling.

Famous athletes, actors, and other celebrities certainly attract curiosity from onlookers, but so do politicians and other well-known leaders. In some ways, fascination with these figures could be rooted in concern for world affairs. After all, while policies and laws become known to citizens after they've been developed, far fewer people have an understanding of or appreciation for how those policies or laws came to be.

This is its own mystery locked behind a figurative fence, though I suppose one could substitute the fence surrounding the White House as a tangible stand-in. When onlookers or commentators think about the people and situations shaping society, the White House naturally comes to mind. What these individuals fail to realize is that quintessential conversations influencing policy happen in innumerable locations, including a specific one that has largely flown under the radar because of its geographic seclusion and utter privacy. After all, Camp David, as it's currently known, is not open to the public.

Camp David has existed for decades, but very few Americans know how integral it has been to US presidents and their policymaking. Not only is it situated in a nondescript place (just far enough away from the nation's capital to offer isolation, yet close enough for ease of transit), but it provides a unique environment compared to that of 1600 Pennsylvania Avenue.

As its name suggests, Camp David offers an informal, recreational setting, which is not an atmosphere most people would associate with a president of the United States. In fact, I'd venture to say that most citizens fail to think of the president as a real person—someone with a life and hobbies outside of sitting behind the Resolute desk. It's understandably jarring to imagine said person partaking in those hobbies in the middle of the wilderness, potentially accompanied by other world leaders. It's even more jarring to think of these meetings facilitating policy discussions that may shape geopolitics for decades to come.

> **Why Riley Would Care:** Stepping onto the grounds of Camp David—figuratively, of course—would help Riley get into the minds of world leaders and understand how they've used strategic secrecy to cement geopolitical deals.

HUNT DOWN THAT HISTORY

In Frederick County, Maryland, located approximately sixty-four miles northwest of Washington, D.C., sits a two-hundred-acre private retreat within Catoctin Mountain Park, a wildlife reserve managed by the US National Park Service. Nearby you'll find several sites of historic significance, including the Gettysburg and Antietam Battlefields. The retreat itself is reserved for use by the current president of the United States, which is why President John F. Kennedy departed from the site to visit the local battlefields during one of his stays at this so-called Camp David.

Camp David's origins are shockingly modest. In 1935, the Works Progress Administration acquired the land to develop a retreat for federal employees and their families. Construction of the original buildings on the multisite property, called the Catoctin Recreational Demonstration Area Project, concluded in 1938. The portion of the property that would eventually become Camp David was known as Camp Hi-Catoctin.

From the outset, the concept of establishing a recreational area for federal employees was certainly an interesting one that we haven't quite seen the likes of since. But at the time, the site was meant to serve as a case study, demonstrating how barren land that had been depleted or degraded by industrialism could be repurposed and made useful once again. Things were off to a swimming start in 1937 when the retreat first opened its proverbial doors to federal employees in the D.C.-Maryland-Virginia area, but the onset of World War II shuttered the facility almost immediately.

> **Riley's Favorite Fact (Probably):** Camp David originated as a short-lived retreat for federal workers; the retreat was established to demonstrate how land depleted by industrialization could be rejuvenated and used productively.

Up until this point, each president had his own preferred method and destination for relaxing and even strategizing beyond the White House grounds. Before World War II, President Franklin Delano Roosevelt, for instance, typically unwound on a presidential yacht, the *USS Potomac*, which sailed along the nearby Potomac River. However, once the war broke out, security officials grew increasingly concerned with the president being a sitting duck on open water (literally and figuratively), since the Germans had proven themselves skilled planners of U-boat attacks.

This prompted President Roosevelt to assign the National Park Service an interesting task: identify suitable properties within one hundred miles of the White House that could theoretically be transformed into a presidential hangout. The National Park Service's survey turned up a few options, including one in Virginia's Shenandoah National Park and two in Maryland's Catoctin Mountain Park. President Roosevelt eventually selected the site at Camp Hi-Catoctin in April 1942.

It was said that President Roosevelt was influenced by his doctors when choosing which of the sites would be the best location for his retreat. To benefit his health, Roosevelt was advised to spend more time in cooler locations and at higher altitudes. Camp Hi-Catoctin certainly fit this description, sitting seventeen hundred feet above sea level and boasting an overall climate that was significantly cooler and less humid than the daily conditions in the nation's capital.

What followed was an all-out retrofitting of the already new facilities, making the camp less tailored to a federal workforce audience and more suitable to the needs of a sitting president. The site was transformed into an official Navy installation (since it was functionally taking the place of the seafaring *USS Potomac*) known as the Naval Support Facility Thurmont; this allowed the US Navy to take over day-to-day operations. The staff that previously tended to the presidential yacht followed President Roosevelt to his new digs on dry land.

The makeover of the site was extensive. President Roosevelt requested more than $18,600 worth of renovations, which included ample accessibility features to permit easy use of his wheelchair. The military installed security measures and communications equipment. Roosevelt gave the site its first name, Shangri-La, based on a tranquil mountain utopia described in British novelist James Hilton's book *Lost Horizon* (1933). Roosevelt also assigned nicknames to Shangri-La's many buildings, such as the Bear's Den (main lodge), Soap Dish (laundry house), and Baker Street Urchins (Secret Service outpost).

Perhaps Roosevelt's comfort at the site was based on its aesthetic familiarity, since he designed the Bear's Den to resemble his family vacation home in Georgia. He would ultimately visit Shangri-La more than twenty times throughout his lengthy presidency, and the site has been utilized by every US president since its establishment. Adding to its mystique is the fact that the US government never spoke publicly about the location until after World War II.

Shangri-La did not become the official retreat of the president until 1945 under the tenure of President Harry S. Truman. It was Truman who had the site designated as a permanent facility of the US government, despite using the site himself only a handful of times throughout his administration. When President Dwight D. Eisenhower took office in 1953, he initiated an effort to offload as many superfluous government-owned properties as possible, and Shangri-La was on the chopping block. But when his attorney general, Herbert Brownell, paid a visit for a routine inspection, he completely fell in love with the place and implored President Eisenhower to reconsider.

In the end, Attorney General Brownell should be given at least some credit for the fact that the site still exists today, because President Eisenhower granted his request. Eisenhower went on to make numerous changes to the retreat, most notably replacing the name Shangri-La (which he deemed too fancy) with Camp David, chosen in honor of his five-year-old grandson, Dwight David Eisenhower II. Additional modifications made to Camp David during Eisenhower's tenure were both pragmatic and luxurious, ranging from construction of a bomb shelter to installation of a three-hole golf course.

Eisenhower also called for the addition of a helipad, as he was the first president to commute from the White House to Camp David by chopper. Taking merely half an hour, this modern means of transportation was significantly more efficient than driving (shout-out to D.C. traffic, a timeless tradition that unites generations). Given that President Eisenhower nearly eliminated the site from existence, it's funny that his administration's fingerprints are all over Camp David. For example, First Lady Mamie Eisenhower bestowed the name "Aspen" upon the presidential cabin, which retains this moniker even today.

As a destination, Camp David is quite different than what most people would expect from a site servicing the president of the United States. Despite its myriad amenities, it is, at its core, a rustic woodland retreat. In addition to the presidential cabin, Camp David includes twelve guest cabins, a swimming pool, and the main lodge (Laurel Lodge), which itself houses meeting rooms, a dining room, and an office. All the site's cabins are single story.

Each building at Camp David has its own unique flavor. Hickory Lodge, for example, contains numerous communal spaces, including a grill, bar, and even a gift shop (which personally blows my mind, since the retreat is not publicly accessible). Recreational space is also available at Holly Cabin alongside its small meeting rooms.

Entertainment opportunities at Camp David are varied and benefit from the fact that the site is located in the middle of nowhere on top of a mountain. Outdoor options include hiking, basketball, horseshoes, skeet shooting, and cycling. But if outdoor activities aren't their vibe, or if the weather is poor, the president can also make use of a private movie theater, game room, pool tables, bowling alley, fitness center, and library.

Based on these ample choices, it's probably obvious that the site is rather large, so golf carts are frequently used to navigate the property. The expansiveness of Camp David also extends below ground, where defenses are said to be so robust that British Prime Minister Harold MacMillan, who was given a sneak peek in 1959, purportedly described them as a "fortress."

Each president has the ability, if they so choose, to suggest additional modifications to the property, and many have taken advantage of this privilege. President Kennedy, for example, was responsible for the addition of a horse stable, while President Ronald Reagan designed a nondenominational chapel to be added. The chapel, named Evergreen, opened its doors during the administration of President George H. W. Bush.

While onlookers might dub Camp David a glorified vacation home, presidents have used the site in many ways since its establishment. Of course, the president, their family, and guests have taken advantage of the site as a private getaway for much-needed relaxation, but presidents have also used the facility as a quiet space for reflection, writing, working, and meeting with advisers. How a president uses the site depends on a given visit, with some visits being more work-oriented and others designated for play.

Since I personally think presidents could benefit from some humanizing, let's examine a few case studies. For starters, President Eisenhower was known to enjoy golfing, painting, and hosting barbecues at the retreat, and he also recovered from his 1956 heart attack within the site's secluded confines. President Reagan enjoyed horseback riding, the first President Bush played tennis, and Presidents Roosevelt and Nixon entertained guests. George H. W. Bush's daughter Doro was married at the Evergreen chapel, while her wedding reception took place on the lawn of Aspen cabin. Holidays have also been spent at Camp David, with President Bill Clinton and President George W. Bush spending Thanksgiving 1994 and Christmas 2003, respectively, at the retreat.

But it was President Roosevelt—right at the onset of Shangri-La's establishment—who set the precedent that important meetings could be held there. And in retrospect, this makes sense: the location is and was little known to the public, and it offers a great deal of privacy. Plus, because of its recreational amenities, it created an ideal setting for world leaders to engage one another as humans. Compared to the stuffiness of the White House, Camp David provides an informal venue that feels comparatively empty (ignoring the fact that about two hundred sailors and marines work there full-time).

As such, the first high-level meeting with a foreign dignitary that took place at the retreat featured President Roosevelt in conversation with Winston Churchill, Prime Minister of Great Britain, in May 1943.

Their chat naturally centered around World War II, and they ultimately discussed plans for the D-Day invasion of Normandy that would occur in 1944. In the afternoons, the two men enjoyed trout fishing at a stream passing through the compound.

World War II wasn't the only conflict to take center stage at Camp David. In 1959 during the Cold War, President Eisenhower met with Soviet Premier Nikita Khrushchev at the retreat. The occasion marked the first time a Soviet leader visited the United States, and the intent of the meeting was to ease tensions brewing between the two nations. Perhaps unsurprisingly, Khrushchev was initially skeptical of the idea of traveling to Camp David; at the time, the suspiciously off-the-grid site was not yet common knowledge.

Khrushchev ultimately acquiesced, and at Camp David he enjoyed steak dinners, time spent at the recreational facilities, and watching classic Westerns. From this meeting came the term "Spirit of Camp David," which is generally used to describe cautiously optimistic—or even unofficial—diplomacy. The Soviets used the oppositional, negative version of the term, "*violating* the Spirit of Camp David," to describe US policies or actions with which they disagreed.

In the end, Khrushchev wasn't the only foreign dignitary to be entertained at the retreat. For instance, President Eisenhower invited President Charles de Gaulle of France, President Lopez Mateos of Mexico, and President Alberto Lleras of Colombia for visits.

Other key moments in the intervening decades also centered Camp David. In April 1961, President Kennedy met with former President Eisenhower, his immediate predecessor, to review the failed Bay of Pigs operation in Cuba. In April 1973, President Nixon meandered through Camp David's tulip garden when he requested the resignation of John Ehrlichman and H. R. Haldeman following the Watergate scandal. And in 2001 after the terrorist attacks of September 11, President George W. Bush brought members of his cabinet and other national security officials to Camp David to begin charting a way forward. At this time, President Bush was said to frequently attend services at the Evergreen chapel.

The largest gathering of world leaders at Camp David occurred in 2012, when President Barack Obama hosted a G8 summit. The convening brought together nine heads of state, in addition to President Obama himself. Today, the summit is memorialized in many ways, but especially via a famous photograph featuring the attendant world leaders gathered around a long table and reacting to a soccer match between Chelsea and Bayern Munich; the leaders had pressed pause on their work to watch the Champions League final.

LISTEN TO RILEY

Much like Blair House, Camp David has hosted myriad important figures in intimate, informal moments, and the public is left wondering about the conversations to which only participants and security cameras are privy. While the details of many meetings remain a mystery to most of the population (and even to the vast majority of those working in a given presidential administration), there's one Camp David-based historical event that has been especially remembered by history. I am referring, of course, to the development of a peace treaty known as the Camp David Accords.

Israel and the Arab States have experienced waves of conflict in the Middle East and North Africa since the establishment of Israel in 1948. During one such war in 1967, Israel would come to occupy territories designated as part of nearby Egypt and Jordan, as well as a portion of Syrian land in the Sinai Peninsula. To oversimplify an exceedingly complex and decades-long story, Egypt—the most powerful Middle Eastern neighbor of Israel at the time—was not pleased, and the US government sought to play a role in negotiating peace between the two nations.

The United States referenced United Nations Resolution 242, which dated back to November 1967 and proposed several actions to create a peaceful solution. First, Israel was meant to retreat from the Arab land it occupied. Second, the Arab nations were to officially recognize Israel as an independent country. Third, the resolution called for the settlement of Palestinian refugees who had been displaced by the creation of Israel and the chaos of the 1967 war.

By the mid-1970s, the United States thought it could reconvene the Geneva Conference, which had initially met in December 1973, to begin making progress on these proposals. But a series of political events, including an election upset in Israel and disagreements between Arab leaders, prevented the convening from moving forward.

Attempts at direct negotiations between Israel and Egypt were less than successful, and tensions increased by the day. The countries were at odds regarding the level of Israeli withdrawal from the region—how complete the withdrawal would be and over what time frame—so President Jimmy Carter threw his hat in the ring to mediate a discussion between the two countries' leaders. Carter would ultimately host Egyptian President Anwar Sadat and Israeli Prime Minister Menachem Begin for the Egyptian-Israeli peace negotiations that lasted a whopping thirteen days, from September 5 through 17, 1978.

Many people believe President Carter was not the one to initially suggest Camp David as the venue for these critical talks. While unconfirmed, it is said that First Lady Rosalynn Carter was the originator of this idea. Wherever the location, President Carter was adamant about mediating the convening, which was an interesting insistence, since presidents rarely dedicated so much time to a single foreign policy priority. To achieve an optimal and untainted result (by preventing the opposing leaders from making public appeals to their citizenry), Carter insisted on excluding the press from the discussions.

Upon their arrival, neither Sadat nor Begin had much intention to negotiate. Begin sought an outcome in which his counterpart conceded to his demands, while Sadat was eager to sway Americans' sympathies from Israel to Egypt. The delegations that accompanied the two leaders were ironically discomforted by Camp David's serene environment, finding the wooded area foreboding and the informality disquieting.

While negotiations were both the impetus and emphasis of the convening, the participants—like so many before them—also utilized Camp David's amenities, famously working their way through fifty-eight movies in total. Perhaps it was believed that creating peace necessitated feeling peace, which led to robust time spent at the site's recreational facilities.

Once negotiations began, however, they were tense and slow-moving. Since President Carter's goal was to broker a peace agreement between Egypt and Israel, he enlisted his expert Middle East advisers to draft a strawman text that would serve as the starting point for their negotiations. While Sadat and Begin were accompanied by a plethora of their own advisers, Carter insisted that meetings take place between the three leaders without middlemen. At an early stage, Sadat privately offered Carter several pages of concessions he was willing to make if and when necessary, though he asked Carter to hold off as long as possible before putting those concessions on the table.

It's a small wonder Carter didn't find the need to utilize them sooner. To say negotiations were strained would be the understatement of the century. After three days of getting absolutely nowhere fast, President Carter and Secretary of State Cyrus Vance were forced to meet with Egypt and Israel in individual meetings to review proposed revisions to the strawman text. In the end, the final ten days of the summit saw Sadat and Begin refusing to speak with each other. Very quickly, Carter's hopes for discussions taking place directly between the three leaders had been flushed down the toilet.

Instead, after consultations, a new version of the text would be delivered to Sadat and Begin individually, they would each provide commentary, and yet another version would be drafted. This process continued, with the proposed peace agreement undergoing around twenty-four rounds of revisions. As the summit neared its conclusion, it was largely believed the convening would be a failure, with no agreement in sight. So likely did this dissatisfying result seem that President Carter's advisers crafted a speech he could deliver to the nation explaining why the meetings had been fruitless.

The last piece of the puzzle—the final point of contention preventing the agreement from coming together—involved Israel's occupation of the Sinai Peninsula. But Begin's team made a last-minute call home to Israel's then-minister of agriculture, who was a leading advocate for Israeli settlements in other territories. In this call, the minister of agriculture supposedly agreed to dismantling Israel's settlements in Sinai if peace with Egypt could be secured as a result. At long last, the two nations were seemingly in lockstep.

To this day, it's widely thought that the summit's setting at Camp David played a quintessential role in the successful drafting of the resultant Camp David Accords, also known by their formal name, Framework for Peace in the Middle East. Camp David offered isolation, keeping focus on the task at hand and preventing any influence from outside forces, including the media. Sadat, Begin, and Carter all signed the accords at the end of the summit. The former two leaders would go on to win the Nobel Peace Prize that same year, with President Carter receiving the accolade in 2002 for his role in developing solutions to international conflicts.

Ultimately, the Camp David Accords did not constitute a legally binding treaty. Instead, they represented an agreed-upon commitment from the three world leaders to pursue a lasting, legal solution. In addition to serving as an overall guide for establishing peace, they offered a framework to set up a Palestinian government in Gaza and the West Bank. It was hoped that the accords might lead to similar peace agreements between Israel and its other Middle Eastern neighbors.

> **Riley's Next Hunt:** Riley and his fellow treasure protectors could conceivably find a treasure buried at Camp David, providing a conspiratorial explanation as to why the site was transformed from a public space to a secluded presidential retreat.

In March 1979, the Camp David Accords were succeeded by the Egypt-Israel Peace Treaty—the *intended* outcome of President Carter's summit—but it did take much longer than expected for this treaty to come to fruition. In the end, the treaty's final look largely resembled what Carter had proposed on those fateful days at Camp David. This included a commitment by Israel to withdraw from the Sinai Peninsula and Egypt opening the Suez Canal and Straits of Tiran to Israeli ships. Another outcome with long-lasting impact was the establishment of diplomatic relations between the two countries. As for its part, the United States agreed to provide foreign assistance, including military aid, to both nations. Despite this perceived success, other Middle Eastern countries opted not to follow Egypt's lead in negotiating with Israel.

World leaders have been hard-pressed to replicate the outcomes of the summit at Camp David despite occasional attempts. For instance, President Clinton hosted Israeli Prime Minister Ehud Barak and Palestine's Yasser Arafat in an attempt to commence peace talks in 2000, but his effort was in vain. Today, the efficacy of the Camp David Accords in progressing peace in the Middle East remains hotly contested. Even the US officials working with President Carter to make the accords possible deemed them imperfect.

Despite this lingering question, which will undoubtedly be debated for years to come, one thing is certain: the Camp David Accords represent the most famous diplomatic outcome borne out of Camp David since the site's unceremonious introduction into US political history. What future meeting or convening—perhaps one that redefines history for all mankind—might one day claim this throne?

-CHAPTER 19-

Myths That Could Be True

If you couldn't tell, I believe the history lessons that would be attractive to Riley—both as a child and as an adult—all have a bit of a twist. Some of the stories are famous, some are infamous, and some you may have never even heard of before, but they all boast at least one unanswered question. Of course, historians have attempted to answer those questions for years, but when a definitive, incontrovertible answer remains elusive, there's an opportunity for students of history (children and adults alike) to develop their own theories.

In my view, the single most interesting aspect of historical mysteries is how opposite they are from scientific ones. As a trained scientist myself, I know firsthand that the best way to tackle a scientific challenge is to relentlessly jab at it using the tried-and-true scientific method; I like to think Riley, who spent his early career at a computer engineering company, can relate. The longer you jab—the more time you spend investigating a hypothesis—the closer you get to the truth. In some scientific disciplines, it can literally take decades to reach sound conclusions.

But history doesn't work like that. The longer it takes to investigate the mystery at hand, the *less* likely we are to find the truth. That's because history relies so heavily on primary sources, and as time passes, so do people. Like in any game of whisper down the lane, the more a story is retold—the more degrees of separation that exist between the original story and its latest retelling—the more inaccuracies it contains.

Yet the passage of time claims not just people. It also claims the artifacts, structures, and other tangible objects that may be quintessential to prove a historical hypothesis. In essence, time is the enemy of history's greatest mysteries—*if* you care enough to solve them.

Whether or not you buy into the various mysteries, intrigues, and controversies elaborated within the preceding pages, and whether or not the truth behind those mysteries is ever revealed, the stories that surround them can tell us a great deal about how our culture has morphed over decades and centuries. Indeed, simply examining how historical accounts, such as those related to the "lost" Roanoke colonists or Seward's "folly," have changed throughout time allows us to reflect on our changing beliefs at local, national, or even global scales.

This begs the question: are mysteries, myths, and legends just truths waiting to be told? While enough time has passed that the reality underpinning so many of these stories may never be uncovered, their persistence and evolution betray facts about society that we would do well to consider. After all, they say those who ignore history are destined—or doomed—to repeat it.

Many people would consider Riley's interest in the unexplained fanciful, failing to understand the beauty of a good historical mystery. If I were to take it upon myself to defend Mr. Poole, I'd point out that an intense interest in myths and mysteries is inherently human. Humans are curious and imaginative, two characteristics that unsuccessful history classes seem to systematically squeeze out of students' brains. Mysteries and myths quench our curious imagination and provide us with an escape from the mundane, exercising our minds as we attempt to conjure up the perfect piece to complete the puzzle.

Mysteries, myths, and legends are the basis of community. If I retained anything from my own history classes, it's that storytelling is one attribute that all cultures—all civilizations—have in common. Myths were literally created so that communities could rationalize the unexplained and teach lessons that would be passed down through generations. And today, our collective interest in mysteries generates a community of armchair investigators who share evidence and brainstorm theories. People who lived hundreds of years ago and those who live today connect with open-ended questions because they allow us to explore something bigger than ourselves.

From a purely practical point of view, mysteries can certainly function as a tool to galvanize interest in history itself. Not to toot my own horn, but I suspect Riley would have paid way more attention in history class if *this* had been his textbook. Traditional history classes focused on memorization of facts are far less effective at creating students who are interested in history and its lessons than classes that entertain the open-ended questions that mysteries provide.

I personally can relate to all these reasons for people's persistent interest in myths and legends. And as Riley would be quick to add, the promise—or at least the possibility—of finding gold surely doesn't hurt.

So, I can't conceive of a better way of concluding this text—the history textbook of the future—than by complementing the past with the future and alluding to some of our favorite *National Treasure* lore in the process. The Templar treasure was a once-in-a-lifetime discovery that Riley would do anything in his power to replicate, if only because Ben Gates assured him that he'd be determining the finders' fee on their next haul. The only thing I can think of that might be worth more than a football field's worth of ancient artifacts is a football *stadium* filled with priceless gold. Good thing there seems to be an unlimited missing supply in the Americas alone—if you believe in legends.

Consider, for example, the City of Gold, rumored to have existed in North America (and, importantly, not yet "discovered" by Riley and team when his *Templar Treasure* book was published). The advent of the legend itself was almost an accident. Following the failed expedition of Spanish conquistador Pánfilo de Narváez in 1527, the expedition's only surviving members traversed the southwestern United States and northwestern Mexico (based on modern borders), encountering innumerable Native American tribes along the way. These tribes shared stories of a prosperous golden city located somewhere in the north.

One of the Narváez expedition's survivors, an enslaved African man named Esteban, was later tasked with guiding Marcos de Niza's expedition in search of this fabled City of Gold. Esteban traveled ahead of de Niza's cohort to converse with tribes and determine the route forward. But in 1539, after sending word that he had finally reached the target city, Esteban was purportedly killed. A spooked de Niza claimed to have spotted a gleaming golden metropolis in the distance but opted to retreat. His account was the impetus for Francisco Vásquez de Coronado's subsequent mission, which ultimately yielded not a golden city, but a swath of pueblos.

It's worth considering what Esteban claimed to have witnessed when he "reached" the city before his supposed death. His message relayed a series of seven distinct communities under a single government. The communities comprised large stone houses adorned with turquoise. For centuries, native tribes in the American Southwest have indeed mined turquoise, incorporating the blue stone into jewelry and other objects.

Today, some people believe the legend of the City of Gold was crafted to occupy the Spanish conquistadors—to encourage them to move on from whatever tribal community they were currently terrorizing. Others believe the Spaniards' unyielding belief in the city was the result of a long string of miscommunications; in other words, the Native American tales were simply mistranslated. In fact, gold wasn't common to the native cultures found north of the Rio Grande; copper was much more readily mined in these parts. That said, gold has certainly been an integral part of pre-Columbian Native American civilizations in Central and South America for millennia, so where did it all go?

This question requires us to depart the supposed City of Gold in the United States and head southward to Mesoamerica. Because if there's one pot of gold, so to speak, that we know existed at one point in history, it's Montezuma's treasure. Montezuma II, as Europeans would come to know him, was the ninth ruler of the Aztec empire, a sophisticated and wealthy civilization based in modern-day Mexico. Like many Latin American Indigenous societies, the Aztec added gold to their jewelry, regalia, and other trinkets. As an emperor, Montezuma owned the lion's share, yet his treasure remains lost to this day.

Legend passed down for centuries has provided hints about where it may be located. In 1520, the Spanish conquistadors finally found themselves on the losing end of a battle with the Aztecs. As the Spanish fled Aztec territory, they carried as much gold and other valuables as they could manage, but the unwieldy stash complicated their escape that claimed the lives of many fellow conquistadors. In self-preservation mode, some conquistadors are believed to have off-loaded the heavy riches into the waterways surrounding the city. Yet when Hernán Cortés returned and searched the same waterways years later, he came up empty.

So, what happened to the sunken treasure? If it ever ended up in the water at all, it's likely the Aztecs retrieved it themselves following the Spaniards' departure. One theory suggests the Aztecs eventually relocated the treasure north—somewhere in the present-day United

States—and subsequently hid it. This story has been passed down through oral tradition, as Native American tribes along the Aztecs' supposed route northward claimed to have observed the caravan and the wealth it carried. If this legend holds (and it's a big "if"), the treasure's most widely accepted final destination is Utah, the Aztecs' possible ancestral homeland.

As of the time of this writing, only one piece of Aztec gold that can be definitively traced to Montezuma's hoard has been found. In 1981, a gold bar was serendipitously recovered from under the streets of Mexico City, and a careful analysis suggested it belonged to the late Aztec empire. It turns out the bar was found along what was once the route Cortés and the conquistadors traversed when departing the kingdom on the night they lost most of their men—spurring hope that gold from that fateful evening may still be rediscovered.

Our discussion of lost gold in the Americas would hardly be complete without navigating still farther south to the empire of the Inca, who, like the Aztec, applied gold liberally to jewelry, objects, and even building décor. In 1533, Francisco Pizarro captured the civilization's emperor, Atahualpa, and instituted a basic ransom scheme, but the Spanish foolishly killed their captive before receiving the gold they demanded. Legend has it that when the Inca learned their ruler had been murdered, they hid the remainder of the gold they were preparing to send to the Spanish.

If you guessed we don't know where that loot is located today, you're quick on the uptake. Considering the heavily forested and mountainous terrain the Inca occupied, the potential hiding places are quite literally endless, but the most popular theories include caves and lakes. An explorer claimed to have found the gold in 1886—his notes indicate the quantity was so large he couldn't even begin extracting it—but he met a mysterious death when he fell (or was pushed) overboard when sailing in the United States.

Another legend of Incan treasure is that of Paititi. If you believe the stories, this golden city is concealed somewhere in the rainforest east of the Andes Mountains, and the Inca may have retreated to this location when Pizarro initially arrived to conquer the great empire. The origins of the Paititi story trace back to the 1600s, when a missionary was told an Indigenous tale about a city of vast riches, and said tale was later conveyed to the Pope. Interest in Paititi was reignited as recently as the early 2000s when an Italian archaeologist rediscovered the missionary's original report.

Innumerable searches have tried and failed to unearth Incan gold cities since the 1500s. But the vast expanse of as-yet uncharted land across South America means ancient structures are still being unearthed on what seems like a daily basis. Paititi has not yet been found, nor is there consensus that it ever existed in the first place. But if it did, it could quite literally be recovered tomorrow, in two decades, or in two centuries. And if you ask me, that alone makes the story worth retelling for years to come.

As we consider the myriad ancient civilizations that prospered in the Americas and beyond, we encounter no shortage of legends suggesting that a once glorious treasure has since been lost to time. Treasure hunters like Riley must then ask a difficult question: is a treasure lost because we don't know where to look, or because it physically no longer exists?

It's almost unbelievable that *National Treasure*'s intrepid heroes were able to recover the complete Templar treasure beneath Trinity Church in the early 2000s. Some of the objects contained within the treasure, like scrolls from the library at Alexandria, should not exist anymore based on the fragile materials of which they're made. You've got to love movie magic.

That's a pragmatic reason why gold makes such an attractive treasure. After all, a convenient characteristic of gold well-known to even novices of chemistry is that it's incredibly resilient, and it lasts a heck of a long time. This means lost gold treasures aren't going anywhere. They aren't corroding or disintegrating or dissolving. They're just sitting there—wherever they're hidden—literally waiting to be found.

And you can bet Riley Poole looks forward to finding them. After all, treasure hunting is the perfect way to combine his technology skills with his passion for the lesser-appreciated tales of history, and it certainly beats slaving away at a cubicle as a cog in a corporate machine. If you buy into the character analysis with which I launched this text, you'll agree that treasure hunting provides the mental stimulation Riley has always longed for, and it probably gives him just enough street cred to impress the ladies. I'm pretty sure Indiana Jones got the girl in the end, even if his marriage didn't last. I think Riley could live with that.

So, fellow treasure protectors and mystery enthusiasts, I leave you with this. While I cannot tell you which treasure Ben Gates, Riley Poole, and Abigail Chase will locate next, I *can* promise that pursuing the niche unknowns of the past will offer great excitement for the future. Riley would be the first to tell you that not everyone will understand your interests; indeed, those who fear what lurks beyond the pages of their textbooks will turn up their noses. But what's the purpose of life without the freedom to imagine and to seek answers that may always lie just out of reach? Even if you fail in your intended quest, you never know what other discoveries you might make along the way.

That's why each of us would do well to take a page out of *National Treasure*'s history book. After all, as someone wise once said, "*Listen to Riley.*"

It's All Connected: The Challenge

Every *National Treasure* fan knows Riley Poole loves urban legends and conspiracy theories, the most popular of which draw unexpected connections between seemingly unrelated people, places, and events. It's not hard to imagine Riley's apartment sporting a prominent evidence board—a series of sticky notes and photographs tacked to a wall and linked with string—as part of an attempt to unravel his conspiracy theory du jour.

Throughout the course of this book, we have considered a variety of topics—spanning many centuries—that are completely unrelated. One event did not necessarily give rise to the next, but even so, commonalities often exist between them. That's because history is, at its core, a web of both contemporaneous and sequential moments influenced by the same evolving set of figures and social conditions.

How many of those shared influences did you identify during your reading? Examine the web below and determine what the two topics connected by each line have in common. The more you think like Riley, the easier your task will be!

Seward's Folly

President's Secret Book

Corps of Discovery

Winchester Mystery House

Mecklenburg Declaration

Blair House

Lincoln Assassination

Camp David

Salem Witch Trials

Templar Treasure

Jack the Ripper

Bermuda Triangle

Headless Horseman

Blackbeard the Pirate

Lost Roanoke Colony

The *Mary Celeste*

Myths That Are True:
National Treasure Location Edition

Interested in exploring the urban legends, curiosities, and other quirks that make a city tick? These are (probably) Riley Poole's favorite lesser-known sites and stories from US cities featured in his hunt for the Templar treasure. You won't find these local legends* in your history textbook!

Boston, Massachusetts

First Spiritualist Temple: This magnificent building, dating back to the 1880s, was the first epicenter of the spiritualist movement, characterized by the use of séances and other practices to facilitate communication with spirits. Though the temple is no longer used for this purpose today, passers-by still notice ghostly faces carved into the building's exterior. *Find it at 26 Exeter Street, Boston.*

Mather Family Tomb: Father-son duo Increase and Cotton Mather, ministers at Old North Church, gained fame from the mid-1600s to early-1700s by publishing several treatises on witchcraft, demons, and related topics that were referenced during the Salem witch trials. The Mather family tomb, a raised, flat structure made of brick, is located in a corner of Copp's Hill Burying Ground. *Find it at 45 Hull Street, Boston.*

Paul Revere's Bell: Paul Revere was more than a one-hit wonder in history. Following his legendary midnight ride and the entirety of the American Revolution, he cast bells professionally under a company named Paul Revere and Son. One of the bells he had a hand in creating, a more than nine-hundred-pound piece sold to a Massachusetts church in 1805, can still be visited at the Paul Revere House historic site. *Find it at 19 N Square, Boston.*

New York, New York

Explorers Club: The Explorers Club, established in 1904 by a small group of polar adventurers, remains an elite organization for those dedicated to exploring land, sea, air, and space. The organization's headquarters boasts artifacts from notorious global expeditions, including tools of the exploration trade and a robust collection of taxidermy animals. *Find it at 46 E 70th Street, New York.*

New York Federal Gold Vault: The New York Federal Reserve Bank houses the largest collection of gold known to mankind in an underground vault. The structure is filled with seven thousand tons of gold bars that are the property of nations around the world; these nations benefit from the centralized storage system that permits easy transfer between countries. The bank maintains detailed records regarding the purity and composition of each bar, so a "customer" can deposit and retrieve the same one. *Find it at 33 Liberty Street, New York.*

Trinity Churchyard: Trinity Churchyard predates its namesake, Trinity Church, whose first structural iteration was completed in 1697. In addition to the tomb of Alexander Hamilton, the churchyard houses the oldest carved gravestone in all of New York City: that of Richard Churcher, a child who passed away in 1681. The 1700s-era grave of James Leeson features Freemason symbols and a pigpen cipher that, when decoded, reads "Remember Death." *Find it at 75 Broadway, New York.*

Philadelphia, Pennsylvania

Eastern State Penitentiary: Upon opening in 1829, the castle-shaped Eastern State Penitentiary featured modern amenities and provisions, but inmates were not permitted to speak or interact with one another or the guards. The system inadvertently drove inmates toward severe mental anguish until more traditional prison practices were eventually adopted. Once home to Al Capone and other notorious criminals, the penitentiary is believed to be haunted today. *Find it at 22nd Street and Fairmount Avenue, Philadelphia.*

Masonic Temple of Philadelphia: Constructed beginning in 1868, Philadelphia's Masonic Temple is arguably the grandest Freemason lodge in the world. Each room is ornately themed, with styles ranging from Egyptian to Corinthian to the Renaissance. The massive structure is overflowing with secret passageways, and each room features one purposeful design flaw as a reminder of humans' fallibility. *Find it at One N Broad Street, Philadelphia.*

Mütter Museum: Based at the College of Physicians of Philadelphia, the Mütter Museum is famous for housing specimens of medical oddities. While the museum boasts several unusual skeletons, including that of the tallest-ever man and several conjoined twins, the most prized item within the collection is a set of microscope slides containing slivers of Albert Einstein's brain. *Find it at 19 S 22nd Street, Philadelphia.*

Washington, District of Columbia

Catacombs: The Catacombs of Washington, D.C., contain only one real skeleton—that of an eight-year-old boy who was supposedly a second-century martyr. Built in the early 1900s as a Holy Land stand-in for Americans to visit closer to home, the Catacombs are located beneath the Franciscan Monastery of the Holy Land in America. Above the tunnel system sits numerous religious replicas, including a copy of Jesus's tomb. *Find it at 1400 Quincy Street NE, Washington, D.C.*

FBI Spy House: Across the street from the Russian Embassy in the US capital is a house made famous for its conspicuous spy activity in the late 1900s. The FBI hid its ownership and use of the house poorly, with agents frequently coming and going, no mail delivery, and cameras peering out the windows. The house may have been the starting point for a tunnel that was part of a failed FBI attempt to install listening devices beneath the embassy. *Find it at 2619 Wisconsin Avenue NW, Washington, D.C.*

Kilroy: During World War II, allied soldiers popularized a small cartoon dubbed "Kilroy" as a means of generating camaraderie and raising morale. Sketches of the innocuous figure were left in bunkers, ships, and other wartime sites to indicate that another allied soldier had previously visited and survived. Two Kilroy etchings can be found at the World War II Memorial; start your search near the Delaware and Pennsylvania pillars. *Find it at 1964 Independence Avenue SW, Washington, D.C.*

*Atlas Obscura was referenced in the development of this appendix.

Selected References

The following book, journal, newspaper, magazine, radio, web, and film sources represent a sampling of those that were referenced in the writing of this text.

"'13 Days in September' Examines 1978 Camp David Accords." 2014. *Morning Edition.* NPR. https://www.npr.org/2014/09/16/348903279/-13-days-in-september-examines-1978-camp-david-conference.

Adam, David. 2019. "Does a New Genetic Analysis Finally Reveal the Identity of Jack the Ripper?" *Science,* March 15, 2019. https://www.science.org/content/article/does-new-genetic-analysis-finally-reveal-identity-jack-ripper.

Andrews, Evan. 2018. "Did North Carolina Issue the First Declaration of Independence?" HISTORY. September 1, 2018. https://www.history.com/news/did-north-carolina-issue-the-first-declaration-of-independence.

Barger, Jennifer. 2022. "How Turquoise Became Synonymous with New Mexico." *National Geographic,* February 3, 2022. https://www.nationalgeographic.com/culture/article/how-turquoise-became-synonymous-with-new-mexico.

Barr, Luke. 2020. "'The President's Daily Briefing': How the Top Secret Intelligence Document Is Put Together." *ABC News,* July 3, 2020. https://abcnews.go.com/Politics/presidents-daily-briefing-top-secret-intelligence-document-put/story?id=71578830.

Belding, Samuel. 2022. "Stanley Meyer: An Infamous Invention and Death." *University of Minnesota Institute on the Environment* (blog). April 29, 2022. https://environment.umn.edu/education/susteducation/stanley-meyer-an-infamous-invention-and-death/.

"Blair House: The President's Guest House." n.d. Accessed June 29, 2024. https://blairhouse.org/.

Blumberg, Jess. 2007. "Abandoned Ship: The Mary Celeste." *Smithsonian Magazine,* November 2007. https://www.smithsonianmag.com/history/abandoned-ship-the-mary-celeste-174488104/.

————. 2022. "A Brief History of the Salem Witch Trials." *Smithsonian Magazine*, October 24, 2022. https://www.smithsonianmag.com/history/a-brief-history-of-the-salem-witch-trials-175162489/.

Bolker, Jamie M. 2023. "America Still Isn't Ready to Acknowledge That a Hero of National Myth Could Have Died by Suicide." *TIME*, December 1, 2023. https://time.com/6340942/meriwether-lewis-suicide-history/.

Bradley, Elizabeth L. 2014. "What 'The Legend of Sleepy Hollow' Tells Us About Contagion, Fear and Epidemics." *Smithsonian Magazine*, October 30, 2014. https://www.smithsonianmag.com/history/what-legend-sleepy-hollow-tells-us-about-contagion-fear-and-epidemics-180953192/.

Catalfamo, Kelly. 2019. "The Myth and Reincarnation of John Wilkes Booth." *Scalawag*, October 30, 2019. http://scalawagmagazine.org/2019/10/john-wilkes-booth-halloween-2019/.

Coutant, Linda. 2023. "The Lost Colony — An Outer Banks Mystery." *National Parks Conservation Association* (blog). October 30, 2023. https://www.npca.org/articles/3604-the-lost-colony-an-outer-banks-mystery.

Cullen, Bob. 2003. "Two Weeks at Camp David." *Smithsonian Magazine*, September 2003. https://www.smithsonianmag.com/history/two-weeks-at-camp-david-88891073/.

Dawson, Scott. 2020. *The Lost Colony and Hatteras Island*. North Carolina: Arcadia Publishing.

Dobson, Jim. 2021. "How the Discovery of Paititi, The Lost City of Gold, May Change Peru Forever." *Forbes*, June 29, 2021. https://www.forbes.com/sites/jimdobson/2016/01/11/move-over-machu-picchu-the-discovery-of-paititi-the-secret-city-of-gold-may-change-peru-forever/.

Dolin, Eric Jay. 2018. "The Most Iconic Episode from the Life of Blackbeard Is How It Ended. Here's How the Pirate Really Died." *TIME*, November 21, 2018. https://time.com/5457008/blackbeard-death/.

Dowd, Katie. 2021. "Everything You Know About the Winchester Mystery House Isn't True." *SFGATE*, October 31, 2021. https://www.sfgate.com/sfhistory/article/the-myth-of-the-winchester-mystery-house-16571653.

Drake, Matt. 2019. "Secret Knights Templar Tunnels 'Leading to a Treasure Tower' Discovered in Israel." *The Independent*, October 28, 2019, sec. News. https://www.independent.co.uk/news/science/knights-templar-secret-tunnels-treasure-tower-israel-acre-a9174776.html.

Farrow, Lee A. 2016. *Seward's Folly: A New Look at the Alaska Purchase*. Fairbanks, Alaska: University of Alaska Press.

Fleming, Thomas. 2010. "When Dolley Madison Took Command of the White House." *Smithsonian Magazine*, March 2010. https://www.smithsonianmag.com/history/how-dolley-madison-saved-the-day/.

Garcia, Kristina. 2022. "Possessed: The Salem Witch Trials." *Penn Today* (blog). March 11, 2022. https://penntoday.upenn.edu/news/possessed-salem-witch-trials.

Goforth, J. Pennelope. 2015. "Debunking a Myth: Enough, Already!" *Alaska Historical Society* (blog). March 17, 2015. https://alaskahistoricalsociety.

org/debunking-a-myth-enough-already/.

Goodall, Jamie L. H. 2020. *Pirates of the Chesapeake Bay: From the Colonial Era to the Oyster Wars*. Gloucestershire, United Kingdom: The History Press.

Greenspan, Jesse. 2020. "Why the Purchase of Alaska Was Far From 'Folly.'" HISTORY. March 24, 2020. https://www.history.com/news/why-the-purchase-of-alaska-was-far-from-folly.

Gustafson, Milton O. 1994. "Seward's Bargain: The Alaska Purchase from Russia." *Prologue Magazine*, 1994. https://www.archives.gov/publications/prologue/1994/winter/alaska-check.

Haag, Pamela. 2016. "The Heiress to a Gun Empire Built a Mansion Forever Haunted by the Blood Money That Built It." *Smithsonian Magazine*, July 7, 2016. https://www.smithsonianmag.com/history/heiress-gun-empire-built-mansion-forever-haunted-blood-money-built-it-180959712/.

Hall, Mark F. 2014. "The Book of Secrets, and Other Secret Books." *From the Catbird Seat* (Library of Congress Blogs) (blog). October 15, 2014. https://doi.org/10/the-book-of-secrets-and-other-secret-books.

Hanna, Mark G. 2017. "A Lot of What Is Known about Pirates Is Not True, and a Lot of What Is True Is Not Known." *Humanities*, 2017. https://www.neh.gov/humanities/2017/winter/feature/lot-what-known-about-pirates-not-true-and-lot-what-true-not-known.

Hapka, Catherine. 2008a. *Uncharted. Gates Family Mystery Series 3*. Disney Press.

———. 2008b. *Westward Bound. Gates Family Mystery Series 4*. Disney Press.

History.com Editors. 2023. "Lewis and Clark: Expedition." HISTORY. March 28, 2023. https://www.history.com/topics/19th-century/lewis-and-clark.

———. 2024. "Knights Templar." HISTORY. May 1, 2024. https://www.history.com/topics/middle-ages/the-knights-templar.

Hoare, Callum. 2021. "Knights Templar's Holy Grail 'Treasure' Pinpointed to 'Labyrinth of Tunnels' in UK." *Daily Express*, July 30, 2021, sec. UK. https://www.express.co.uk/news/uk/1469843/knights-templar-holy-grail-treasure-bible-sinai-park-house-burton-abbey-spt.

Holland, Brynn. 2023. "The Knights Templar Rulebook Included No Pointy Shoes and No Kissing Mom." HISTORY. October 2, 2023. https://www.history.com/news/the-knights-templar-rulebook-included-no-pointy-shoes-and-no-kissing-mom.

Iggiagruk Hensley, William L. 2017. "There Are Two Versions of the Story of How the US Purchased Alaska from Russia." *Smithsonian Magazine*, March 29, 2017. https://www.smithsonianmag.com/history/why-russia-gave-alaska-americas-gateway-arctic-180962714/.

Jacques, Jenise L. 2020. "Computer Science Professor's Photo Sleuth Software Helps Investigate 150-Year Mystery of John Wilkes Booth." Virginia Tech. December 9, 2020. https://news.vt.edu/content/news_vt_edu/en/articles/2020/12/cseng_historychannel.html.

Johnson, Mark. 2023. "The Plot Thickens: Did DNA Settle a Centuries-

Old Conspiracy?" Davidson College. September 18, 2023. https://www.davidson.edu/news/2023/09/18/plot-thickens-did-dna-settle-centuries-old-conspiracy.

Klin, Richard. 2022. "The True History Behind 'The Legend of Sleepy Hollow.'" *Westchester Magazine*, October 12, 2022. https://westchestermagazine.com/life-style/irving-legend-sleepy-hollow/.

Knight, Andrew, and Katherine D. Watson. 2017. "Was Jack the Ripper a Slaughterman? Human-Animal Violence and the World's Most Infamous Serial Killer." *Animals 7* (4): 30. https://doi.org/10.3390/ani7040030.

Koncius, Jura. 2018. "Inside Blair House, Where the President's Guests Get the VIP Treatment." *The Washington Post*, June 19, 2018. https://www.washingtonpost.com/lifestyle/magazine/blair-house-in-the-presidents-guesthouse-everyone-is-treated-like-royalty/2018/06/12/51bff808-3f5b-11e8-974f-aacd97698cef_story.html.

La Vere, David. 2010. *The Lost Rocks: The Dare Stones and the Unsolved Mystery of Sir Walter Raleigh's Lost Colony*. 2nd ed. Wilmington, North Carolina: Burnt Mill Press.

Lawler, Andrew. 2018. *The Secret Token: Myth, Obsession, and the Search for the Lost Colony of Roanoke*. New York: Doubleday.

———. 2018. "Three Centuries After His Beheading, a Kinder, Gentler Blackbeard Emerges." *Smithsonian Magazine*, November 13, 2018. https://www.smithsonianmag.com/history/three-centuries-after-his-beheading-kinder-gentler-blackbeard-emerges-180970782/.

Leonnig, Carol. 2021. *Zero Fail: The Rise and Fall of the Secret Service*. New York, New York: Random House.

"Lincoln's Assassination." n.d. Ford's Theatre. Accessed June 29, 2024. https://fords.org/lincolns-assassination/.

Luckhurst, Roger. 2016. "The Horror of the Headless Horseman." BBC. November 17, 2016. https://www.bbc.com/culture/article/20161118-the-horror-of-the-headless-horseman.

Machemer, Theresa. 2020. "Spanish Conquistadors Stole This Gold Bar from Aztec Emperor Moctezuma's Trove." *Smithsonian Magazine*, January 14, 2020. https://www.smithsonianmag.com/smart-news/gold-bar-once-belonged-aztec-emperor-moctezuma-180973959/.

"Marilyn Monroe." n.d. Folder. FBI Records: The Vault. Accessed June 29, 2024. https://vault.fbi.gov/Marilyn%20Monroe.

Mark, Joshua J. 2021. "Cibola - The Seven Cities of Gold & Coronado." World History Encyclopedia. May 11, 2021. https://www.worldhistory.org/article/1754/cibola---the-seven-cities-of-gold--coronado/.

Odell, Robin. 2006. *Ripperology: A Study of the World's First Serial Killer and a Literary Phenomenon*. Kent, Ohio: The Kent State University Press.

Owen, James. 2017. "Lost Inca Gold." *National Geographic*, January 21, 2017. https://www.nationalgeographic.com/history/article/lost-inca-gold.

Pearce, Jr., Haywood J. 1938. "New Light on the Roanoke Colony: A Preliminary Examination of a Stone Found in Chowan County, North

Carolina." *The Journal of Southern History* 4 (2): 148–63.

Priess, David. 2017. *The President's Book of Secrets: The Untold Story of Intelligence Briefings to America's Presidents*. PublicAffairs.

Prologue Magazine. 2008. "Camp David," 2008. https://www.archives.gov/publications/prologue/2008/winter/camp-david.html.

Pruitt, Sarah. 2023. "How the Salem Witch Trials Influenced the American Legal System." HISTORY. June 29, 2023. https://www.history.com/news/salem-witch-trials-justice-legal-legacy.

"Queen Anne's Revenge Project." n.d. Accessed June 29, 2024. qaronline.org/.

Ramesar, Vernon. 2023. "A N.S. Ghost Ship Is Fading from Memory—150 Years After Its Crew Disappeared." *CBC News*, May 6, 2023. https://www.cbc.ca/news/canada/nova-scotia/mary-celeste-ghost-ship-nova-scotia-history-1.6830855.

Robinson, Joanna. 2018. "*Winchester*: The True Ghost Story Behind Helen Mirren's Haunted House Thriller." *Vanity Fair*, February 2, 2018. https://www.vanityfair.com/hollywood/2018/02/winchester-helen-mirren-haunted-house-san-jose.

Rosenberg, Howard L. 1974. "Exorcizing the Devil's Triangle." *Sealift*, June 1974.

Rossmo, Kim. 2016. "Jack the Ripper." Texas State University Center for Geospatial Intelligence and Investigation. Texas State University. December 14, 2016. https://www.txst.edu/gii/projects/jack-the-ripper.html.

Runnells, Charles. 2023. "Was Serial Killer H. H. Holmes Also Jack the Ripper? His Relative Makes a Case in Fort Myers." *The News-Press*, February 24, 2023. https://www.news-press.com/story/life/2023/02/24/serial-killer-jack-the-ripper-and-hh-holmes-the-same-person-american-monster/69924371007/.

Sadler, Dave. 2021. "Lost Relics of the Knights Templar: A Review." *The Archaeology and Metal Detecting Magazine*, May 2021. https://archmdmag.com/lost-relics-of-the-knights-templar-a-review/.

Sayare, Scott. 2023. "The Secrets of the JFK Assassination Archive." *Intelligencer*, November 9, 2023. https://nymag.com/intelligencer/article/jfk-assassination-documents-national-archives.html.

Scharping, Nathaniel. 2024. "What Is the Scientific Mystery Behind the Bermuda Triangle?" *Discover Magazine*, March 25, 2024. https://www.discovermagazine.com/planet-earth/the-bermuda-triangle-what-science-can-tell-us-about-the-mysterious-ocean.

Sneff, Emily. 2016. "The Mecklenburg Declaration of Independence." *Declaration Resources Project: Delegate Discussions* (blog). June 16, 2016. https://declaration.fas.harvard.edu/blog/dd-meckdec.

Stephey, M. J. 2009. "Blair House: World's Most Exclusive Hotel." *TIME*, January 15, 2009. https://time.com/archive/6913913/blair-house-worlds-most-exclusive-hotel/.

Tangredi, Sam J. 2023. "The Elusive Fleet of the Knights Templar." *Naval History Magazine,* April 2023. https://www.usni.org/magazines/naval-history-magazine/2023/april/elusive-fleet-knights-templar.

"The Journals of the Lewis and Clark Expedition." n.d. University of Nebraska Press / University of Nebraska-Lincoln Libraries-Electronic Text Center. http://lewisandclarkjournals.unl.edu.

"The Mecklenburg Declaration of Independence." 1775. https://www.loc.gov/item/2020775438/.

Thompson, Jonathan. 2005. "Dating of Wreck's Timbers Puts Wind in Sails of the 'Mary Celeste.'" *The Independent*, January 23, 2005, sec. News. https://www.independent.co.uk/news/uk/this-britain/dating-of-wreck-s-timbers-puts-wind-in-sails-of-the-mary-celeste-mystery-487927.html.

"Thoughts from an Assassin: The Journal of John Wilkes Booth." 2021. Ford's Theatre (US National Park Service). June 27, 2021. https://www.nps.gov/foth/learn/historyculture/thoughts-from-an-assassin-the-journal-of-john-wilkes-booth.htm.

Tucker, Abigail. 2009. "Meriwether Lewis' Mysterious Death." *Smithsonian Magazine*, October 2009. https://www.smithsonianmag.com/history/meriwether-lewis-mysterious-death-144006713/.

———. 2011. "Did Archaeologists Uncover Blackbeard's Treasure?" *Smithsonian Magazine*, March 2011. https://www.smithsonianmag.com/history/did-archaeologists-uncover-blackbeards-treasure-215890/.

Turteltaub, Jon, dir. 2004. *National Treasure*. Walt Disney Pictures, Jerry Bruckheimer Films, Junction Entertainment.

———, dir. 2007. *National Treasure: Book of Secrets*. Walt Disney Pictures, Jerry Bruckheimer Films, Junction Entertainment.

"Uncovering Presidential Secrets, From Washington to Trump." 2017. *Fresh Air*. NPR. https://www.npr.org/2017/02/20/515803768/uncovering-presidential-secrets-from-washington-to-trump.

"Washington Irving's Headless Horseman of Sleepy Hollow Turns 200." 2020. *Weekend Edition Saturday*. NPR. https://www.npr.org /2020/10/24/927384409/washington-irvings-headless-horseman-of-sleepy-hollow-turns-200.

Waxman, Olivia B. 2023. "What We Know and Still Don't Know About JFK's Assassination." *TIME*, November 21, 2023. https://time.com/6338396/jfk-assassination-conspiracy-culture/.

"Who Was John Wilkes Booth Before He Became Lincoln's Assassin?" 2015. *Morning Edition*. NPR. https://www.npr.org/2015/04/15/399579416/historian-john-wilkes-booth-not-a-deranged-lone-madman.

Williams, Victoria. n.d. "Culper Spy Ring." George Washington's Mount Vernon. Accessed June 3, 2022. https://www.mountvernon.org/library/digitalhistory/digital-encyclopedia/article/culper-spy-ring/.

"Winchester Mystery House." n.d. Accessed June 2024. winchestermysteryhouse.com/.

Wolff Scanlan. 2022. "The Salem Witch Trials According to the Historical Records." *Humanities*, 2022. https://www.neh.gov/article/records-salem-witch-trials.

Yates, Ronald. 1982. "Mystery Still Lingers on Marilyn Monroe." *Chicago Tribune*, August 6, 1982.

Suggested Readings

The following texts offer further insight into the historical figures, locations, events, and—most importantly—legends and mysteries explored throughout this book. Inclusion in this list does not necessarily represent endorsement of the texts' analyses or conclusions. Recent publications, and those representing diverse interpretations, have been included whenever possible.

National Treasure Franchise
Hapka, Catherine. 2007. *Changing Tides*. Gates Family Mystery Series 1. Disney Press.
————. 2008a. *Midnight Ride*. Gates Family Mystery Series 2. Disney Press.
————. 2008b. *Uncharted*. Gates Family Mystery Series 3. Disney Press.
————. 2008c. *Westward Bound*. Gates Family Mystery Series 4. Disney Press.
Lloyd, Ann. 2007. *National Treasure: Book of Secrets*. Disney Press.
Paris, Aubrey R., and Emily M. Black. 2023. *National Treasure Hunt: One Step Short of Crazy*. Tucker DS Press.

Alaska Purchase
Black, Lydia. 2004. *Russians in Alaska, 1732-1867*. 1st ed. Fairbanks, Alaska: University of Alaska Press.
Farrow, Lee A. 2016. *Seward's Folly: A New Look at the Alaska Purchase*. Fairbanks, Alaska: University of Alaska Press.
Stahr, Walter. 2013. *Seward: Lincoln's Indispensable Man*. Reprint. New York, New York: Simon & Schuster.

American & European Witch Trials
Barstow, Anne L. 1995. *Witchcraze: A New History of the European Witch Hunts*. Reprint. San Francisco, California: HarperOne.
Foulds, Diane. 2013. *Death in Salem: The Private Lives Behind the 1692 Witch Hunt*. 1st ed. Essex, Connecticut: Globe Pequot Press.
Godbeer, Richard. 2005. *Escaping Salem: The Other Witch Hunt of 1692*. 1st

ed. New York, New York: Oxford University Press.

Norton, Mary Beth. 2003. *In the Devil's Snare: The Salem Witchcraft Crisis of 1692*. 1st ed. New York, New York: Vintage.

Roach, Marilynne K. 2004. *The Salem Witch Trials: A Day-by-Day Chronicle of a Community Under Siege*. Lanham, Maryland: Taylor Trade Publishing.

Blair House & Camp David

Garten, Jeffrey E. 2022. *Three Days at Camp David: How a Secret Meeting in 1971 Transformed the Global Economy*. Reprint. New York, New York: Harper Paperbacks.

Giorgione, Michael. 2020. *Inside Camp David: The Private World of the Presidential Retreat*. Reprint. New York, New York: Back Bay Books.

Seale, William. 2016. *Blair House: The President's Guest House*. White House Historical Association.

Wilroy, Mary Edith. 1982. *Inside Blair House: An Intimate Look at Life Behind the Door of the President's Guest House*. 1st ed. New York, New York: Doubleday & Company, Inc.

Wright, Lawrence. 2014. *Thirteen Days in September: Carter, Begin, and Sadat at Camp David*. 1st ed. New York, New York: Knopf.

Ghost Ships & the Bermuda Triangle

Konstam, Angus. 2005. *Ghost Ships: Tales of Abandoned, Doomed, and Haunted Vessels*. 1st ed. Guilford, Connecticut: Lyons Press.

Quasar, Gian. 2005. *Into the Bermuda Triangle: Pursuing the Truth Behind the World's Greatest Mystery*. 1st ed. International Marine/Ragged Mountain Press.

———. 2014. *A Passage to Oblivion: The Last Voyage of the USS Cyclops*. Brodwyn, Moor & Doane.

Winer, Richard. 2000. *Ghost Ships: True Stories of Nautical Nightmares, Hauntings, and Disasters*. Reprint. New York, New York: Berkley.

Golden Age of Piracy

Dolin, Eric Jay. 2019. *Black Flags, Blue Waters: The Epic History of America's Most Notorious Pirates*. New York, New York: Liveright.

Head, David, ed. 2018. *The Golden Age of Piracy: The Rise, Fall, and Enduring Popularity of Pirates*. Athens, Georgia: University of Georgia Press.

Konstam, Angus. 2024. *The Pirate Menace: Uncovering the Golden Age of Piracy*. Oxford, England: Osprey Publishing.

Marquis, Samuel. 2018. *Blackbeard: The Birth of America*. Mount Sopris Publishing.

Simon, Rebecca. 2023. *The Pirates' Code: Laws and Life Aboard Ship*. London, England: Reaktion Books.

Jack the Ripper

Begg, Paul. 2006. *Jack the Ripper: The Facts*. Rev Ed. Sun Lakes, Arizona:

Robson Books.

Rubenhold, Hallie. 2019. *The Five: The Untold Lives of the Women Killed by Jack the Ripper*. 1st ed. Boston, Massachusetts: Houghton Mifflin Harcourt.

Russo, Stan. 2011. *The Jack the Ripper Suspects: Persons Cited by Investigators and Theorists*. Reprint. Jefferson, North Carolina: McFarland.

Sugden, Philip. 2002. *The Complete History of Jack the Ripper*. 2nd ed. Robinson Publishing.

Knights Templar

Barber, Malcolm. 1993. *The Trial of the Templars*. Reprint. Cambridge, England: Cambridge University Press.

———. 2012. *The New Knighthood: A History of the Order of the Temple*. Reprint. Cambridge, England: Cambridge University Press.

Martin, Sean. 2004. *The Knights Templar: The History and Myths of the Legendary Military Order*. New York, New York: Basic Books.

Newman, Sharan. 2005. *The Real History Behind the Da Vinci Code*. New York, New York: Berkley.

Ralls, Karen. 2007. *Knights Templar Encyclopedia: The Essential Guide to the People, Places, Events, and Symbols of the Order of the Temple*. 1st ed. Newburyport, Massachusetts: Weiser.

Lewis & Clark Expedition

Ambrose, Stephen. 1997. *Undaunted Courage: Meriwether Lewis, Thomas Jefferson, and the Opening of the American West*. 1st ed. New York, New York: Simon & Schuster.

Ambrose Tubbs, Stephenie. 2008. *Why Sacagawea Deserves the Day Off and Other Lessons from the Lewis and Clark Trail*. 1st ed. Lincoln, Nebraska: Bison Books.

Lewis, Meriwether, and William Clark. 2018. *The Essential Lewis and Clark*. Edited by Anthony Brandt. Reprint. Washington, D.C.: National Geographic.

Morris, Larry E. 2005. *The Fate of the Corps: What Became of the Lewis and Clark Explorers After the Expedition*. New Haven, Connecticut: Yale University Press.

Raymond Hebard, Grace. 2002. *Sacajawea: Guide and Interpreter of Lewis and Clark*. Reissue. Mineola, New York: Dover Publications.

Lincoln Assassination

Bogar, Thomas A. 2013. *Backstage at the Lincoln Assassination: The Untold Story of the Actors and Stagehands at Ford's Theatre*. Illustrated. Washington, D.C.: Regnery History.

Hutchinson, Robert J. 2020. *What Really Happened: The Lincoln Assassination*. 1st ed. Washington, D.C.: Regnery History.

Kauffman, Michael W. 2005. *American Brutus: John Wilkes Booth and the Lincoln Conspiracies*. New York, New York: Random House Publishing

Group.

Steers, Edward. 2005. *Blood on the Moon: The Assassination of Abraham Lincoln*. Lexington, Kentucky: University Press of Kentucky.

Swanson, James L. 2007. *Manhunt: The 12-Day Chase for Lincoln's Killer*. Reprint. New York, New York: William Morrow Paperbacks.

Lost Treasure & Treasure Hunts in the Americas

Honigsbaum, Mark. 2005. *Valverde's Gold: In Search of the Last Great Inca Treasure*. 1st ed. London, England: Picador.

Jameson, W. C. 2006. *Lost Treasures of American History*. Lanham, Maryland: Taylor Trade Publishing.

———. 2013. *The Silver Madonna and Other Tales of America's Greatest Lost Treasures*. Lanham, Maryland: Taylor Trade Publishing.

Jenks, Daniel. 2021. *The Lost Gold Rush Journals: Untold Tales of Gold Rush Adventure*. Edited by Larry Obermesik. Larry Obermesik.

Mecklenburg Declaration of Independence

Fleming, David. 2023. *Who's Your Founding Father?: One Man's Epic Quest to Uncover the First, True Declaration of Independence*. New York, New York: Hachette Books.

Hoyt, William Henry. 1907. *The Mecklenburg Declaration of Independence: A Study of Evidence Showing That the Alleged Early Declaration of Independence by Mecklenburg County, North Carolina, on May 20th, 1775, Is Spurious*. New York, New York: G. Putnam's Sons.

Plumer, Richard. 2014. *Charlotte and the American Revolution: Reverend Alexander Craighead, the Mecklenburg Declaration and the Foothills Fight for Independence*. Gloucestershire, United Kingdom: The History Press.

Syfert, Scott. 2014. *The First American Declaration of Independence?: The Disputed History of the Mecklenburg Declaration of May 20, 1775*. Jefferson, North Carolina: McFarland.

Presidential Secrets & Other Conspiracies

Dunning, Brian. 2018. *Conspiracies Declassified: The Skeptoid Guide to the Truth Behind the Theories*. Stoughton, Massachusetts: Adams Media.

Graham, Mary. 2017. *Presidents' Secrets: The Use and Abuse of Hidden Power*. New Haven, Connecticut: Yale University Press.

O'Brien, Cormac. 2004. *Secret Lives of the US Presidents: What Your Teachers Never Told You About the Men of the White House*. Philadelphia, Pennsylvania: Quirk Books.

Priess, David. 2017. *The President's Book of Secrets: The Untold Story of Intelligence Briefings to America's Presidents*. PublicAffairs.

Walker, Jesse. 2014. *The United States of Paranoia: A Conspiracy Theory*. Reprint. New York, New York: Harper Perennial.

Roanoke Colony

Dawson, Scott. 2020. *The Lost Colony and Hatteras Island.* North Carolina: Arcadia Publishing.

Ewen, Charles R., and E. Thomson Shields, Jr. 2024. *Becoming the Lost Colony: The History, Lore and Popular Culture of the Roanoke Mystery.* Jefferson, North Carolina: McFarland.

Klingelhofer, Eric, ed. 2023. *Excavating the Lost Colony Mystery: The Map, the Search, the Discovery.* Chapel Hill, North Carolina: The University of North Carolina Press.

Lawler, Andrew. 2018. *The Secret Token: Myth, Obsession, and the Search for the Lost Colony of Roanoke.* 1st ed. New York, New York: Doubleday.

Miller, Lee. 2002. *Roanoke: Solving the Mystery of the Lost Colony.* Reprint. New York, New York: Penguin Books.

Washington Irving & the Hudson Valley

Daughan, George C. 2017. *Revolution on the Hudson: New York City and the Hudson River Valley in the American War of Independence.* Reprint. New York, New York: W. W. Norton & Company.

Guertin Marchese, Allison. 2017. *Hudson Valley Curiosities: The Sinking of the Steamship Swallow, the Poughkeepsie Seer, the UFOs of the Celtic Stone Chambers and More.* Gloucestershire, United Kingdom: The History Press.

Irving, Washington. 2009. *The Sketch-Book of Geoffrey Crayon, Gent.* Reissue. New York, New York: Oxford University Press.

———. 2015. *Knickerbocker's History of New York, Complete.* Reprint. CreateSpace Independent Publishing Platform.

Jones, Brian Jay. 2011. *Washington Irving: The Definitive Biography of America's First Bestselling Author.* 1st ed. New York, New York: Arcade.

Winchester Mystery House

Haag, Pamela. 2016. *The Gunning of America: Business and the Making of American Gun Culture.* 1st ed. New York, New York: Basic Books.

Ignoffo, Mary Jo. 2012. *Captive of the Labyrinth: Sarah L. Winchester, Heiress to the Rifle Fortune.* 1st ed. Columbia, Missouri: University of Missouri.

It's All Connected: Secrets Revealed

The following connections might have come to mind if you based your answers on a close read of the preceding chapters. But if you truly transform into Riley Poole—pairing your hoodie and Converse with the latest and greatest conspiracy theory—you may find that even more links undoubtedly exist!

Blackbeard the Pirate & Bermuda Triangle: The Bermuda Triangle is situated within the <u>Caribbean Sea</u>, the same waters that Blackbeard frequented during his heyday.

Blackbeard the Pirate & Lost Roanoke Colony: <u>British colonies</u> like Roanoke had complex and evolving relationships with pirates like Blackbeard.

Blackbeard the Pirate & Templar Treasure: Both stories center on <u>rumored treasures</u> that many historians agree never existed.

Blair House & Camp David: These landmarks have been used to facilitate <u>diplomatic</u> convenings, such as a G8 summit and peace negotiations between Egypt and Israel.

Blair House & Headless Horseman: Both are synonymous with <u>American ghost stories</u>, as President Wilson's spirit is said to haunt Blair House and the headless horseman features in *The Legend of Sleepy Hollow*.

Blair House & Lincoln Assassination: The topics share a theme of <u>presidential assassination</u>—an event that claimed President Lincoln's life and nearly took President Truman's as well.

Blair House & President's Secret Book: The media once accused the US government of conducting <u>espionage</u> by installing surveillance equipment at Blair House, while the Culper Spy Ring may have originated the president's secret book legend.

Blair House & Winchester Mystery House: These sites eventually found themselves on the national <u>register of historic places</u>.

Bermuda Triangle & The *Mary Celeste*: The *Mary Celeste* represents one of the most famous discoveries of a <u>ghost ship</u>, plenty of which have been found sailing in the Bermuda Triangle.

Bermuda Triangle & President's Secret Book: Both rely on <u>supernatural rationale</u> to explain events such as ship disappearances and unidentified aerial phenomena.

Bermuda Triangle & Seward's Folly: The <u>Alaska</u> Triangle, a terrestrial Bermuda Triangle analog, is situated in the state that Seward infamously purchased.

Bermuda Triangle & Templar Treasure: Conspiracy theorists suggest that <u>Christopher Columbus</u> followed the Templar treasure to the New World, where he was the first to record strange phenomena in the Bermuda Triangle.

Camp David & President's Secret Book: President Nixon was at Camp David when he requested his staffers' resignations after <u>Watergate</u>, a scandal Riley believes would be explored in the president's secret book.

Camp David & Templar Treasure: The Knights Templar amassed their rumored treasure through operations in the <u>Middle East</u>, while Camp David hosted a famous meeting between leaders from this region.

Corps of Discovery & Lost Roanoke Colony: Both missions relied on <u>Native American support</u> to ensure their adventurers' survival.

Corps of Discovery & Mecklenburg Declaration: <u>Thomas Jefferson</u>, who commissioned the Corps of Discovery, came under scrutiny for plagiarism thanks to the Mecklenburg Declaration story.

Corps of Discovery & President's Secret Book: According to legend, the president's secret book is a result of <u>journaling</u>, a key responsibility of the Corps of Discovery's leaders.

Corps of Discovery & Seward's Folly: Both were inspired by a desire for US westward expansion justified using the concept of <u>manifest destiny</u>.

Headless Horseman & Jack the Ripper: The stories of the headless horseman and Jack the Ripper have <u>European roots</u>.

Headless Horseman & The *Mary Celeste*: These tales have been preserved by <u>famous authors</u>, including the Brothers Grimm, Washington Irving, and Sir Arthur Conan Doyle.

Headless Horseman & Mecklenburg Declaration: The Mecklenburg Declaration was supposedly a response to the onset of the <u>Revolutionary</u>

<u>War</u>, which claimed the life of the soldier who inspired America's first headless horseman story.

Jack the Ripper & Salem Witch Trials: Both sets of infamous legal cases featured at least one—if not multiple—<u>false confessions</u>.

Lincoln Assassination & Mecklenburg Declaration: Rumors swirling around the deaths of John Wilkes Booth and Peter Stewart Ney include suspicions of <u>mistaken identity</u>.

Lincoln Assassination & Salem Witch Trials: <u>Controversial trials</u> were held to convict the accused conspirators and witches.

Lincoln Assassination & Seward's Folly: Secretary of State <u>William Seward</u>, who committed the eponymous "folly," was a second assassination target on the night of President Lincoln's murder.

Lost Roanoke Colony & The *Mary Celeste*: Each case features the mysterious <u>disappearance</u> of a large group of people.

Mecklenburg Declaration & Salem Witch Trials: <u>Colonial tensions</u> gave rise to both the Salem witch trials and the Mecklenburg Declaration (or the Mecklenburg Resolves, depending on your beliefs).

President's Secret Book & Seward's Folly: While one is an urban legend and the other an infamous event, both were born out of <u>government secrecy</u>.

Salem Witch Trials & Templar Treasure: <u>Religious influence</u> underpins both the legend of the Templar treasure and the string of witchcraft accusations that rocked New England.

Seward's Folly & Winchester Mystery House: A severe case of <u>misunderstanding</u> caused the Alaska acquisition to be dubbed a "folly" and Sarah Winchester to be remembered as an unstable recluse.

Acknowledgments

For years it has bothered me that *The Templar Treasure and Other Myths That Are True*, the text written by Riley Poole that features in *National Treasure: Book of Secrets*, doesn't exist. But as Benjamin Franklin Gates eloquently reminded us in 2004, "Those who have the ability to take action have the responsibility to take action." So, it became my job to right a rare wrong within the *National Treasure* franchise by writing a book—this book—to celebrate the moments in history that may have inspired Riley on his own publication journey.

I must begin by thanking director Jon Turteltaub for not only penning the foreword to this book, but also for offering constant encouragement with a dash of grounding realism. To Jon, as well as screenwriters Marianne and Cormac Wibberley and Ted Elliott, and story writers Charles Segars and Oren Aviv: your prowess in creating a truly relatable character like Riley made this book possible. But more importantly, these individuals have been incredibly supportive of my academic work related to their fictional world, and I am grateful for the trust they have placed in my efforts to keep the franchise alive and well in the public consciousness. For helping me realize that goal, David Bushman and Scott Ryan at Tucker DS Press have my utmost gratitude.

Thank you to Emily Black, my colleague, friend, and partner in crime on the *National Treasure Hunt* project. Her collaboration on our myriad *National Treasure*-themed activities (another of which will have undoubtedly cropped up by the time this is published) has enabled me to write this text. I don't know what I'd be doing today if she hadn't picked up the phone when I called with a "one step short of crazy" idea to start a *National Treasure* podcast, but I'm certainly not looking back. And on that note, I would be remiss if I failed to thank my partner, Bryan Kudisch, for his unquestioning support of each and every one of my new projects (which some might call antics), no matter how niche they seem.

It turns out that delving into the mind of Riley Poole—understanding what might drive his various pursuits—was more challenging than I initially anticipated, perhaps because I've always related more to his counterpart, Ben Gates. Changing perspectives forced me to examine the depths of my own personality and find kinship with Riley in ways that I hadn't previously. Just like my envisioning of Riley in childhood, I too was a "science fair kid," and I must thank my parents, June and Ken Paris, for their encouragement (and funding) of my increasingly complex science projects.

Riley's character analysis also prompted me to reflect on my own experience with history as a subject, which further implicates my parents as inspirations for this book. My mom injected enviable passion into her lessons as a sixth-grade teacher of ancient civilizations (and is also the reason hundreds of New Jersey middle schoolers grew up watching *National Treasure* in the classroom). Because of my dad, I knew how to use a metal detector (probably better than Ben Gates, actually) and developed a passion for digging up antique glass bottles starting at a young age. My creative work related to the *National Treasure* franchise is a homage to them both.

About the Author

AUBREY R. PARIS, PhD is the cofounder of National Treasure Hunt LLC. She cohosts and executive produces *National Treasure Hunt*, the independent podcast providing an interdisciplinary examination of *National Treasure* and sharing both retrospective and forward-looking interviews with the franchise's cast and creative team. Her interviews have broken *National Treasure* news that has been covered by media outlets such as Gizmodo, Screen Rant, MovieWeb, CBR, and more. Dr. Paris coauthored the book *National Treasure Hunt: One Step Short of Crazy* (Tucker DS Press), which is sold at numerous national landmarks featured in the franchise. She has engaged diverse audiences during live shows at the US National Archives, the Library of Congress, and Independence National Historical Park. Screenwriters Marianne and Cormac Wibberley have called her a "historian of the *National Treasure* franchise." Follow *National Treasure Hunt* at @NTHuntPodcast or NTHuntPodcast.com.

Dr. Paris is a policy adviser, public speaker, and multimedia producer who has worked on topics ranging from the nexus of women's empowerment and climate change to emerging technologies. Previously, her academic research focused on the development of electrocatalysts for carbon dioxide utilization, and she also contributed to interdisciplinary projects examining the future of US nuclear energy, implications of energy generation on water security, and impacts of climate change on national security. Dr. Paris received her PhD in chemistry and materials science from Princeton University (2019), M.A. in chemistry from Princeton University (2017), and B.S. in chemistry and biology from Ursinus College (2015). Follow her on X and Instagram at @BelleTucker11.

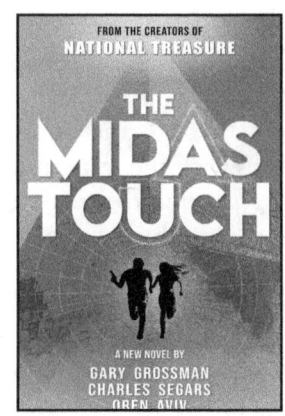

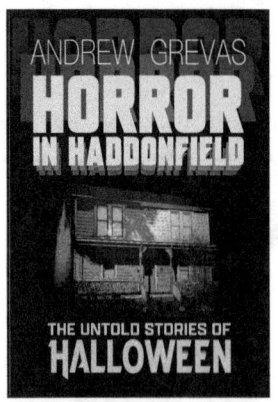

134-8-8 91-1-7 35-28-11 51-9-27 193-17-28 221-24-1 99-21-8

62-3-10 22-8-7 104-11-7 181-26-25 78-2-5 15-22-19' 84-21-2

56-24-35 9-12-35 185-8-29 147-4-11, 245-9-8 48-11-24 30-21-4

37-5-14 125-33-11 75-16-18 237-8-20 162-28-20 13-31-5 68-6-3

128-8-12 22-38-16 2-11-13 96-13-18 69-21-21 143-3-17 233-26-11

178-3-3 68-32-3 262-1-11 95-28-5 205-13-33 172-15-5 15-33-1

27-22-10 118-25-47 100-9-56 195-13-13 58-1-10' 82-25-32 117-18-1

117-29-23 197-12-14 73-13-47 57-1-4 209-29-42 168-28-8 101-20-34

144-10-13 40-10-3 163-12-14 34-12-44 107-8-17 175-14-23 211-16-21

240-29-44 2-8-10 31-33-27 104-3-11 96-28-5 161-13-25 7-13-6

79-27-21* 127-3-29 47-8-15 164-10-28 91-9-7 107-1-49 86-38-1

158-4-28 222-21-2 221-5-54 71-8-3 110-19-13 242-30-36 19-11-42

39-8-17 87-18-30 45-10-41 166-32-25 251-4-18 150-9-27 73-16-35

78-10-43 148-7-1 20-23-28 121-14-13 56-28-36 163-15-29 234-8-13

28-23-8 66-16-41 268-14-15 15-24-7 199-5-47 162-23-12 64-19-16

33-1-30 147-13-36 241-10-33 9-25-29 108-19-3 110-15-14 205-14-6

175-14-57 49-9-1 118-10-37 182-11-40 54-23-26 178-17-16 142-30-8

260-2-7 58-6-9 171-20-10 93-10-57 189-7-20 237-29-2 60-7-26

112-10-25 34-3-5 194-2-25 162-10-38 265-3-8 226-13-6 12-11-43

42-6-14 14-18-1 84-15-13.

www.ingramcontent.com/pod-product-compliance
Lightning Source LLC
Chambersburg PA
CBHW061606120626
46550CB00004B/1627